TAKING SIDES

Clashing Views on Controversial

Issues in Human Sexuality

EIGHTH EDITION

Clashing Views on Controversial
Issues in Human Sexuality

EIGHTH EDITION

Selected, Edited, and with Introductions by

William J. Taverner
Fairleigh Dickinson University

McGraw-Hill/Dushkin
A Division of The McGraw-Hill Companies

To my wife, Denise, and my son, Robert, for their kind patience, support, and encouragement

Photo Acknowledgment
Cover image: © 2002 by PhotoDisc, Inc.

Cover Art Acknowledgment
Charles Vitelli

Manufactured in the United States of America

Eighth Edition

123456789BAHBAH5432

Library of Congress Cataloging-in-Publication Data
Main entry under title:
Taking sides: clashing views on controversial issues in human sexuality/selected, edited, and with introductions by Robert T. Francoeur and William J. Taverner.—8th ed.
Includes bibliographical references and index.
1. Sex. 2. Sexual ethics. I. Taverner, William J., *comp.*
612.6
0-07-248062-9
ISSN: 1098-5387

Printed on Recycled Paper

Preface

In few areas of American society today are clashing views more evident than in the area of human sexual behavior. Almost daily, in the news media, in congressional hearings, and on the streets, we hear about Americans of all ages taking completely opposite positions on such issues as abortion, contraception, fertility, homosexuality, teenage sexuality, and the like. Given the highly personal, emotional, and sensitive nature of these issues, sorting out the meaning of these controversies and fashioning a coherent position on them can be a difficult proposition. The purpose of this book, therefore, is to encourage meaningful critical thinking about current issues related to human sexuality, and the debates are designed to assist you in the task of clarifying your own personal values and identifying what society's are or should be in this area.

For this eighth edition of *Taking Sides: Clashing Views on Controversial Issues in Human Sexuality,* we have gathered 38 lively and thoughtful statements by articulate advocates on opposite sides of a variety of sexuality-related questions. For the questions debated in this volume, it is vital that you understand and appreciate the different positions other people take on these issues, as well as your own. You should respect other people's philosophical biases and religious beliefs and attempt to articulate your own. Democracies are strongest when they respect the rights and privileges of all citizens, be they conservative, liberal, or middle-of-the-road, religious or humanistic, of the majority or in the minority. Although you may disagree with one or even both of the arguments offered for each issue, it is important that you read each statement carefully and critically. Since this book is a tool to encourage critical thinking, you should not feel confined to the views expressed in the articles. You may see important points on both sides of an issue and may construct for yourself a new and creative approach, which may incorporate the best of both sides or provide an entirely new vantage point for understanding.

To assist you as you pursue the issues debated here, each issue has an issue *introduction,* which sets the stage for the debate, tells you something about each of the authors, and provides some historical background to the debate. Each issue concludes with a *postscript* that briefly ties the readings together and gives a detailed list of *suggested readings,* if you would like to further explore a topic.

Changes to this edition This edition has five completely new issues: *Should Sexuality Education Be Comprehensive?* (Issue 1); *Does the G-Spot Really Exist?* (Issue 3); *Should Federal Funding of Stem Cell Research Be Restricted?* (Issue 11); *Is Cohabitation Before Marriage a Bad Idea?* (Issue 13); and *Should Same-Sex Marriage Be Legal?* (Issue 15). In addition, for one of the issues retained from the previous edition—*Should Sexual Relationships Between Professors and Students Be Banned?* (Issue 9)—one of the selections has been replaced to provide a different perspective on the issue and to bring the issue up to date. In all, there are

11 new selections in this edition. In addition, the introductions and postscripts have been revised and updated where necessary.

A word to the instructor An *Instructor's Manual With Test Questions* (multiple-choice and essay) is available through the publisher for the instructor using *Taking Sides* in the classroom. A general guidebook, *Using Taking Sides in the Classroom*, which discusses methods and techniques for integrating the pro-con approach into any classroom setting, is also available. An online version of *Using Taking Sides in the Classroom* and a correspondence service for *Taking Sides* adopters can be found at http://www.dushkin.com/usingts/.

Taking Sides: Clashing Views on Controversial Issues in Human Sexuality is only one title in the Taking Sides series. If you are interested in seeing the table of contents for any of the other titles, please visit the Taking Sides Web site at http://www.dushkin.com/takingsides/.

Acknowledgments The task of tracking down the best essays for inclusion in this collection is not easy, and we appreciate the useful suggestions from the many users of *Taking Sides* across the United States and Canada who communicated with the publisher. Special thanks go to those who responded with specific suggestions for the this title:

Vincent Alfonso
Fordham University

Charles Mancil
Texas A & M University

Peter Anderson
University of New Orleans

Elizabeth Schroeder
Montclair State University

Debra Berke
Messiah College

Jilline G. Seiver
Green River Community College

Linda Hendrickson
East Stroudsburg State University

John Whitaker
Chapman University

I appreciate the great ideas that came from members of the HEDIR and SEXNET list servs. Please continue to write in care of McGraw-Hill/Dushkin with comments and suggestions for issues and readings.

I would also like to thank two colleagues who are both mentors and friends: Peggy Brick and Robert T. Francoeur. Peggy is a sexuality education consultant with whom I have collaborated on numerous projects, and whose advice I value greatly. She is a patient and generous mentor who constantly inspires me to think critically about all matters, not just those related to sexuality education. Bob edited or coedited the first seven editions of *Taking Sides: Clashing Views on Controversial Issues in Human Sexuality*. I have had the pleasure of working with Bob on the previous three editions of this book, and was introduced to both *Taking Sides* and Bob when I took his international studies course in Copenhagen, Denmark, ten years ago. I am grateful for his kind guidance over the years. Every young sexuality educator should have the privilege of working with such knowledgeable and caring mentors.

Benjamin Franklin once remarked that democracies are built on compromises. But you cannot have healthy compromises unless people talk with each other and try to understand, appreciate, and respect their different ways of reasoning, their values, and their goals. Open and frank discussions of controversial issues is what this book is all about. Without healthy controversy and open exchange of different views, intolerance and bigotry could easily increase to the point where our democratic system could no longer function. Democracy thrives on controversy.

William J. Taverner
Fairleigh Dickinson University

Contents In Brief

Contents

Sexuality educator Deborah M. Roffman expresses support for the surgeon general's report calling for comprehensive sexuality education. Roffman states that young people need to be taught about abstinence as well as other methods to avoid pregnancy and sexually transmitted infections. Editorialist Don Feder argues that comprehensive sexuality education is not effective, and criticizes the methods used to compile the surgeon general's report, which includes interviews with commercial sex workers.

Researchers Sally Guttmacher et al. maintain that their study of New York City high school students who received both condoms and an HIV/AIDS education program versus Chicago high school students who received only HIV/AIDS education proves that distributing condoms in schools does not increase sexual activity but does result in students using condoms more often when they are sexually active. Professor of education Edwin J. Delattre rejects the argument that there is a moral obligation to save lives by distributing condoms in schools. He asserts that distributing condoms in schools promotes morally unacceptable casual sexual relationships.

Sexologist Gary Schubach states that the G-spot exists and describes his own research examining the chemical makeup of female ejaculatory fluid. Schubach argues for a better understanding of the G-spot among the medical community so that medical professionals can help women avoid feelings of guilt or shame when they experience ejaculation. Psychologist Terence M. Hines counters that the widespread acceptance of the G-spot as real goes well beyond the available evidence. Hines maintains that the existence of the G-spot has never been verified by empirical, objective means and that women may have been misinformed about their bodies and their sexuality.

Loretta M. Kopelman, a professor of medical humanities, argues that certain moral absolutes apply to all cultures and that these, combined with the many serious health and cultural consequences of female circumcision, require that all forms of female genital mutilation be eliminated. P. Masila Mutisya, a professor of multicultural education, contends that we should allow the simplest form of female circumcision, nicking the clitoral hood to draw a couple of drops of blood, as part of the rich heritage of rite of passage for newborn and pubertal girls in those cultures with this tradition.

Diane D. Aronson, executive director of RESOLVE, the National Infertility Association's consumer-advocacy and patient-support organization, argues that infertility is a disease of the reproductive system that strikes people in all walks of life. She concludes that requiring insurance companies to pay for proven medical treatments for infertility is the right thing to do in a country that places great value on healthy families. Merrill Matthews, Jr., a medical ethicist and vice president of domestic policy at the National Center for Policy Analysis, maintains that requiring all health insurance plans to pay for infertility treatments could significantly increase insurance costs for everyone.

PART 2 SOCIAL ISSUES 81

Janice Weinman, executive director of the American Association of University Women (AAUW), states that, while there has been some progress since the AAUW published its study entitled *How Schools Shortchange Girls* in 1991, its 1998 review of 1,000 research studies entitled *Gender Gaps: Where Schools Still Fail Our Children* found that girls still face a gender gap in math, science, and computer science. Psychologist and author Judith Kleinfeld argues that despite appearances, girls still have an advantage over boys in terms of their future plans, teachers' expectations, and everyday school experiences. Furthermore, minority males in particular are at a disadvantage educationally.

Issue 7.　Should Public Libraries Provide Sexuality Information?　94

Martha Cornog, editor of *Libraries, Erotica, and Pornography,* maintains that public libraries have a responsibility to preserve all literature that is part of our cultural heritage for patrons and future generations. Public libraries that preserve and make available materials, including controversial sexuality materials, facilitate and promote debate, which is essential in the democratic process. James L. Sauer, a librarian at Eastern College in Phoenixville, Pennsylvania, states that free speech is not unlimited—it is governed by and must serve the moral order. Thus, it is proper for libraries to use their censorship power to curb unfettered expression that violates or attacks the moral values of society.

Issue 8.　Is Pornography Harmful to Women?　108

Researchers Elizabeth Cramer et al. state that their study of abused women shows that the use of pornography by males is directly linked with the physical and sexual abuse of women. Professor of law Nadine Strossen argues that misguided assaults on pornography have resulted in the naive belief that pornography is a major weapon that men use to degrade and dominate women.

Issue 9.　Should Sexual Relationships Between Professors and Students Be Banned?　122

Professor Brian Martin asserts that sexual relationships between professors and students are inappropriate and constitute an abuse of trust. He contends that universities need to establish clear and firm policies against such abuse. Professor of sociology Barry M. Dank and author Joseph S. Fulda counter that efforts to ban all romances between students and faculty on college campuses feed off unrelated notions of sexual harassment and pedophilia, treat female students as incompetent children incapable of giving informed consent, and are fueled by a resentment toward societal norms about older men dating and marrying younger women.

Issue 10. Does Recent Pedophilia Research Threaten Accepted Moral Standards?   138

Radio commentator Laura Schlessinger denounces a study, published by the American Psychological Association (APA), that reexamined the results and conclusions from 59 earlier studies of child sexual abuse (CSA) in more than 37,000 college students. Schlessinger views this study as a "pseudo-scientific" attempt to convince people to accept pedophilia as normal. Sharon Lamb, a *Boston Globe* commentator, argues that solid, scientific research on child sexual abuse should be accepted, even when it calls into question common assumptions about CSA and its consequences.

Issue 11. Should Federal Funding of Stem Cell Research Be Restricted?   152

President George W. Bush explains his decision to permit limited federal funding of embryonic stem cell research for the purpose of seeking treatments for serious diseases. Douglas F. Munch, a management consultant to the pharmaceutical and biotechnology industries, criticizes President Bush's decision for not fully reflecting the will of the people and for being too restrictive to have any meaningful impact on medical science and the lives of people affected by serious diseases.

Issue 12. Should States Fund Sexuality Research?   166

John Bancroft, a medical doctor, sexologist, and director of the University of Indiana's Alfred Kinsey Institute for Research in Sex, Gender, and Reproduction, argues that public funding for scientific research on sexuality issues is vital in order to solve some of the major sexual problems that plague the United States. Beverly R. Newman, a counselor of sexual abuse survivors and a teacher at Ivy Tech College in Indianapolis, Indiana, opposes any public funding of sexuality research by the Kinsey Institute or any other alleged scientific research group because she fears that researchers will follow Alfred Kinsey (1894–1956), whom she calls "a callous, maniacal scientist."

Issue 13.   Is Cohabitation Before Marriage a Bad Idea?   178

David Popenoe and Barbara Dafoe Whitehead, directors of the National Marriage Project, http://marriage.rutgers.edu, contend that living together before marriage is not a good way to prepare for marriage or avoid divorce. They maintain that cohabitation weakens the institution of marriage and poses serious risks for women and children. Dorian Solot and Marshall Miller, founders of the Alternatives to Marriage Project, http://www.unmarried.org, state that while marriage may be a good choice for some people, it should not be pushed as the only acceptable option. They criticize a report by the National Marriage Project for misrepresenting social science research on cohabitation and marriage.

Issue 14.   Is the Model of Normal and Vandalized Gendermaps/Lovemaps Biased?   202

Pat Califia, a feminist and self-described sex radical, argues that John Money's concept of lovemaps reflects a high-handed, moralistic division of the world into "normal" and "abnormal" sexuality. She maintains that many "differently pleasured" persons, including homosexuals, are at risk because of the moralistic distinctions implicit in Money's model of lovemaps. John Money, an expert on gender development, contends that every society has taboos and establishes its own sexual ethic. Money suggests that

Califia's idea of a sexual democracy where people can love whomever they please, in whatever fashion they please, is unachievable because of those taboos.

PART 3 LEGAL ISSUES 221

Jonathan Rauch, senior writer for the *National Journal,* argues that the proposed constitutional amendment to define marriage sidesteps the democratic process and violates conservatives' own principles regarding states' rights. Rauch maintains that the legalization of same-sex marriage would benefit all of society. Robert H. Bork, former federal appeals court judge, contends that the proposed constitutional amendment to define marriage is necessary to stop gay activists from redefining marriage. Bork asserts that gay activists have misused liberal lower courts to gradually redefine the traditional, heterosexual institution of marriage.

Professor of law Katherine Shaw Spaht states that the main benefit of allowing couples to commit to stricter covenant marriages will be to reduce the devastating, long-term damage that divorce inflicts on America's children. She maintains that there are other "compelling values" that counterbalance "the siren song of self-improvement." Author Ashton Applewhite counters that repealing or rewriting U.S. no-fault divorce laws and championing a stricter covenant marriage will not reduce the divorce rate because divorce is the "result of sweeping social changes that cannot be wished away with a piece of sanctimonious and punitive legislation." She concludes that covenant marriages are sexist, will hurt children, and will raise the economic and emotional cost of divorce.

Author James Bovard asserts that legalizing sex work would help stem the spread of AIDS and free up the police to focus on controlling violent crime. Anastasia Volkonsky, founding director of PROMISE, an organization dedicated to combating sexual exploitation, maintains that decriminalizing prostitution would only cause more social harm, particularly to women.

Douglas J. Besharov, a resident scholar at the American Enterprise Institute in Washington, D.C., argues that carefully conducted research in Europe and the United States shows that chemical castration is effective, more humane, and much less expensive than imprisonment for some convicted compulsive sex offenders. Andrew Vachhs, a juvenile justice advocate and novelist, asserts that chemical and surgical castration both fail to address aggression as an underlying motive for repeat sex offenders.

Bernice Sandler, a senior scholar at the National Association for Women in Education, maintains that schools should pay damages for student-on-student sexual harassment. She cites several cases in which school authorities ignored blatant and pervasive sexual harassment of students by other students until the parents of the harassed students forced action by filing lawsuits seeking compensation for damages. Author Sarah J. McCarthy objects to schools paying damages for student-on-student sexual harassment, stating that Congress and lawmakers often jump to legislation as a quick-fix solution. She asserts that new laws authorizing the filing of lawsuits would empty taxpayers' pockets, bankrupt school districts, and lead to centralized thought control, an Americanized version of Chairman Mao's cultural revolution in China.

Introduction

Sexual Attitudes in Perspective

Robert T. Francoeur

William J. Taverner

As you examine the nineteen controversial issues in human sexuality in this volume you will find yourself unavoidably encountering the values you have absorbed from our society, your ethnic background, and your religious heritage and traditions. Because these values will influence your decisions, often without being consciously recognized, it is important to remind you of the role these undercurrent social, ethnic, and religious values play in the positions you take on these issues.

How Social and Ethnic Factors Influence Our Values

American society is not homogeneous. People who grow up in rural, suburban, and large urban environments often have subtle differences in their values and attitudes when it comes to gender roles, marriage, and sexuality. Growing up in different areas of the United States can influence one's views of sex, marriage, and family. This is even more true for men and women who were born, and raised, in another country and culture.

Also, many studies have shown how values are affected by one's family income level and general socioeconomic status. In general, there is more mutuality and sharing between men and women in the middle class than in the blue-collar working class. Working-class males are more reluctant to share in household duties and are more apt to segregate themselves from women at social functions. Working-class women tend toward passivity and nurturing and are more emotionally volatile than their middle-class counterparts. Studies have also indicated that one's occupation, educational level, and income are closely related to one's values, attitudes, role conceptions, child-rearing practices, and sexual identity.

Our values and attitudes about sex are also influenced by whether we are brought up in a rural, suburban, or large urban environment. Our ethnic background can be an important, if subtle, influence on our values and attitudes. In contrast to the vehement debates among white, middle-class Americans about pornography, for instance, Robert Staples, a professor of sociology at the University of California, San Francisco, says that among African Americans, pornography is a trivial issue. "Blacks," Staples explains, "have traditionally had a more naturalistic attitude toward human sexuality, seeing it as the normal expression of sexual attraction between men and women.... Rather than seeing the depiction of heterosexual intercourse or nudity as an inherent debasement of women, as a fringe group of [white] feminists claims, the black community would see women as having equal rights to the enjoyment of sexual stimuli.... Since the double [moral] standard has never attracted many American blacks, the claim that women are exploited by exhibiting their nude bodies or engaging in heterosexual intercourse lacks credibility" (quoted in Philip Nobile and Eric Nadler, *United States of America vs. Sex* [Minotaur Press, 1986]). While middle-class whites may be very concerned about pornography promoting sexual promiscuity, many African Americans are much more concerned about issues related to poverty and employment opportunities.

Similarly, attitudes toward homosexuality vary among white, African American, and Latino cultures. In the macho tradition of Latin America, male homosexual behavior is a sign that one cannot find a woman and have sexual relationships like a "real" man. In lower socioeconomic African American cultures, a similar judgment prevails, and lesbian relationships are often unrecognized. Understanding this ethnic value becomes very important in appreciating the ways in which African Americans and Latinos respond to the crisis of AIDS and the presence of males with AIDS in their families. Often the family will deny that a son or husband has AIDS until the very end because others might interpret this admission as a confession that the person is homosexual.

Another example of differing ethnic values is the issue of single motherhood. In ethnic groups with a strong tradition of extended matrilineal families, the concept of an "illegitimate" child born "out-of-wedlock" may not even exist. Unmarried mothers in these cultures do not carry the same stigma often associated with single mothers in other, less-matrilineal cultures. When "outsiders" who do not share the particular ethnic values of a culture enter into such a subculture, they often cannot understand why birth control and family life educational programs do not produce any substantial change in attitudes. They overlook the basic social scripting that has already taken place.

Gender roles also vary from culture to culture. Muslim men and women who grow up in the Middle East and then emigrate to the United States have to adapt to the much greater freedom women have in the States. Similarly, American men and women who served in the armed forces in Saudi Arabia during the 1990 Persian Gulf War and American and European military assigned to bases in Muslim countries during the Afghanistan war found they had to adapt to very different Muslim cultures that put many restrictions on the movement and dress of women in the military.

A boy who grows up among the East Bay Melanesians in the Southwestern Pacific is taught to avoid any social contact with girls from the age of three or four, even though he may run around naked and masturbate in public. Adolescent Melanesian boys and girls are not allowed to have sex with each other, but boys are expected to have sex both with an older male and with a boy of his own age. Their first heterosexual experiences come with marriage. In the Cook

Islands, Mangaian boys are expected to have sex with many girls after an older woman teaches them about the art of sexual play. Mangaians also accept and expect both premarital and extramarital sex.

But one does not have to look to exotic anthropological studies to find evidence of the importance of ethnic values. Even within the United States, one can find subtle but important differences in sexual attitudes and values among people of French, German, Italian, Polish, Spanish, Portuguese, Dutch, Scandinavian, Irish, and English descent.

Religious Factors in Our Attitudes Toward Sex

In the Middle Ages Christian theologians divided sexual behaviors into two categories: behaviors that were "natural" and those that were "unnatural." Since they believed that the natural function and goal of all sexual behavior and relations was reproduction, masturbation was unnatural because it frustrated the natural goal of conception and continuance of the species. Rape certainly was considered illicit because it was not within the marital bond, but since it was procreative, rape was considered a natural use of sex. The same system of distinction was applied to other sexual relations and behaviors. Premarital sex, adultery, and incest were natural uses of sexuality, while oral sex, anal sex, and contraception were unnatural. Homosexual relations, of course, were both illicit and unnatural. These religious values were based on the view that God created man and woman at the beginning of time and laid down certain rules and guidelines for sexual behavior and relations. This view is still very influential in our culture, even for those who are not active in any religious tradition.

In recent years several analysts have highlighted two philosophical or religious perspectives that appear throughout Judeo-Christian tradition and Western civilization.[1] Understanding these two perspectives is important in any attempt to debate controversial issues in human sexuality.

Let me introduce these two distinct worldviews by drawing on a non-Western example from recent history—the Islamic or Muslim cultures of the Middle East and the politics of Islamic fundamentalists. On one side of the spectrum are Muslims, who see the world as a process, an ever-changing scene in which they must struggle to reinterpret and apply the basic principles of the Koran (the sacred book of the teachings of Allah, or God) to new situations. On the opposing side of the spectrum are fundamentalist Muslims who believe that the Muslim world needs to return to the unchanging, literal words of Mohammed and the Koran. This means purging all Western and modern influences that have assimilated into Islamic society. The September 11, 2001, terrorist attacks against the United States' World Trade Center and the Pentagon represent the rejection of Western influences at its ultimate, deadliest extreme.

Two decades ago, Islamic fundamentalists overthrew the shah of Iran, who had encouraged the country's modernization. Anwar Sadat, the late president of Egypt, was assassinated by Muslim fundamentalists who opposed his tolerance of Muslim women being employed outside the home and wearing Western dress instead of the traditional black, neck-to-ankle chador. These fundamentalists were also repulsed by the suggestion made by Sadat's wife that Muslim women should have the right to seek divorce and alimony. Nowadays women do have the right to divorce their husbands in some Muslim countries, but new issues that raise conflicts between the two worldviews continually arise in the Middle East. Typical of these new conflicts was the 1993 election of Tansu Ciller as Turkey's first female prime minister.

These same two worldviews are equally obvious in the ongoing history of American culture. Religious fundamentalists, New Right politicians, and the various members of the American Family Association, the Family Research Council of America, Focus on the Family, and the Eagle Forum believe that we need to return to traditional values. These distinct groups often share a conviction that the sexual revolution, changing attitudes toward masturbation and homosexuality, a tolerance of premarital and extramarital sex, sexuality education in the schools instead of in the homes, and the legality of abortion are contributing to a cultural decline and must be rejected. A classic expression of this value system surfaced on nationwide television in the aftermath of the September 11, 2001, terrorist attacks when former presidential candidate Pat Robertson and the Reverend Jerry Falwell agreed that the destruction of the towers of the World Trade Center and the Pentagon were caused in part by the immoral activism of the American Civil Liberties Union and advocates for abortion and gay rights.

At the same time, other Americans argue for legalized abortion, civil rights for homosexuals, decriminalization of prostitution, androgynous sex roles in child-rearing practices, and the abolition of all laws restricting the right to privacy for sexually active, consenting adults.

Recent efforts to analyze the dogma behind the fundamentalist and the "changing-world" value systems have revealed two distinct worldviews, or philosophies, tenuously coexisting for centuries within the Judaic, Christian, and Islamic traditions. When Ernst Mayr, a biologist at Harvard University, traced the history of biological theories, he concluded that no greater revolution has occurred in the history of human thought than the radical shift from a fixed worldview of cosmology rooted in unchanging archetypes to a dynamic, evolving cosmogenic worldview based on populations and individuals. While the process or evolutionary worldview may have gained dominance in Western cultures and religious traditions, the influences felt by such groups as the Moral Majority and religious New Right in the United States, the rise of Islamic fundamentalism in Iran and the Near East, and the growing vitality of orthodox Judaism provide ample evidence that the fixed worldview still has clear influence in moderating human behavior.

These two worldviews characteristically permeate and color the way we look at and see everything in our lives. One or the other view colors the way each of us approaches a particular political, economic, or moral issue, as well as the way we reach decisions about sexual issues and relationships. However, one must keep in mind that no one is ever fully and always on one or the other end of the spectrum. The spectrum of beliefs, attitudes, and values proposed here is an intellectual abstraction. Real life is not that simple. Still, it is a useful model that can help us to understand each other's positions on controversial issues provided we realize that the fixed and process worldviews are at the two ends of a continuum that includes a wide range of approaches to moral and sexual issues. While individuals often take a fixed position on one issue and a process position on a second issue, they generally tend to adopt one or the other approach and maintain a fairly consistent set of intertwined religious values and attitudes with respect to sexuality.

Either we view the world as a completely finished universe in which human nature was perfectly and completely created by some supreme being, unchanging in essence from the beginning, or we view the world as continually changing with human nature constantly evolving as it struggles to reach its fuller potential, or what is called "to become by the deity." Either one believes that the first human beings were created by God as unchanging archetypes, thus determining standards of human behavior for all time, including our fixed roles as males and females, or one believes that human nature, behavior, and moral standards have been evolving since the beginning of the human race. In the former view, a supreme being created an unchanging human nature. In the latter view, the deity created human nature, then let it transform under human influences.

Coming out of these two views of the world and human nature, one finds two distinct views of the origins of evil and sexuality. If one believes that human nature and the nature of sexual relations were established in the beginning, then one also finds it congenial to believe that evil results from some original sin, a primeval fall of the first humans from a state of perfection and grace. If, on the other hand, one believes in an evolving human nature, then physical and moral evils are viewed as inevitable, natural growth pains that come as humans struggle toward the fullness of their creation.

Facing Some Clashing Views of Controversial Issues in Human Sexuality

As you plunge into the nineteen controversial issues selected for this volume, try to be sensitive to the kinds of ethnic, religious, social, economic, and other factors that may be influencing the position a particular author takes on an issue. Understanding the roots that support a person's overt position on an issue will help you to decide whether or not you agree with that position. Understanding these same factors in your own thinking will help you to articulate more clearly and convincingly your own values and decisions.

Note

1. Details of the perspectives offered in this introductory essay can be found in the author's chapter "Religious Reactions to Alternative Lifestyles," in E. D. Macklin and R. H. Rubin, eds., *Contemporary Families and Alternative Lifestyles: A Handbook on Research and Theory* (Sage Publications, 1983). That chapter summarizes and gives a complete comparison of seven models developed by researchers working independently in quite distinct disciplines. Included are a behavioral model based on a comparison of chimpanzee, baboon, and human social behavior by the British primatologist Michael Chance; a cultural/moral model based on an

analysis of British and French arts, fashions, politics, lifestyles, and social struc-tures proposed by British science writer and philosopher Gordon Rattray Taylor; a cross-cultural comparison based on child-rearing nurturance patterns and adult lifestyles by neuropsychologist James W. Prescott; a model relating lifestyles and values with technological and economic structures by economist/engineer Mario Kamenetzky; a model of open and closed marriages created by George and Nena O'Neill, authors of the 1972 best-seller *Open Marriage*; and Robert T. Francoeur's model of "Hot and Cool Sexual Values," which was adapted from an insight by Marshall McLuhan and George B. Leonard.

On the Internet . . .

The Sexuality Information and Education Council of the United States (SIECUS)

The Sexuality Information and Education Council of the United States (SIECUS) is a national, nonprofit organization that is dedicated to affirming that sexuality is a natural and healthy part of life. SIECUS develops, collects, and disseminates information, promotes comprehensive education, and advocates the right of individuals to make responsible sexual choices.

http://www.siecus.org

The Abstinence Clearinghouse

The Abstinence Clearinghouse is a national, nonprofit organization that promotes the practice of sexual abstinence through the distribution of educational materials and by providing speakers on the topic.

http://www.abstinence.net

Rising Daughters Aware

The Rising Daughters Aware Web site is dedicated to the existence of support and culturally sensitive, qualified medical and advocacy assistance for women who are seeking to avoid, or who have already been subjected to, female genital mutilation (FGM).

http://www.fgm.org

RESOLVE: The National Infertility Association

RESOLVE: The National Infertility Association provides information and advocacy related to infertility.

http://www.resolve.org

PART 1

Sexual Health Issues

*S*exuality has been called a "bio-psycho-socio and cultural phenomenon." Humans are sexual beings from birth through death, and
our sexual health is shaped by our physical makeup (biological); our
thoughts, feelings, and perceptions of our sexuality (psychological); and
the way we interact with our environment (sociological and cultural).
This section examines five aspects of human sexuality that are connected
to sexual health from the early years through the adult years. It explores
fundamental questions about the way we understand and experience
our sexuality.

- Should Sexuality Education Be Comprehensive?

- Should Schools Make Condoms Available to Students?

- Does the G-Spot Really Exist?

- Should All Female Circumcision Be Banned?

- Should Health Insurers Be Required to Pay for Infertility
  Treatments?

ISSUE 1

Should Sexuality Education
Be Comprehensive?

YES: Deborah M. Roffman, from "Abstain, Yes. But With Your Eyes Wide Open," *The Washington Post* (September 2, 2001)

NO: Don Feder, from "Devil Is in the Details of Surgeon General's Sex Report," *Insight on the News* (August 6, 2001)

ISSUE SUMMARY

YES: Sexuality educator Deborah M. Roffman expresses support for the surgeon general's report calling for comprehensive sexuality education. Roffman states that young people need to be taught about abstinence as well as other methods to avoid pregnancy and sexually transmitted infections.

NO: Editorialist Don Feder argues that comprehensive sexuality education is not effective, and criticizes the methods used to compile the surgeon general's report, which includes interviews with commercial sex workers.

In the summer of 2001, United States surgeon general David Satcher released a report titled "A Call to Action to Promote Sexual Health and Responsible Sexual Behavior." In his report Satcher called for a comprehensive approach to sexuality education for America's children. Comprehensive sexuality education includes the teaching of abstinence, as well as other methods for preventing unwanted pregnancy and sexually transmitted infections. By contrast, abstinence-only education forbids any discussion of methods other than sexual abstinence. The surgeon general's report clashed with President George W. Bush's own call for $67 million in new federal spending on abstinence-only education, which would be added to the $250 million abstinence-only education funds already allocated by Congress. Bush's administration immediately distanced itself from the report.

The subject of abstinence-only education versus comprehensive sexuality education has been debated for many years and in many past editions of *Taking Sides*. Abstinence-only education proponents are concerned that any message other than "abstain" is confusing to young people. They fear that teaching about other methods for preventing pregnancy and infection gives a mixed message to young people. Many abstinence-only education proponents also believe that sexual behavior outside of marriage is immoral and that young people must be guided strongly to abstain from intercourse until marriage. Abstinence-only education efforts often seek to discredit the reliability of condoms and other methods.

Proponents of comprehensive sexuality education believe that sexuality education should not be limited to discussions of abstinence but should include information about other methods in recognition of the realities young people face. They state that failing to teach about all methods does a disservice to the 70 percent of young people who will have had intercourse by the time they finish high school. Further, proponents indicate that young people who are *currently* abstaining need information for decisions they may make *later.* Young people, on average, become sexually active eight years before they become married.

The United States is unique in its battle over sexuality education, compared to most other developed nations. Most European nations not only embrace comprehensive sexuality education but also integrate it into government-sponsored pregnancy and sexually transmitted infection prevention campaigns. The resulting teen pregnancy rates are substantially lower than those in the United States, despite similar levels of sexual activity.

In the following selections, Deborah M. Roffman comments favorably on the surgeon general's call to action. Roffman states that young people need education that encourages them to reason and take responsibility for their decisions. Don Feder argues that Satcher's conclusions were formed long before the report was developed, as they are congruent with his prior work heading the Centers for Disease Control (CDC). Feder criticizes the report for its methodologies and conclusions about sexuality education.

Deborah M. Roffman

 **YES**

Abstain, Yes. But With Your Eyes Wide Open

As a sexuality educator, I felt my spirits lift in June [2001] when Surgeon General David Satcher issued his "Call to Action" on sexual health. In this groundbreaking report, the nation's chief doctor made the case for a comprehensive approach to sex education in the schools, combining an emphasis on abstinence with information on preventing pregnancy and sexually transmitted diseases. Here at least, I allowed myself to hope, was an event that could stimulate an unprecedented national dialogue on an issue that hits us where it matters most—the lives and health of our children.

Then, within a day, the Bush administration distanced itself from the report, and conservatives began to talk about a replacement for Satcher. The White House made clear that it would aggressively seek to increase funding for public school "abstinence-only" programs, which by statute prohibit discussion of other methods of disease and pregnancy prevention.

And I thought, here we go again.

Welcome to the latest skirmish in the nation's "abstinence wars." This fierce subsidiary of the much touted "culture wars" has stalled realistic and creative policy-making in the field of sex education for more than three decades. Satcher's attempt notwithstanding, it became clear to me that we weren't about to make any progress soon when I received a call asking me to participate in a Baltimore talk-radio program. The topic: "Traditional approaches to sex education vs. the abstinence-until-marriage approach."

No, thanks, I said, as I always do whenever the issue is framed in this way. That's because I believe that pitching comprehensive sex education as the opposite, in fact the enemy, of abstinence is false, misleading and counterproductive, and that as long as we in the United States continue to polarize this issue, we're kidding ourselves if we think we're doing well by our kids.

Despite the fact that more than 80 percent of American adults say they favor a comprehensive approach to sex education, this either/or standoff persists. What is the justification for it? Abstinence-only proponents argue that giving a clear and unequivocal directive is the best and most effective strategy. Adults must insist that refraining from sex until marriage is the only safe and moral course; providing additional information about protection lends unacceptable credibility to any other choice. In any case, they say, the need for such information becomes moot, because kids who abstain will not be putting themselves in a situation where they need protection.

But there's something missing from this argument. Adolescents need clear messages—most definitely—but as my experience over more than 30 years in the classroom has taught me, clarity by itself is never enough. Consider this example. Some time ago, a nationally prominent abstinence-only educator came to the all-girls school where I teach, one that works particularly hard at turning out girls who are skilled critical thinkers. The woman gave the girls unequivocal messages about how damaging premarital intercourse would be in their lives, but her moralizing tone infuriated many of the eighth-graders who heard her presentation. By the time they came to my class, they were ready to kill the messenger—and her messages. Said one student: "There will be girls who go out and 'do it' just to spite her!"

Once I got the girls to settle down and refocus, I was able to reframe the conversation in a manner that felt more respectful. "If you were presenting the abstinence argument, what would you say, and how would you say it?" I asked. From then on, these 13- and 14-year-olds were more than able on their own to articulate and seriously consider all of the points the speaker had been trying to make. "Contraceptives might not work 100 percent," one said, "and a baby would change your whole life." Added another, "Even if you were able to avoid physical effects, we're too young to handle the emotions."

The students even made some excellent points the speaker had not brought up, based on their own life experiences. One, for instance, noted that boys usually aren't as socially mature as girls, and might not want the same things from a relationship. The girl next to her nodded and added, "Besides, if you had to hide things you were doing from your parents, you wouldn't feel good about yourself." I remember driving home that day and thinking to myself: how ironic. I—the supposed "anti-abstinence" lady, because I also talk about contraception and STD [sexually transmitted disease] prevention—had saved the day for the abstinence message!

In truth, the kinds of false polarities that have been set up in the sex education debate only serve the needs of adults. They enable politicians who hold up the pro-abstinence/anti-education banner, for example, to sound noble and moral and to give the appearance that their side is holding down the fort at the entrance to the moral high ground. And this tactic is neither liberal nor conservative, Democratic nor Republican: Federal involvement in promoting abstinence-only education—$250 million in matching funds to the states—was originally signed into law in 1996 on the watch of the Clinton administration.

Regardless of our personal politics, the guidance we deliver our young people must take into account the harsh realities of adolescent sexual health in this country today: Every year, nearly 10 percent of teenage girls become pregnant; teens acquire an estimated 3 million sexually transmitted infections every year; 25 percent of new HIV cases occur in people under the age of 20; 50 percent of all ninth- through 12th-grade students have already had sexual intercourse.

There is no scientific evidence that abstinence-only curricula in schools are effective, either in delaying onset of first intercourse or preventing pregnancy and STDs. On the other hand, multiple studies show that the combination of a strong abstinence message and information about methods of protection does work and therefore makes the most logical sense.

My guess as to why it works is that the underlying message is the developmentally correct one. The message communicated to teenagers is that we adults recognize them as maturing individuals who are learning to take responsibility for themselves, and that we will not treat them as though they lack the ability to reason on their own. We can tell them that we will do our very best to provide appropriate limits and help guide their choices, but we know that we cannot ultimately make all of those choices for them.

This is an approach that adolescents will hear—and buy. We can all remember from our own adolescence how teenagers resist and resent adults who attempt to control their lives, but respect those who set clear limits while showing respect for them and their developing sense of autonomy.

It's ironic, and frightening to me as an educator, that the underlying message in the abstinence-only approach is actually the same as the one young people get from the popular media. The words sound diametrically opposed ("Don't do it!" vs. "Do it now!") but the underlying message is exactly the same: "When it comes to sex, there's nothing for you to think about." In neither case are we training teenagers to do what they must learn to do for themselves: Think. Here's what I aim for in my classrooms: teenagers with lightbulbs over their heads and a look in their eyes that says, "This issue is a lot more complicated than I realized. I'd better think this one through very carefully."

Thinking responsibly and correctly about an issue as complicated as sex is hard. Quite frankly, adults have difficulty thinking through all that it entails themselves, let alone helping kids do so. Too many of us are tempted to hide behind the false argument that talking about abstinence and condoms amounts to sending a mixed message. "Wait!" and "Protect yourself!" are not mixed messages. Both are about protection. If it sounds like a mixed message when it comes out of our mouths, we need to keep fixing it until it's clear.

What I know from listening to thousands of parents over the years is that all of them love their children and want them to become prudent, caring, ethical and fulfilled people. All want their children eventually to embrace their sexuality and learn to enjoy it as a positive life force. And all want their children to understand that sexual behavior, especially sexual intercourse, is extraordinarily powerful, and that only people who are capable of mature, responsible conduct should ever consider engaging in it.

These are immensely important shared values, the enormous and fertile common ground upon which we all stand, even as our areas of disagreement may blind us to it.

Many parents view abstinence as an issue of postponement; they want their children to abstain at least until they are developmentally ready and want schools to help make them ready for that time. Others view abstinence as an end in itself, and sex as something to be reserved for the holy sacrament of marriage; they want assurance that schools will present that, too, as a legitimate and viable option.

But promoting abstinence as the only option is to negate the critical needs of millions of young people, the wishes of the majority of American parents, and the universality of our fundamental hopes and dreams for our children.

Don Feder

 **NO**

Devil Is in the Details of Surgeon General's Sex Report

Along with his predecessor, Joycelyn Elders (the mullah of masturbation education), U.S. Surgeon General David Satcher was appointed by President Clinton. It shows, especially in his new report, *A Call to Action to Promote Sexual Health and Responsible Sexual Behavior.*

There's a telling item buried in a *Washington Post* story on the report's release. In compiling his manifesto, he consulted a variety of sources, the surgeon general disclosed, including those who would "qualify as commercial sex workers."

"Now, wait a minute," I said to Damon Thompson, a Satcher spokesman. "Are you telling me the surgeon general asked prostitutes how to teach our children about sex?" After checking with his boss, Thompson assured me that "commercial sex workers" would indeed include ladies of the night. The lunatics haven't just taken over the asylum; they're franchising the operation!

That was not the most incredible aspect of the report. Besides hookers, Satcher received sage advice from their colleagues at Planned Parenthood, the Alan Guttmacher Institute and the Sex Information and Education Council of the United States. Somehow, he overlooked the Penthouse Forum.

Armed with this input, Satcher concluded there is no "scientific evidence" that teaching abstinence until marriage alone is effective. Consequently, he urged schools to adopt curricula that praise self-control and pass out contraceptives.

Imagine a violence-prevention program where kids are given automatic weapons or courses promoting tolerance where students are lectured by white supremacists and Afrocentrists.

Only in the never-never land of sexual pedagogy is "wait until you're married, but here's a condom in case you have an uncontrollable urge in the meantime" considered anything but self-defeating.

Actually, Satcher isn't telling America's youth to wait until marriage. Any old "mutually monogamous" relationship will do. That's because our surgeon general understands that "marriage is not perfect."

From Don Feder, "Devil Is in the Details of Surgeon General's Sex Report," *Insight on the News*, vol. 17, no. 29 (August 6, 2001). Copyright © 2001 by News World Communications, Inc. Reprinted by permission of *Insight on the News*.

So, instead of asking adolescents to exercise restraint (with a pocketful of condoms) until they say, "I do," Satcher wants them to refrain from getting hot and heavy until they achieve a "mutually monogamous" relationship.

How long is this mutuality to exist before couples hop between the sheets? How is a commitment to exclusivity to be manifested, absent vows exchanged before God and man?

Quite coincidentally, Satcher's report endorses conclusions he long has held. In 1994, when Satcher headed the Centers for Disease Control and Prevention (CDC), the agency ran an $800,000 national advertising campaign aimed at America's youth. One ad helpfully advised: "Latex condoms are available in different sizes, colors and textures. Find one that's right for you." And if you have trouble making a selection, consult your friendly, neighborhood commercial sex worker. That's where the surgeon general goes for advice.

Satcher and the rest of the safe-sex crowd neglect to mention that condoms frequently fail. Leslie Unruh of the National Abstinence Clearinghouse says she attended a conference of sex educators where a speaker asked the audience if they would have sex with the man or woman of their dreams knowing that person had HIV/AIDS using only a condom for protection. In a crowd of several hundred, no one raised a hand.

We've had comprehensive sex education (erotic indoctrination, really) for more than 30 years. Children are given instruction in copulation that is comprehensive by the *Kama Sutra's* standards. They've warned continually of the perils of nasty microbes and unwanted pregnancy and are drilled in contraception. Still, each year, there are 1.4 million abortions and 12 million new cases of sexually transmitted diseases. The out-of-wedlock birthrate is 33 percent. Since this carnal explosion parallels the triumph of sexual instruction, could cause and effect be at work here?

Streetwalkers often cruise urban areas with strip clubs and adult bookstores. Might there be a connection between stimulation and gratification? Perhaps Satcher should consult informed sources in the commercial sex industry. No self-respecting parakeet would want the bottom of his cage lined with the pages of the good doctor's report.

POSTSCRIPT

Should Sexuality Education Be Comprehensive?

A 2000 study by the Kaiser Family Foundation documented overwhelming support for comprehensive sexuality education among American parents. The study, "Sex Education in America: A View From Inside the Nation's Classrooms," revealed that parents thought sexuality education should include:

- How to use condoms (85 percent of parents)
- How to use other forms of contraception (84 percent of parents)
- How to talk about condoms and other methods with partners (88 percent of parents)

Parents also wanted sexuality education to include "real-life" issues, like sexual peer pressure (94%), the emotional consequences of becoming sexually active (94%), abortion (79%), and sexual orientation (76%). The report also indicated that most parents (74%) wanted these issues to be presented in a balanced way that reflects different views in society.

In mid-1997 the National Campaign to Prevent Teen Pregnancy, a private, nonpartisan initiative, found no evidence that abstinence-only education delays sexual activity. The campaign concluded, "Some abstinence programs are probably inadequate, and others probably do a fair amount of good." According to the campaign's research review, there is some evidence that comprehensive sexuality education programs are more helpful to teens than abstinence-only education.

As a contraceptive method, abstinence has been recorded to have a failure rate of 26 percent; that is, of 100 women who begin a given year declaring abstinence as her method, 26 will become pregnant by the end of that year. This statistic led some sexuality educators to comment, "Unfortunately, vows of abstinence break more frequently than condoms do." What do you think of this observation? What skills are needed to make abstinence "work" effectively? How does one define abstinence? Abstinence is often defined *individually*. One person's abstinence definition may exclude any sexual contact or body touching, while another person's definition may exclude vaginal intercourse only. Furthermore, how does a gay or lesbian person handle the message "abstinence until marriage" in a country that forbids gay and lesbian marriages?

Think of the sexuality education that was provided when you attended high school. Was the approach comprehensive, or did it emphasize abstinence as the only option? What characteristics of the program were most or least helpful? How did you or other students respond to the messages given by the educator? What would you change about the formal sexuality education you received? How can sexuality education best meet the needs of young people?

Suggested Readings

P. Brick and B. Taverner, *Positive Images: Teaching Abstinence, Contraception, and Sexual Health,* 3rd ed. (Planned Parenthood of Greater Northern New Jersey, 2001).

R. Brown et al., eds., "Opinions in Pediatric and Adolescent Gynecology: Opinions on Abstinence Programs for Adolescents," *Journal of Pediatric and Adolescent Gynecology* (vol. 9, 1996).

J. R. Diggs, "Support of Sex Ed Challenged by Mass. Doctor: John Diggs Disputes Surgeon General's Report," *The Massachusetts News* (August 2001).

J. J. Frost and J. D. Forrest, "Understanding the Impact of Effective Teenage Pregnancy Prevention Programs," *Family Planning Perspectives* (September 1995).

D. Haffner, "What's Wrong With Abstinence-Only Sexuality Education Programs?" *SIECUS* Report (April 5, 1997).

D. Haffner, "Abstinence-Only Education Isn't Enough: Teens Need a Wide Range of Information," *Insight on the News* (September 1997).

Kaiser Family Foundation, *Sex Education in America: A View From Inside the Nation's Classrooms* (The Henry J. Kaiser Family Foundation, September 2000).

J. F. Keenan, "Talking About Sex: The Surgeon General's Invitation to a Conversation," *America* (August 13, 2001).

T. Lickona, "Where Sex Education Went Wrong," *Educational Leadership* (vol. 51, no. 3, 1993).

J. McIlhaney, " 'Safe Sex' Education Has Failed: It's Time to Give Kids the Good News About Abstinence," *Insight on the News* (September 1997).

K. L. Nelson, "The Conflict Over Sexuality Education: Interviews With Participants on Both Sides of the Debate," *SIECUS Report* (August/ September 1996).

J. Stryker, "Abstinence or Else!" *Nation* (June 16, 1997).

B. D. Whitehead, "The Failure of Sex Education," *Atlantic Monthly* (October 1994).

ISSUE 2

Should Schools Make Condoms Available to Students?

YES: Sally Guttmacher et al., from "Condom Availability in New York City Public High Schools: Relationships to Condom Use and Sexual Behavior," *American Journal of Public Health* (September 1997)

NO: Edwin J. Delattre, from "Condoms and Coercion: The Maturity of Self Determination," *Vital Speeches of the Day* (April 15, 1992)

ISSUE SUMMARY

YES: Researchers Sally Guttmacher et al. maintain that their study of New York City high school students who received both condoms and an HIV/AIDS education program versus Chicago high school students who received only HIV/AIDS education proves that distributing condoms in schools does not increase sexual activity but does result in students using condoms more often when they are sexually active.

NO: Professor of education Edwin J. Delattre rejects the argument that there is a moral obligation to save lives by distributing condoms in schools. He asserts that distributing condoms in schools promotes morally unacceptable casual sexual relationships.

Research shows that nationwide, 70 percent of American high school seniors have engaged in sexual intercourse. In the larger cities and suburbs, the percentage of sexually active students is even higher.

With the highest rate of teenage pregnancy and abortion in North America and Europe, and with young people fast becoming the highest risk group for HIV (human immunodeficiency virus) infection, American parents, educators, and health care professionals have to decide how to deal with these problems. Some advocate teaching abstinence-only sex education and saying nothing about contraceptives and other ways of reducing the risk of contracting sexually transmitted infections (STIs) and HIV infections. Others advocate educating and counseling: "You don't have to be sexually active, but if you are, this is what you can do to protect yourself." Making free condoms available in school takes this one step further. School boards in New York, Baltimore, Chicago, Los Angeles, San Francisco, Philadelphia, Miami, and other cities are convinced that school nurses and school-based health clinics should be allowed to make free condoms available to students, usually without requiring parental notification or permission.

Dr. Alma Rose George, president of the National Medical Association, opposes schools giving condoms to teens without their parents knowing about it. She asserts, "When you give condoms out to teens, you are promoting sexual activity. It's saying that it's all right. We shouldn't make it so easy for them." Faye Wattleton, former president of the Planned Parenthood Federation of America, approves of schools distributing condoms and maintains that requiring the students to obtain written permission from their parents "would be counterproductive and meaningless."

Some detect an overtone of racism in condom availability programs. "When most of the decisions are made, it's by a White majority for schools predominantly Black," says Dolores Grier, noted African American historian and vice chancellor of community relations for the Catholic Archdiocese of New York. "They introduce a lot of Black and Hispanic children to this like they're animals. I consider it racist to give condoms to children." Elijah Mohammed, founder of the Black Nation of Islam, also condemned condom availability programs as racist genocide.

In the following selections, Sally Guttmacher and her colleagues report on their study comparing the sexual activity and condom use of 7,000 students in New York City high schools who received free condoms and 4,000 similar high school students in Chicago who did not have access to condoms at school. Both school systems had similar HIV/AIDS education programs. This study, they maintain, shows that making condoms available in schools does not promote teen sex but does increase condom use by sexually active teens. Edwin J. Delattre opposes condom education because he maintains that it encourages teen sex and does not save lives.

Sally Guttmacher et al.

 **YES**

Condom Availability in New York City Public High Schools

Introduction

Human immunodeficiency virus (HIV) infection is a major threat to the health of adolescents in the United States. Several recent surveys suggest that the majority of today's high school students are sexually active, do not use condoms consistently, and are unaware of their own serostatus, their partners' serostatus, or both. As condoms are the only effective method of preventing HIV transmission among the sexually active, increasing access to condoms and reducing the barriers to condom use may be an effective method for decreasing the risk of HIV transmission among adolescents.

Condoms are readily available at drugstores, but many adolescents may not have the financial resources or self-confidence to purchase them. Although family planning clinics are a cheaper source of condoms, distance and lack of foresight may prevent teens from obtaining them there. School-based condom availability programs reduce financial and psychological barriers and present opportunities for the discussion of condom use and other safer sex practices.

In the few years that school condom availability has become an acceptable public health strategy, more than 400 schools in the United States have implemented such programs. Program variations include differences in where and when condoms are made available, who distributes condoms, who is eligible to receive them, whether counseling is mandatory or voluntary, and the extent of parental involvement. Some of the existing programs are pilot projects that use clinic staff through preexisting school-based clinics, but the majority of schools with condom availability programs do not have school-based clinics. In this [selection] we report on an analysis of data from an evaluation of New York City's systemwide school-based condom availability program.

Condom Availability in New York City

In 1991 the New York City (NYC) Board of Education implemented one of the first non-clinic-based, systemwide school condom availability programs. Each

From Sally Guttmacher, Lisa Lieberman, David Ward, Nick Freudenberg, Alice Radosh, and Don Des Jarlais, "Condom Availability in New York City Public High Schools: Relationships to Condom Use and Sexual Behavior," *American Journal of Public Health*, vol. 87, no. 9 (September 1997). Copyright © 1997 by The American Public Health Association. Reprinted by permission. References omitted.

public high school was mandated to do the following: (1) assemble an HIV/ acquired immunodeficiency syndrome (AIDS) team, composed of the principal, assistant principal, teachers, parents, students, health resource staff, and other interested personnel, to oversee the condom availability program; (2) teach a minimum of six HIV/AIDS lessons in each grade; (3) designate and maintain at least one site at the school as a resource room where condoms and AIDS prevention materials are available; (4) staff this site no less than 10 periods a week and post the hours that the site is open; (5) identify at least one male and one female staff member as condom resource room volunteers and apprise students of the names of these individuals; and (6) arrange for an HIV/AIDS information session for parents.

To receive condoms, students must give their student identification numbers to the condom resource volunteer. The volunteer is not supposed to distribute condoms to students whose parents have notified the school that they do not want their children to be eligible for the program. (Less than 2% of parents citywide have exercised this option.)

Despite the public health advantages of this program, controversy erupted over its initiation. At the heart of the debate were two recurring issues—the fear that the program would increase adolescent sexual activity, and the role of parents vs schools in matters of teen sexuality. While both proponents and opponents of the program held fast to their beliefs, neither could draw upon the support of empirical evidence. After a lengthy struggle, the program was approved by the school board and, in conjunction with expanded AIDS education, condoms were made available. In spite of the appearance of substantial opposition to condom availability, 69% of parents, 89% of students, and 76% of teachers ultimately supported the program.

Methods

A total of 7119 students from 12 randomly selected NYC schools and 5738 students from 10 Chicago schools participated in a cross-sectional survey in the early fall of 1994. The Chicago public school system, a large, unified urban system that, like the NYC system, is ethnically diverse and has a high dropout rate, provides HIV/AIDS education but does not make condoms available to students. The NYC condom availability program was implemented in every public high school before the evaluation began. Thus, the study was a quasi-experimental design with a post hoc–only comparison.

The 12 schools in the NYC sample were randomly selected after all 120 schools in the system were stratified by type of school (comprehensive, vocational, alternative) and socioeconomic status of the student body, as measured by eligibility for free or reduced-price school lunches. Post-sample selection analysis determined that the sample of 12 schools represented the proportions of the student population in the NYC school system with respect to type of school, family income, and borough location. Ten Chicago public high schools were chosen to match the resulting NYC sample of students on relevant demographic characteristics.

In both NYC and Chicago, students completed self-administered questionnaires during required school classes, such as English or physical education. The required classes were randomly selected, using a quota designed to ensure distribution of students across grades 9 through 12. Students had to be in the classroom at the time the survey was conducted to be included in the sample. Trained data collectors administered the survey in both cities. While teachers remained in the classroom, as required by law, they were not involved in the data collection in any way, nor did they observe the responses of individual students.

The survey was designed to measure students' knowledge, attitudes, and self-reported behavior related to sexual activity, condom use, and HIV risk reduction. Demographic comparisons between the NYC sample and all students in the NYC public high school system revealed that the sample did not differ from the systemwide student population on most characteristics. Girls and Latinos, however, were slightly overrepresented in the sample. The NYC data were then weighted to estimate the age, ethnic, and gender distribution of the NYC public high school system; Chicago data were weighted to approximate the resultant NYC sample; and weighted data were used for all subsequent analyses.

Sexual activity was measured by response to the question, "Have you ever had any form of sex? (Mark all that apply.)" Possible answers were (1) oral intercourse (mouth); (2) vaginal intercourse (vagina); (3) anal intercourse (anus); (4) I have "fooled around" but have not had oral, vaginal, or anal intercourse; (5) I have never had sexual intercourse. Pilot tests focused on ensuring that the students who identified themselves as sexually active would include those who had engaged in nonvaginal (i.e., oral or anal) intercourse. Students who marked choices 1, 2, or 3 were considered sexually active for all subsequent analyses. Condom use was explored for those students who reported having had sex within the past 6 months. Condom use was measured by response (yes or no) to the question, "The *last time* you had sexual intercourse (oral, vaginal, or anal), did you or your partner use a condom?"

Responses to several condom-related questions on the survey were correlated with and supported the validity of the question regarding condom use at last intercourse, for both the NYC and Chicago samples....

We compared NYC students with Chicago students on variables related to sexual behavior and condom use, using weighted and unweighted data and controlling for age, gender, ethnicity, and psycho-social factors. Students who were new to their high school system (i.e., students who had been in an NYC or Chicago public high school for less than 1 year) were categorized as "new students." As new students, they were unlikely to have been exposed to their school's HIV/AIDS prevention strategies prior to participating in the survey and thus served as a proxy baseline measure. In an effort to establish a clean baseline, new students in NYC who had obtained a condom at school..., indicating direct exposure to the program, were eliminated from the analyses. (Eliminating these students did not affect any of the subsequent analyses.) Students who had been in an NYC or Chicago public high school for 1 year or more were categorized as "continuing students." Continuing NYC students were then compared with continuing Chicago students.

Multivariate logistic models were used to compare continuing Chicago students with continuing NYC students on condom use at last intercourse, overall sexual activity rates, and other outcome variables. Subgroup analyses were performed to determine the relationship between the program and condom use by gender, ethnic group, and HIV risk status. "High-risk" students were those who reported having had three or more sexual partners within the past 6 months.

For all but the demographic comparisons, logistic regression models were tested on the weighted samples with condom use at last intercourse as the dependent variable. In additional models, sexual behavior, drug use, and HIV risk status were used as the dependent variables. The logistic models controlled for age, gender, ethnicity, age at first intercourse, number of partners, and frequency of sexual intercourse. In addition, the models controlled for a range of other variables that might influence condom use: *salience of HIV/AIDS*, defined as knowing someone who is HIV positive; *self-efficacy*, defined as the degree of confidence students had in their ability to negotiate a series of situations related to sexual activity and condom use . . . ; *assessments of peer risk*, defined as students' perceptions of the proportion of their friends engaging in risky sexual behaviors . . . ; *depression* . . . ; *locus of control*, which measures the extent of control students felt they had over their lives . . . ; and *parental support*, which measures how comfortable students felt talking to their parents about a variety of problems. . . .

Finally, to explore the mechanisms by which condom availability might influence condom use, a series of additional models were tested, to which two predictor variables were added: (1) *use of the condom availability program*, defined as a "yes" response to the question, "In the past 6 months, have you gotten condoms from a teacher or staff person at your school?" and (2) *exposure to HIV/AIDS lessons*, defined as a "yes" response to the question, "In the last semester, were you taught about AIDS/HIV infection in school?" At the time of the survey, only 42% of Chicago students and 53% of NYC students reported having been exposed to the mandatory HIV/AIDS lessons.

For all logistic models, students missing responses on dependent variables were excluded from the analyses. Nonresponses on independent variables showed no correlation with dependent variables and were therefore replaced with appropriate sample means.

Results

. . . The majority of students in the sample were between 15 and 17 years of age. There were slightly more girls than boys. More than a quarter (28%) of the sample were of Hispanic/Latino origin and almost half the sample (47%) were African Americans or Blacks from English-speaking Caribbean countries. These two categories of Blacks are combined because preliminary analyses revealed no differences between the two in sexual activity or other relevant variables.

The two samples were virtually identical with respect to the percentage of students who reported that they had ever had any form of sexual intercourse (new students, 46%; continuing students, 60%). When types of sexual intercourse (vaginal, oral, anal) were compared, the samples were again surprisingly similar. As expected, sexual activity increased with age, and the NYC and Chicago students were remarkably similar in this respect as well as in many other variables related to sexual activity, including age at first intercourse and age of first partner. They were also similar in the percentage of students who reported having had three or more partners in the past 6 months (new students, 23%; continuing students, 19%).

More NYC students than Chicago students (37% vs 25%) ... reported that they knew someone with HIV infection or AIDS. Because the prevalence of HIV/AIDS is noticeably higher in NYC than in Chicago ... students' opportunities for interactions with people with HIV/AIDS are significantly greater in NYC. Despite this difference, students in both cities were equally unlikely to feel vulnerable to HIV infection; 91% of students in both cities said it was "unlikely" or "not at all likely" that they would become infected with HIV in the next 5 years....

In both cities a higher proportion of boys than girls were sexually active and a higher proportion of African-American or Caribbean students than students from other ethnic groups reported having had sex. A slightly higher proportion of NYC Hispanic/Latino students than Chicago Hispanic/Latino students reported having had sex.... These bivariate analyses are descriptive and present only a preliminary view.

...[T]he proportions of new students and continuing students who were sexually active were the same in both NYC and Chicago (47% for new students and 60% for continuing students). For condom use at last intercourse, however, a different pattern emerged. A similar percentage of new students in NYC and Chicago (58% and 60%, respectively) reported using condoms at last intercourse, but among continuing students condom use at last intercourse was significantly higher in NYC.

... [R]eported condom use at last intercourse varied by

- age ..., indicating that older students were less likely to use condoms;
- gender ..., indicating that girls were less likely than boys to use condoms;
- ethnicity ..., indicating that African-American and Caribbean students were more likely than White students to use condoms;
- age at first intercourse ..., indicating that those who became sexually active at a later age were more likely to use condoms;
- number of partners ..., indicating that those who had more partners were more likely to use condoms;
- frequency of sex ..., indicating that those who had sex more frequently were less likely to use condoms;
- self-efficacy ..., indicating that students who felt more confident in their ability to refuse to have sex without a condom were more likely to use condoms;
- peer risk ..., indicating that students who reported having friends who took a variety of HIV-related risks were less likely to use condoms;

- locus of control..., indicating that students who felt they had little control over their lives were less likely to use condoms;
- depression..., indicating that students who were more depressed were less likely to use condoms....

Discussion

We used a variety of analytic strategies to examine the relationship between condom availability and sexual behavior. Clearly, making condoms available at school does not lead to increases in sexual activity. New students (the proxy baseline measure for this study) in New York City had the same sexual activity rates as new students in Chicago. In both cities the rate of increase of sexual activity associated with age was the same. A similar study of Latino adolescents in a community-based condom availability program in Boston also found no effect of condom availability on sexual behavior. Thus, the fear that making condoms available will increase sexual activity, a primary political obstacle to making condoms available to high school students, appears to be unfounded.

Additionally, these results suggest that making condoms available in high schools increases condom use. Notably, the impact of exposure to the program on condom use was significantly greater for those students who reported having had three or more partners in the past 6 months (the higher-risk group).

A range of psychosocial, behavioral, and demographic variables also influence condom use at last intercourse, including depression, self-efficacy, age at first intercourse, and gender. For example, although the NYC program is made available to both male and female students, the multiple determinants of condom use vary between males and females. Thus, logistic models, such as those presented in the Results section, were examined separately for males and females and for higher-risk males and higher-risk females. Exposure to the program continued to make an independent, significant contribution to condom use at last intercourse in each of these subgroups, although the relationships between other explanatory variables and condom use differed between males and females.

The major methodological limitation of this study is that there was no baseline measurement of condom use among NYC public high school students prior to the implementation of the condom availability program. Because the program was systemwide, there could be no random assignment to intervention or comparison groups. Thus the comparison group, by definition, had to be another school system. This raised the question of whether some unexplained differences between NYC and Chicago, rather than the condom availability program itself, might account for any observed differences in condom use. A variety of analytic strategies were used to account for these limitations. No single method or analytic strategy could overcome all the limitations, but as others have suggested, these methodologies used together build a case for the overall results.

Conclusions

Other studies have suggested that HIV education alone appears to have little impact on behavior and that most adolescents do not perceive themselves to be at risk for HIV infection, despite the fact that they are engaging in unprotected sex. Classroom-based programs alone have had limited success in delaying the onset of sexual activity, increasing the use of contraceptives and condoms, and decreasing rates of pregnancy and sexually transmitted disease, while programs that include additional enabling or service provisions have been somewhat more successful. The data presented in this [selection] suggest that making condoms available does not encourage students who have never had sex to become sexually active. In addition, adding condom availability to an HIV/AIDS education program has a significant though modest relationship with condom use, particularly among students with multiple partners, whether through direct use of the program or through other, indirect, means.

School may not be the place to reach adolescents at highest risk for HIV infection, yet the school population does include a substantial proportion of students at high risk; nearly 1 in 10 (8.7%) of all NYC public high school students reported that they had had three or more sexual partners in the past 6 months. In fact, while less than one fifth of sexually active NYC students reported actually getting a condom from school, higher-risk students reported getting a condom from school in significantly higher proportions than lower-risk students. Our findings suggest that school-based condom availability, a low-cost, harmless addition to classroom HIV/AIDS prevention education efforts, merits policy consideration because it can lower the risk of HIV infection and other sexually transmitted diseases for urban teens in the United States.

NO

Edwin J. Delattre

Condoms and Coercion:
The Maturity of Self Determination

We [are] told... by condom distribution advocates that school distribution of condoms is not a moral issue but rather an issue of life and death. We [are] told, by the same people, that we have a moral obligation to do everything in our power, at all times, to save lives. The incoherence—indeed, contradiction—between these claims reflects the failure of condom distribution advocates to perceive the fact that *all* life-and-death issues are morally consequential; that questions of what schools have the right and the duty to do in the interest of their students are irreducibly moral questions; and that *how* schools should endorse and sustain the honorable conduct of personal life is a moral issue of the most basic and profound sort.

The plain fact is that if our only moral duty were to save lives—at whatever cost to other ideals of life—on statistical grounds, we would have to raise the legal age for acquiring a driver's license to at least twenty-five; we would have to reduce interstate highway speed limits to 35 mph or less; we would have to force everyone in America to undergo an annual physical examination; we would have to outlaw foods that contribute to bad health; we would have to prohibit the use of tobacco and advertisements for it, and spend huge resources to enforce those laws; we would have to eliminate rights of privacy in the home in order to minimize the possibility of domestic violence; we would have to establish laws to determine who can safely bear children, and therefore who is allowed to become pregnant; we would have to make AIDS and drug testing mandatory for all citizens at regular intervals; we would have to do away with the rights of suspects to due process in order to eliminate open-air drug marketplaces in our cities; we would have to incarcerate, on a permanent basis, all prostitutes who test HIV positive; we would have to announce publicly the name of every person who tests HIV positive in order to safeguard others from possible exposure through sexual activity. And so on.

Saving lives is not the only moral concern of human beings. The prevention of needless suffering among adults, youths, children, infants and unborn babies; the avoidance of self-inflicted heartache; and the creation of opportunities for fulfilling work and for happiness in an environment of safety and

From Edwin J. Delattre, "Condoms and Coercion: The Maturity of Self Determination," *Vital Speeches of the Day,* vol. 58, no. 13 (April 15, 1992). Copyright © 1992 by Edwin J. Delattre. Reprinted by permission.

justice all merit moral attention as well. And even if saving lives were our only moral concern, there is no reason to believe that distributing condoms in schools is the best way to save lives. Certainly, the distribution of condoms is an unreliable substitute for the creation of a school environment that conveys the unequivocal message that abstinence has greater life-saving power than any piece of latex can have.

Furthermore, even if condoms were the best means of saving lives, there would be no compelling reason for schools rather than parents to distribute condoms; no reason for schools to be implicated in the distribution of condoms when others are willing and eager to do so; no reason for schools to assent to the highly questionable claim that *if* they distribute condoms, they will, in fact, save lives.

We have a duty to make clear to our students ... the implications of sexual involvement with other people who are ignorant of the dangers of sexual transmission of diseases or uncaring about any threat they may pose to the safety of the innocent. Our students need to grasp that if any one of us becomes sexually involved with someone and truly needs a condom or a dental dam because neither we nor the other person knows how much danger of exposure to AIDS that person may be subjecting us to, then we are sleeping with a person who is either staggeringly ignorant of the dangers involved or else is, in principle, willing to kill us. Such a person has not even the decency to wait long enough for informative medical tests to be conducted that would have a chance of disclosing an HIV positive condition; not even the decency to place saving our lives, or anyone else's, above personal gratification. Obviously, if we behave in this way, we, too, are guilty of profound wrongdoing.

This is so inescapably a moral issue—about saving lives—that its omission by condom distribution advocates astounds the imagination. They have said nothing about the kinds of people who are unworthy of romantic love and personal trust, who conceal or ignore the danger they may pose to another's life, even with a condom. These considerations prove yet another fundamental fact of human life: the only things casual about casual sex are its casual indifference to the seriousness of sexual life, its casual dismissal of the need for warranted trust between one individual and another, and its casual disregard and contempt for our personal duty to protect others from harm or death.

We have a duty to explain to students that there is no mystery about discovering and saying what is morally wrong. It is morally wrong to cause needless suffering, and it is morally wrong to be indifferent to the suffering we may cause by our actions. On both counts, sexual promiscuity is conspicuously wrong.

Sexual promiscuity, casual sexual involvement, whether in youth or adulthood, is an affront to all moral seriousness about one's own life and the lives of others. Exposing oneself and others to possible affliction with sexually transmitted diseases is itself morally indefensible, but even where this danger is not present, sexual promiscuity reveals a grave failure of personal character.

A person who is sexually promiscuous inevitably treats other people as mere objects to be *used* for personal gratification, and routinely ignores the possibility of pregnancies that may result in unwanted children whose lot in life will be unfair from the beginning. This is morally wrong; it is an affront to the dignity of human beings, an affront to their right to be treated with concern for their feelings, hopes, and happiness, as well as their safety.

Where promiscuity is shrewdly calculated, it is crudely exploitative and selfish; where promiscuity is impulsive, it is immature and marks a failure of self-control. In either case, promiscuity is incompatible with moral serious-ness, because wherever there is promiscuity, there is necessarily an absence of the emotional and spiritual intimacy that anchor genuine love among hu-man beings, love that is healthfully expressed among morally mature people in nonpromiscuous sexual intimacy.

Those who are sexually promiscuous—or want to become promiscuous by successfully persuading others to gratify their desires—routinely seek to exert peer pressure in favor of sexual indulgence, as surely as drug users seek to im-pose peer pressure in favor of drug and alcohol consumption. Anyone who believes that such persons will not try to overcome resistance to sexual involve-ment by insisting that the school distributes condoms; that the Health Center says condoms increase your safety, or at least make sex "less dangerous"; that sexual activity is *only* a health issue and not a moral issue, and that condoms eliminate the health problem—anyone so naive ignores entirely, or does not know, the practices of seduction, the manipulativeness among people who treat others as objects to be used for their own pleasure, or the coercive power of adverse peer pressure.

We also have a duty to describe to our students the very real dangers of promiscuity even with condoms. According to research conducted by Planned Parenthood, condoms have a vastly greater rate of failure in preventing preg-nancy when used by young unmarried women—36.3 percent—than has been re-ported by condom distribution advocates. The Family Research Council stresses that this figure is probably low where condom failure may involve possible ex-posure to AIDS, since the HIV virus is $1/450$ the size of a sperm and is less than $1/10$ the size of open channels that routinely pass entirely through latex products such as gloves.

The behavior of health professionals with respect to "less dangerous" sex ought to be described to students as well. As reported in the Richmond, Virginia. *Times-Dispatch* ten days ago:

> "Dr. Theresa Crenshaw, a member of the national AIDS Commission and past president of the American Association of Sex Education, Counselors, and Therapists, told a Washington conference of having addressed an inter-national meeting of 800 sexologists: 'Most of them,' she said, 'recommended condoms to their clients and students. I asked them if they had available the partner of their dreams, and knew that person carried the virus, would they have sex, depending on a condom for protection? No one raised their hand. After a long delay, one timid hand surfaced from the back of the room. I told them that it was irresponsible to give advice to others that they would not follow themselves. The point is, putting a mere balloon between a healthy body and a deadly disease is not safe.'" [January 4, 1992, p. A-10]

These reasons of principle and of fact ought to be sufficient to show the hazards. . . . But there is more to the moral dimension of school distribution of condoms, and those who have claimed otherwise deserve a further account with respect to sexual life itself.

In being forced to distribute condoms... to children and adolescents whose emotional and intellectual maturity remain, for the most part, in the balance—we are made to convey to the young the false message that we do not know these things about basic decency, about safety, about the high price of putting everything at risk for instant pleasure. And we are also giving youths whose judgment is still being formed the impression that we do not particularly care about the moral dimensions of sexual life, and that there is no particular reason for them to do so either.

Remember: we have been told... by adults and youths alike that there *is* no moral issue at stake. The acquiescence of the School... in condom distribution tacitly affirms that pronouncement. Their message betrays fidelity to high standards of ethics in education and sensitivity to more comprehensive dimensions of respect for justice, self-control, courage, and regard for persons in the articulation of institutional policy and the conduct of personal life.

Those who have told us that we are not faced with a moral issue transparently lack understanding of the fundamentals of moral maturity and character excellence. Their judgement, shallow as it is, betrays the young to a supposed, but implausible, expediency.

We will be told that all this will be covered by conscientious counseling of youths who request condoms. But, despite the best efforts of our well-intentioned health care professionals, it will not be adequately covered—and it will certainly not be covered for the students, and their former classmates who have dropped out of school, who are subject to peer pressure but never seek condoms themselves.

Condom distribution in the schools, even under the most carefully considered conditions, lends itself to the theme we have heard here: that profound dimensions of moral life, including decent treatment of others, have nothing to do with morality. It is not simply that this position is morally incompetent; it is also cruel in its licensing of peer pressure to become sexually active, peer pressure that can be, and often is, selfish, intolerant, even downright vicious.

The School... has sanctioned such peer pressure and has thereby given approval to forms of behavior and manipulation that cause, among the young, enormous suffering. Condom distribution advocates behave as though they know nothing of human nature and nothing of the unfair pressures to which the young are routinely subjected. The School['s] decision has now implicated us in teaching the young that we, too, are ignorant of these facts of life as they apply in youth.

The reply of condom distribution advocates to my reasoning is predictable. Sexual activity among the young is inevitable, they will say, even natural, and for reasons of birth control, avoidance of unwanted teenage pregnancies and protection from sexually transmitted diseases, including AIDS, it is better that students should use condoms than not. They will insist that the availability of condoms does not increase the likelihood of sexual activity and that, in any case, many students who use the condoms will be selectively active rather than promiscuous.

The counterarguments are equally straightforward. If we teach the young that sexual activity is what we expect of them, at least some of them will come to expect it of themselves. We have no right to exhibit, or to have, such low expectations—especially toward those whose decisions about whether to become sexually active remain in the balance or who hope to live in an environment where restraint is not only respected but genuinely admired.

And for those who *are* sexually promiscuous—for whatever motives—whether they act in this way to aggrandize themselves; or to exert power over others; or to gain prestige, or physical pleasure, or peer approval; whether they are sexually active because of a desperate and doomed hope of securing affection and attention; or from failure to grasp alternatives; or from ignorance of consequences of promiscuity; or from a mistaken belief that intercourse and intimacy are the same—for all of them, if it is better that they should use condoms than not, how does it follow that *we* should give them the condoms *in* the High School?

In logic—and in fact—it does *not* follow. Even if it is true that promiscuity with condoms and dental dams is physically less dangerous than promiscuity without them, this ostensible fact in no way suggests or implies that *we* should be in the business of distributing condoms—as surely as the fact that filtered cigarettes are less harmful than unfiltered ones does not imply that we should be distributing free filtered cigarettes in the... Public Schools. We should instead be standing on the side of peer pressure against casual sex, and we should be providing resolute support for such peer pressure because it is morally right and because it has a distinctive and irreplaceable power to save lives.

Some condom distribution advocates insist that because we now have a health clinic in the High School, we are obliged to defer to the judgment of experts in health care on this subject. They claim that these experts do not try to tell us what we should do as educators, and we should not tell them what to do in matters of health and health-related services.

This artificial and illusory bifurcation of education and health is based on the false premise that what health officials do in the High School contains no educational lessons and teaches nothing about institutional policy or the decent conduct of personal life.

In this particular matter, health experts have clearly attempted to teach the public—including students—that the High School is an appropriate condom distribution site, while dismissing as irrelevant questions of educational mission and duty; and social service agency leaders have advocated that policy by pandering to and proselytizing for the view naively expressed by the students that there are no moral issues implicit in the policy. They have exceeded their competence in questions of morals.

Furthermore, it is well understood by all of us that condoms are fallible. We have not adequately addressed problems of potential legal liability for... the City..., the... Public Schools, and the School Committee. Yet both health professionals and social service personnel have... explicitly dismissed as trivial the prospect of legal liability for our institutions, as though they were qualified not only in matters of ethics but also in matters of law. In both respects, they have acted as educators—miseducators.

In doing so, they have potentially undermined the achievement of healthy levels of self-assertion by students, putting that achievement at risk from dangerous peer pressure. They have likewise jeopardized the achievement of self-respect among students by teaching them that even a questionable expediency is more important than mature judgment, personal restraint, and respect for the well-being of other people.

These are the facts of our present situation. We have been brought to a moment when we are no longer able to do what we ought to do in the High School, but are forced to do what is educationally wrong. We have been driven to this condition by a collection of flawed arguments about educational policy, about ethical life, and about law.

POSTSCRIPT

Should Schools Make Condoms Available to Students?

The debate over whether or not public schools should make free condoms available to students clearly reflects the opposing philosophical and moral positions of *fixed* versus *process* value systems. The fixed worldview places a top priority on opposing all sexual activity outside marriage. A process worldview maintains that sexual abstinence for teens should be encouraged but that teens should also be provided with the knowledge and ways of reducing the health risk when they do decide to engage in sex.

This debate can be political and heated, especially when the teenagers who are affected by any decision on this issue speak for themselves. In St. Clair Shores, Michigan, five high school students were suspended for wearing buttons promoting condom usage. In Seattle, Washington, activists handing out condoms and risk-reduction pamphlets at local high schools were threatened with arrest for public obscenity.

Approximately one-quarter of all Americans who currently have AIDS were infected during their teen years. In some areas, the rate of HIV infection among teens is doubling every 16 to 18 months. One in four sexually active teens has a sexually transmitted infection.

Despite this debate, which began 10 years ago, a growing number of students in high schools expect to have free condoms available in their schools. For these teenagers the question of whether or not free condoms promote promiscuity is misguided and ignores the reality of their high school lives.

Suggested Readings

D. Kirby et al., "The Impact of Condom Distribution in Seattle Schools on Sexual Behavior and Condom Use," *American Journal of Public Health* (February 1999).

P. O'Campo et al., "Distribution Along a Stages-of-Behavioral-Change Continuum for Condom and Contraceptive Use Among Women Accessed in Different Settings," *Journal of Community Health* (February 1999).

L. Richardson, "When Sex Is Just a Matter of Fact: To High School Students, Free Condoms Seem Normal, Not Debatable," *The New York Times* (October 16, 1997), pp. B1, B6.

ISSUE 3

Does the G-Spot Really Exist?

YES: Gary Schubach, from "The G-'Crest' and Female Ejaculation," *Tools and Education for a Better Sex Life,* http://www.doctorg.com/FemaleEjaculation.htm (1997)

NO: Terence M. Hines, from "The G-Spot: A Modern Gynecologic Myth," *American Journal of Obstetrics and Gynecology* (August 2001)

ISSUE SUMMARY

YES: Sexologist Gary Schubach states that the G-spot exists and describes his own research examining the chemical makeup of female ejaculatory fluid. Schubach argues for a better understanding of the G-spot among the medical community so that medical professionals can help women avoid feelings of guilt or shame when they experience ejaculation.

NO: Psychologist Terence M. Hines counters that the widespread acceptance of the G-spot as real goes well beyond the available evidence. Hines maintains that the existence of the G-spot has never been verified by empirical, objective means and that women may have been misinformed about their bodies and their sexuality.

In late 2001 Sexnet, an online discussion community of sexologists, was stirred by the news that the G-spot may not be real. For twenty years most sex researchers, educators, counselors, and therapists had accepted the existence of the G-spot, even while they acknowledged there were many unanswered questions. Female ejaculation has also been accepted as factual, widely documented by the work of Beverly Whipple and others. The article by Terence M. Hines, from which one of the following selections has been excerpted, led to much debate and discussion on Sexnet about a tenet that had been largely unchallenged.

The G-spot is named for Dr. Ernest Gräfenberg, who first described it in a 1950 article in the *International Journal of Sexology.* The term *G-spot* was coined in 1982 by Alice Kahn Ladas, Beverly Whipple, and John D. Perry in "The G-spot and Other Discoveries About Human Sexuality." The G-spot made its way into most modern college sexuality textbooks, described as being located on the anterior wall of the vagina, with its stimulation leading to ejaculation in some women.

Before the work of Ladas, Whipple, and Perry (and the research that followed), the expulsion of fluid during orgasm was believed to be the result of urinary stress incontinence. During the past 20 years concern has abounded among the professional sexological community that this dysfunctional label might lead women to feel shameful about an experience that is intended to be pleasurable—and unrelated to urination. Research in recent years has focused on the chemical consistency of female ejaculatory fluid to determine that the fluid is not urine. This is an important distinction for many women, and their partners, who do not believe themselves to be urinating at the height of orgasm.

In the following selections, Gary Schubach describes the history of the G-spot and the importance of correctly identifying the chemical makeup of the ejaculatory fluid associated with the G-spot. Furthermore, Schubach makes an argument for renaming the G-spot the "G-crest." Hines critically examines research on the G-spot, highlighting the limitations, methodological flaws, and inability of the research to conclusively determine the existence of the G-spot.

Gary Schubach  **YES**

The G-"Crest" and Female Ejaculation

Introduction

The question of the sexual phenomenon known as female ejaculation and whether there exists a female erogenous zone popularly known as the "G spot" have been major areas of continued controversy and debate among sex researchers, gynecologists and sex educators. Perhaps no two sexual issues, including the question of clitoral vs. vaginal orgasms, have created so much public interest.

These subjects are continuing to attract the attention of the public, particularly of women, as well as the so-called experts in human sexuality, because they are biological issues that have significant social ramifications. What would be the potential impact on our collective sexual belief systems (and actual behaviors/activities) if female ejaculation and the existence of the G spot achieved widespread legitimacy?

Since the 1920's the conventional medical establishment has dismissed "female ejaculation" as actually being a condition known as urinary stress incontinence. This condition is considered to be an undesirable bodily dysfunction in which urine is involuntarily expelled from the urethras of women due to physical straining such as might also occur with coughing or sneezing as well as sexual arousal or orgasm. Women have generally considered such expulsions to be a source of personal shame or embarrassment that also frequently elicited disapproval from their sexual partners. Physicians usually attempt to correct the condition, either by the use of Kegel exercises or by surgery.

Furthermore, noted experts in the field of human sexuality such as Alfred Kinsey and Masters and Johnson dismissed female ejaculation as being an "erroneous but widespread concept."[1] Masters and Johnson also argued against the existence of the erogenous zone known as the "Go-spot" and stood steadfastly for the premise that the clitoris alone was responsible for triggering female orgasm.

However, if it should turn out that these experts had underestimated the sexual capabilities of women's bodies by portraying pleasurable sexual activities like female ejaculation as abnormal and/or imagined, it could have a significant effect on women's views of their sexuality. If the new evidence about these expulsions demonstrated that they are natural sexual bodily functions then many women could be free of guilt and shame about expelling fluid during sex.

Other benefits of a public recognition of female ejaculation as a natural event (and the so-called G spot as an erogenous zone, capable of producing orgasm in a woman) could be the creation of additional sexual activities that might not just be a prelude to intercourse but an end unto themselves. It could lead to a broadening of peoples' sensual experiences and their sexual repertoire. New pleasurable behaviors, with no goal other than pleasure from those activities, could be learned with the added benefits that they have very low risk in terms of AIDS, STDs [sexually transmitted diseases] and unwanted pregnancy.

All of these social issues become a backdrop for new evidence I discovered during my doctoral research project that, as a result of advanced and heightened states of sensual/sexual arousal, some women do expel fluid. In the past, the assumption has been that the expulsions originated *either* in the bladder or from the urethral glands and ducts. My study indicated that *both* may be the case in that a small amount of fluid may be released from the urethral glands and ducts in some instances *and* mixed in the urethra with a clear fluid that originates in the bladder.

The Nature of Female Orgasm

For the last 40 years, modern science has generally accepted first Kinsey's and then Masters and Johnson's premise that the clitoris alone was responsible for triggering female orgasm. They saw the creation of an "orgasmic platform" that underwent a buildup of muscle tension and sexual energy what was then released during orgasm."[2]

However, in 1981, Perry and Whipple, two of the co-authors of the book, The G Spot and Other Recent Discoveries About Human Sexuality, presented a theory of a second form of orgasm. This "uterine" orgasm" included the Gräfenberg Spot (presumed to be the female prostate) as its major source of stimulation..."[3]

Singer and Singer then went on, in 1978, to describe a blended orgasm which "combines elements of the previous two kinds... characterized by contractions of the orgasmic platform, but the orgasm is subjectively regraded as *deeper* than a vulval orgasm."[4]

Now there is new evidence from urology textbooks that heightened stimulation during sensual arousal can indeed create an involuntary opening of the bladder sphincter. This involuntary opening can occur from stimulation of either the clitoris, or from stimulation of the pelvic nerve through the upper wall of the vagina, or from both simultaneously.[5] Stimulation of the urethral glands can be accomplished either by manual stimulation or intercourse, utilizing a correct angle of penetration. Stimulation of the G Crest of some women can also be produced by pressing downward from the outside of the body, slightly above the public bone. Other studies indicated that "stimulation of the anterior vaginal wall is clearly not a prerequisite to ejaculation, although the data suggest it may be facilitated by this type of stimulation."[6]

All of this highlights how subjective and personal a woman's experience of orgasm can be. There is much yet to learn about the intricacies of female orgasm, including the emotional and intellectual components. The experience of orgasm for many women is a continuum of experience, not one way or another, correct or incorrect. There can be a blending of different types of orgasmic experiences that are unique to the individual.[7] This point was made over and over in the comments of the female subjects in my study. One woman participant indicated that she had categorized and kept notes on 126 different types of orgasm to date and she is constantly finding new and more subtle variations.

Historical References to Female Ejaculation

Throughout time there have been reports of the expulsion of fluid from the vagina by women during sexual arousal and/or orgasm. There were references to this by historic scientific figures such as Aristotle and Galen, discussing and identifying vaginal expulsions which did not seem to have the appearance or smell of urine and did not stain bed sheets.

There were also many references to vaginal expulsions in classical literature. However, it is impossible to determine whether these passages are simple reporting of what the writer actually saw or a dramatization of popular male sexual fantasies of the times.[8]

The first modern description both of female genitalia and the question of vaginal expulsions came from the 17th century Dutch physician, Regnier De Graaf. He stated: "The urethra is lined internally by a thin membrane. In the lower part, near the outlet of the urinary passage, this membrane is pierced by large ducts, or lucunae, through which pituito-serous matter occasionally discharges in considerable quantities. Between this very thin membrane and the fleshy fibers we have just described there is, along the whole duct of the urethra, a whitish, membranous substance about one finger-breadth thick which completely surrounds the urethral canal . . . the substance could be called quite aptly the female *prostatae* or *corpus glandulosum*, 'glandulous body.' "[9]

De Graaf's description of the "prostate" in women in reference to the glands surrounding the female urethra represented conventional medical thought for almost 200 years. In 1880, Dr. Alexander Skene, professor of gynecology in the Long Island College Hospital in Brooklyn, New York, wrote a paper describing and diagramming various glands and ducts surrounding the female urethra. Modern science then began to refer to them as Skene's glands, a term that is still in use today.

In 1953, Dr. Samuel Berkow, a urologist, came to the conclusion that the tissue of Skene's glands was erectile when stimulated. However, Berkow's primary interest was in urination and he believed that the function of the "erectile tissue" was to pinch off the urethra in order to control urination. He never explored the question of whether it could become erect during sexual activity.[10]

In 1950, the German obstetrician, Ernst Gräfenberg, wrote of observing the expulsion of fluid from the urethra during sexual arousal. "If there is the opportunity to observe the orgasm of such women, one can see that large quantities of a clear, transparent fluid (that) are expelled not from the vulva, but out of the urethra in gushes. At first, I thought that the bladder sphincter has become defective by the intensity of the orgasm. Involuntary expulsion of urine is reported in sex literature. In the cases observed by us, the fluid was examined and it had no urinary character. I am inclined to believe that 'urine' reported to be expelled during female orgasm is not urine, but only secretions of the intraurethral glands correlated with the erotogenic zone along the urethra in the anterior vaginal wall. Moreover, the profuse secretions coming out with the orgasm have no lubricating significance, otherwise they would be produced at the beginning of intercourse and not at the peak of orgasm."[11]

At the same time, the medical and scientific establishment was highly resistant to considering evidence of a cause for female ejaculation other than urinary stress incontinence. Again, they (and presumably their female patients) tended to consider ejaculation as an undesirable bodily dysfunction, generally resulting in the women experiencing guilt and shame. There have also been frequent reports of disapproval and recriminations from sexual partners of women who "ejaculate" that have often led to painful relationship issues and even dissolution of marriages.

At this point, it should be noted that doctors, who may be very knowledgeable in the areas of urology and reproductive biology, have had little training or experience in human sexuality. If a woman patient were to have evidence of an expulsion of fluid during sensual/sexual activity, a doctor would be unlikely to check for sensitivity through the anterior wall of the vagina. Even if the physician were to suspect a possible expulsion from Skene's glands, ethics would prevent most doctors from engaging in an Ob/Gyn exam in which the patients was sexually aroused so as to duplicate the conditions of the expulsions.

In the early 1980s's, there were several studies that concluded that what had been called Skene's glands and/or paraurethral ducts and glands were, in fact, not a vestigial homologue of the male prostate but, instead, a "small, functional organ that produces female prostatic secretion and possesses cells with neuroendocrine function, comparable to the male prostate."[12]

The G "Crest"

The so called G "Spot" is perhaps the most misunderstood area of three seemingly interconnected subjects: female ejaculation, the urethral glands and ducts, and the G "spot."

This term was first introduced to the public at large in the book, *The G Spot and Other Recent Discoveries About Human Sexuality*. It referred to the previously mentioned 1950 article in the *International Journal of Sexology* in which Gräfenberg also wrote about erotic sensitivity along the anterior vaginal wall. Gräfenberg clearly stated that it was his opinion that what he felt through the anterior vaginal wall was erectile tissue.

He stated that during sexual arousal "the female urethra begins to enlarge and can be felt easily. It swells out greatly at the end of orgasm. The most stimulating part is located at the posterior urethra where it arises from the neck of the bladder."[13] Others have noted that the size and development of these tissues will vary greatly from woman to woman and may change during arousal.

The area on the upper wall of the vagina has been popularly but erroneously called the G spot and would be better labeled as the G Crest. It is the popular media that has promulgated the notion of a "spot" on the anterior wall of the vagina itself. The search for a "spot" *on* the anterior wall of the vagina, as opposed to searching for the urethral glands *through* the anterior wall may be contributing to the difficulty of finding the G "spot" and the controversy as to whether it exists at all.

There is great potential value in renaming the G "spot" as the G "Crest." In that terminology, the "G" would be retained, as reference to and as credit to the important work of Gräfenberg. The word "Crest" is also more useful as a description than "spot" because the swollen female urethral glands feel more like a protruding ridge than a spot (thus enabling her partner to locate the area more readily with less confusion) thus lessening some of the confusion there seems to be in finding it. Furthermore, the word "Crest" also invokes an image of rising sensual/sexual pleasure.

There have been studies that have indicated that the stimulation of the "G Crest" by itself may induce an orgasm that feels very pleasurable, although different than a clitoral orgasm. As Gräfenberg previously observed, this may induce an expulsion of fluid through the urethra at orgasm. In 1988, Milan Zaviacic, M.D., Ph.D., head of the Institute of Pathology of the Comenius University in Bratislava, Slovakia, examined and stimulated the "G Crests" of 27 women patients who volunteered for his study. Ten of the 27 women (37%) were induced to have urethral expulsions, with a wide variation in the amount of stimulation required before the expulsion."[14]

The Experiment

I became interested in the controversy about the source and cause of female ejaculation during the course of my doctoral studies. My doctoral research project was an exploratory experiment designed to provide information about some of the key issues in this controversy by collecting precise data during a medical procedure. The procedure I chose involved placing a Foley catheter through the urethra and into the bladder of seven women who reported that they regularly expelled fluid during sensual and/or sexual arousal. The purpose of the catheter was to effectively segregate the bladder from the urethra and collect vaginal expulsions in a controlled, medically supervised environment.

It was an interesting experiment that had been conceived previously by researchers but never actually performed. I was moved to do this research mainly because I was intrigued by the fact that it had never been done before and fortunately I was acquainted with women ejaculators who were potential and willing subjects. Following a considerable amount of time screening and preparing the applicants, I assembled and managed the necessary research team, including medical personnel, and we created a relaxed and comfortable environment that was conducive to the experiment.

After urine specimens were collected from each of the female subjects, they were aroused for a period of at least an hour in whatever manner was preferable to them before the actual insertion of the catheter. The stimulation choices that were utilized were manual self-stimulation, manual stimulation by a partner and/or use of a nonmechanical acrylic device known as a Crystal or G spot wand.

After the subjects indicated that they felt properly stimulated and ready for the ejaculatory demonstration part of the experiment, the catheter was inserted. Their bladders were drained and the collection bag was changed. The bag with the drained fluid was saved for later analysis (of levels of urea and creatinine, the two main ingredients of urine).

Then, with the catheter in place, the subjects were asked to resume their stimulation of choice and achieved what they (and the medical team) considered to be an ejaculatory orgasm. Any method that the woman preferred was acceptable, although intercourse was not possible, due to the presence of the catheter tube. The primary conclusion from the experiment was that, at least for these seven women, all knowledgeable and experienced ejaculators, the vast majority of the fluid expelled unquestionably came from their bladders. Even though their bladders were drained by the catheter, they still expelled from 50 ml to 900 ml of fluid post-drained through the tube and into the catheter bag, the only reasonable conclusion for which seemed to be that the liquid came from a combination of fluid from the walls of the bladder and from new kidney output.

We also noted a consistency of results between our study and the earlier studies that also showed a greatly reduced concentration of urea and creatinine (the primary components of urine). The clear inference was that the expelled fluid is an altered form of urine, meaning that there appears to be a process that goes on during sensual or sexual stimulation and excitement that affects the chemical composition of urine.

Conclusions

The evidence of this experiment is clear and groundbreaking that the vast majority of the fluid expelled by women during sexual arousal originates in the bladder. Furthermore, that fluid, which passes through the urethra, may be "deurinized" liquid from the bladder. Additionally, in some women and at some times, a small discharge may be added from the female equivalent of the prostate gland, medically known as Skene's glands and long thought to be dormant and no longer functional, and which may be neither.

It has not yet been proven for certain whether women can expel at least a small amount of fluid from their urethral (prostate) glands, during a very deep and intense orgasm, but I sense that it is very close to being proven. Past research has indicated that most women have urethral glands and ducts about a third the size of the prostate gland of the average man, so the amount of fluid that might be emitted would naturally be likely to be less.

In my study, having segregated the urethra from the bladder, we observed, at least for our seven subjects, that more than 95% of the fluid expelled during sexual arousal originated in the bladder. However, that fluid contained an average of only 25% of the amounts of urea and creatinine found in the subjects' baseline urine samples. We theorized that it may lose the appearance and smell of urine due to the secretion of the hormone aldosterone during sensual/sexual arousal, causing the re-absorption of sodium and the excretion of potassium by the kidneys.[15] Furthermore, I found research material indicating that an involuntary opening of the bladder sphincter can be triggered with stimulation of either the G Crest or the clitoris or both simultaneously."[16]

Moreover, on five occasions we observed a small milky discharge from the urethra which may mix in the urethra with the fluid from the bladder. So it is possible that the ejaculatory fluid originates not from *either* the bladder *or* the urethral glands, but from *both*.

For the scientific community to keep saying that the fluid originating in the bladder is solely the result of urinary stress incontinence is a vast oversimplification. The same muscles, nerves, sphincters and reflexes may be involved in female ejaculation as in urinary stress incontinence but this is not urination and we do not want to leave women nor their partners with the impression that they are inappropriately urinating during sexual arousal. It should also be noted that, at least in American culture, there are strong negative associations with urination and defecation even though urine, or course, is sterile and not all cultures have the same biases regarding it.

However, if female ejaculation is viewed as natural and pleasurable, then a woman can feel good about her body as well as all fluids that come out of it. She can then experience these expulsions during sexual arousal more positively than in a situation in which these expulsions are considered "dirty," or a malfunction of the bladder, urogenital system or any of its components.

Desmond Heath, a New York psychiatrist, offered an interesting hypothesis on the question of whether all women can ejaculate and, if so, why don't they? Basically, it is his premise that little girls often become excited in their lives and this may result in their dribbling a few drops of urine. He theorizes that this is probably followed by some form of displeasure by their parents or other adults, along with an admonition that this is bad and wrong, possibly accompanied by feelings of shame on the part of the child. Often punishment follows. Subsequently, women learn to keep their pubococcygeal muscles contracted and don't allow the pelvic floor to relax. Later on, when they become sexually active, it is natural that most women find it difficult to feel emotionally safe enough to allow themselves to become aroused sufficiently to ejaculate."[17]

For women, relaxation and emotional safety are crucial in order to become aroused and stimulated enough so that at orgasm they can ejaculate. At such moments a woman might expel voluminous amounts of fluid from a nearly empty bladder, the fluid having only a tinge of the odor, smell or appearance of normal urine. However, for this to happen to women naturally and normally, our society will have to abandon its puritanical ancestry and celebrate this event as a symbol of a woman fully enjoying bodily pleasure.

A New Possibility for Mutual Pleasure

Despite the fact that scientists and sexologists have underestimated the capabilities of women's bodies to experience pleasure, female ejaculation is now beginning to be accepted as a natural and very pleasurable activity. With stimulation of the G Crest, there is another source of pleasure and orgasm available for women. In light of this potentiality, what current sexual activities may need to be reconsidered? Sensual activities such as oral or manual stimulation of the genitals and/or simple caressing (which are now regarded as pleasurable but are relegated to being just "foreplay" or a prelude to intercourse of "real" sex) may provide an orgasm that is easier to facilitate, more intense and more gratifying than is possible with intercourse itself.

In many modern relationships both partners work at full time jobs. By the time they get home from work and take care of family needs, it is often unrealistic to expect that they will have the time or energy for mutually satisfying intercourse. However, their emotional and physical needs might be served by sensual and/or sexual contact that is not simply a precursor to intercourse but is rather a pleasurable end unto itself.

It's a cliché in our society that men are primarily focused on sexual intimacy, while women principally seek emotional intimacy. My experience is that both men and women find sex and sensuality to be pleasurable physical, emotional and even spiritual expressions of their love and caring for each other. Because of male conditioning in our society and the hypersensitivity of the adolescent penis, it has been easier for men to give themselves permission to be sexually aroused. However, for a woman to feel safe enough to become fully aroused, she must feel that she is emotionally as well as physically safe. Once she feels that safety—along with emotional closeness—she is more willing to explore sexual expressions of intimacy.

So where is the common ground? How can men and women be together in ways where men can enjoy physical contact and women can feel safe and comfortable? One new sexual activity that couples could experience might be referred to as a *focalized pleasure ceremony*. This ritual could be pleasurable and, at the same time, an expression of love and caring between loving partners. It would not necessarily have to be enormously time consuming, nor terribly strenuous, so it can be done even when one or both parties are somewhat tired. The activity would not necessarily be a prelude to intercourse, but it is possible that intercourse might follow if that were a mutual decision. This is how the ceremony might proceed...

The male partner could learn to gently explore different areas of the vagina to see where the woman has a strong response. He could then make short excursions away from that area to give it a chance to rest, then return to it for further stimulation. The woman could give him positive feedback on what makes her feel the best as they proceed slowly from one degree of pressure to the next, from one area to another. In this way, the man would know where the woman is most sensitive and discover how best to pleasure her.

Each time the partners engage in a pleasure ceremony, it's important to discover what is really appealing to the woman at that moment. Woman are all different in wondrously unique and varied ways. The same woman may even have different sensitivities within the same lovemaking session. It is important to know how her sensitivities are changing and shifting in small and subtle ways during a period of time.

Men, being achievement and results-oriented, tend to want to find a formula that works and then stay with it. They feel good when they achieve results. Thus, equipped with the knowledge about the G-Crest, men will achieve far better results in lovemaking and sex play if they realize that there are times when women want direct hands-on stimulation more than they want intercourse, just as men themselves sometimes prefer to be orally or manually stimulated to orgasm.

If the man is familiar with several methods of stimulation and several areas in the woman's body where she often feels pleasure then he can go to one of those areas, manually stimulate it and see if it's sensitive at the moment. If it is not, he can go to each of the other areas that were really pleasurable or orgasmic for her in the past until he finds the one that is pleasurable today, right now. Or he can ask her to let him know what area she wants touched and in what way. That way a man can always feel that he has several alternatives to stimulate a woman and to make her feel wonderful. The woman feels appreciated because the man is not focused on only one spot or method while ignoring the others, thinking that exactly the same thing is going to work all the time, based on the erroneous assumption that she always "feels" in the same way.

A full understanding of the potential of female ejaculation and the nature of the G Crest can create a wide range of sensual opportunities, as long as there is no pressure on the woman to perform in any particular way. Not all women ejaculate and even women who are capable of it will not ejaculate every time. The best perspective for a man to hold is "it's all right if you do or don't . . . I just want to give you whatever pleasure you desire." Most of all, it is valuable for the male, as her lover, to look for the different approaches to pleasuring her and the different ways to excite her, so as to express love and caring.

References

1. Masters, W. and Johnson, V. *Human Sexual Response*. Boston: Little, Brown, 1966. pg. 135.
2. Whipple, Beverly, Komisaruk, Barry. "The G spot, orgasm and female ejaculation: Are they related?" *The First International Conference on Orgasm presentation,* February 1991, pg. 230.
3. Perry, John D. and Whipple, Beverly. "Pelvic muscle strength of female ejaculation," *Journal of Sex Research,* 17, 1981, pg. 32.
4. Singer, Josephine and Singer, Irving. "Types of female orgasm," in LoPiccolo, J. & LoPiccolo, L. (Eds.) *Handbook of Sex Therapy.* New York: Plenum Press, 1978, pg. 179.
5. Tanagho, E. A., M.D. and McAninch, J. W., M.D. *Smith's General Urology.* Norwalk, Connecticut: Appleton & Lange, 1995, Table 30-5, pg. 539.

6. Bullough, B., David, M., Whipple, B., Dixon, J., Algeier, E. R. and Drury, K. C. "Subjective reports of female orgasmic expulsion of fluid," *Nurse Practitioner*, March, 1984, pg. 59.

7. Ladas, Alice K., Whipple, Beverly and Perry, John D. *The G Spot and Other Recent Discoveries About Human Sexuality*. New York: Dell Publishing, 1982, pg. 152.

8. Sevely, J. Lowndes and Bennett, J. W. "Concerning female ejaculation and the female prostate," *Journal of Sex Research*, 14: 424–427, 1978, pg. 5.

9. De Graaf, Regnier. (1672) "New treatise concerning the generative organs of women." In *Journal of Reproduction and Fertility*, Supplement No. 17, 77-222. H. B. Jocelyn and B. P. Setchell, eds. Oxford, England: Blackwell Scientific Publications, 1972, pgs. 103–104.

10. Berkow, Samuel G. "The corpus spongeosum of the urethra: its possible role in urinary control and stress incontinence in women," *American Journal of Obstetrics and Gynecology*, 65: 1953, pg. 350.

11. Gräfenberg, Ernst. "The role of urethra in female orgasm," *International Journal of Sexology*, 3: 1950, pg. 147.

12. Zaviacic, M., Whipple, B. "Update on the female prostate and the phenomenon of female ejaculation," *The Journal of Sex Research*, 1993, pg. 149.

13. Gräfenberg, pg. 146.

14. Zaviacic, M., Zaviacicova, A., Holoman, I. K. and Molcan, J., "Female urethral expulsions evoked by local digital stimulation of the G-spot: Differences in the response patterns," *The Journal of Sex Research*, 24: 311–318, 1988, pg. 311.

15. Normal Renal Function, pg. 88, in *Smith's General Urology*. Norwalk, Connecticut: Appleton & Lange, 1995.

16. Tanagho, E. A., M.D. and McAninch, J. W., M.D. *Smith's General Urology*. Norwalk, Connecticut: Appleton & Lange, 1995, Table 30-5, pg. 539.

17. Heath, D. "Female ejaculation: its relationship to disturbances of erotic function," *Medical Hypotheses*, 24(1): 103–106.

 **NO**

The G-Spot: A Modern Gynecologic Myth

The G-spot is an allegedly highly erogenous area on the anterior wall of the human vagina. Since the concept first appeared in a popular book on human sexuality in 1982, the existence of the spot has become widely accepted, especially by the general public. This article reviews the behavioral, biochemical, and anatomic evidence for the reality of the G-spot, which includes claims about the nature of female ejaculation. The evidence is far too weak to support the reality of the G-spot. Specifically, anecdotal observations and case studies made on the basis of a tiny number of subjects are not supported by subsequent anatomic and biochemical studies.

— (Am J Obstet Gynecol 2001; 185: 359–62.)

The term *G-spot* or *Grafenberg spot* refers to a small but allegedly highly sensitive area on the anterior wall of the human vagina, about a third of the way up from the vaginal opening. Stimulation of this spot is said to result in high levels of sexual arousal and powerful orgasms.[1] The term *G-spot* was coined by Addiego et al[2] in 1981 to recognize Dr Ernest Grafenberg who, they said, was the first to propose the existence of such an area in a 1950 paper.[3] The G-spot broke into public consciousness in 1982 with the publication of the popular book on human sexuality "The G Spot and Other Recent Discoveries About Human Sexuality."[1] One survey study[4,11] suggests that the reality of the G-spot is widely accepted at least by professional women. A 192-item questionnaire on sexuality was mailed to "a random sample of 2350 professional women in health-related fields in the United States and Canada."[11] The response rate was 55% with a total of 1289 questionnaires being returned. Of this sample, 84% responded that they "believed that a highly sensitive area exists in the vagina."[4] Most popular books on sexuality take it for granted that the G-spot is real. Even a leading college-level sexuality text[5] uncritically reports that the spot is "located within the anterior (or front) wall of the vagina, about one centimeter from the surface and one-third to one-half the way in from the vaginal opening."

Given the widespread acceptance of the reality of the G-spot, one would expect to find a considerable body of research confirming the existence of such a structure. In fact, such supporting evidence is minimal at best. Two types of evidence have been used to argue for the existence of the G-spot and will be reviewed in turn. The first is behavioral, the second is based on claims of female ejaculation. This issue of female ejaculation is relevant to the G-spot for 2 reasons. First, the two are often considered together in the popular literature with the strong implication that the reality of ejaculation supports the reality of the G-spot. Second, some authors[4] mistake the presence of glands that may produce a female ejaculate with the G-spot, a topic discussed in detail later.

Behavioral Evidence

Ladas, Whipple, and Perry[1] reported anecdotes about women who had powerful orgasms when their G-spot was stimulated. Anecdotes aside, there are only 2 published studies of the effects of specific stimulation of this area. The first study[2] reported a single case of a woman who experienced "deeper" orgasms when her G-spot was stimulated. During one session with the subject during which digital stimulation of the anterior vaginal wall was administered, it was reported that the area "grew approximately 50%."

Two years later, Goldberg et al[6] examined 11 women, both to determine whether they had a G-spot and to examine the nature of any fluid they ejaculated during orgasm. The latter aspect of this article will be discussed later. To determine whether the subjects possessed G-spots, 2 gynecologists examined each subject. Both had been given a 3-hour training session on how to examine for the presence of a G-spot. This training consisted of "a special type of bimanual exam as well as a sexological exam where they palpated the entire vagina in a clockwise fashion." Using this technique, they judged that 4 of the 11 women had G-spots.

Even if a G-spot had been found by using techniques such as those described in a much larger sample, this would still have provided little real evidence for the existence of the spot. Almost any gentle, manual stimulation of any part of the vagina can, under the right circumstances, be sexually arousing, even to the level of orgasm.[7,8] The fact that manual stimulation of the putative G-spot resulted in real sexual arousal in no way demonstrates that the stimulated area is anatomically different from other areas in the vagina. The subjects in these studies knew that researchers were searching for an allegedly sexually sensitive area, as did the individuals who performed the stimulation. Under these conditions, it is highly likely that the demand characteristics of the situation played a major role in the responsiveness of the female subjects.

One might think that Grafenberg's original 1950 paper,[3] which is credited with introducing the concept, would contain significant evidence for the spot. It does not. In that paper, Grafenberg discusses no evidence for a G-spot. Rather, he reports anecdotes about some of his female patients. Some he terms *frigid*. Others, he says, derived sexual pleasure from inserting objects, such as hat pins, into their urethras. Just how later writers (ie., 2) transformed these reports into evidence for a G-spot is unclear.

Grafenberg[3] does make some mention of the innervation of the vagina. He cites Hardenbergh[9] whom, he says, "mentions that nerves have been demonstrated only inside the vagina in the anterior wall, proximate to the head of the clitoris." Hardenbergh does indeed make this statement, but provides no citation. Hardenbergh then goes on to rather dismiss claims of vaginal sensitivity in the course of his discussion of his questionnaire study of female sexual experience, the actual topic of his paper.

Female Ejaculation

The second source of evidence for the existence of a G-spot is the claim that women sometimes ejaculate a non-urine fluid during orgasm. Initially, the relationship between female ejaculation and the G-spot was tenuous and nonanatomic. Grafenberg[3] noted the possible existence of such ejaculation. Ladas, Whipple, and Perry[1] devoted an entire chapter to the topic in their book. The chapter consists largely of anecdotes about ejaculation.

Belzer[10] concluded that "female ejaculation... is theoretically plausible" based on a brief literature review and interview-generated anecdotes. The interviews were conducted by students taking a graduate level course on sexuality. Six students interviewed "about 5" people each, male or female. Included in the interview was a question about female ejaculation. Of the 6 students, each "found at least 1 person who reported that she herself, or, in the case of a male informant, his female partner, had expelled fluid at orgasm." Three of these women were then interviewed at length about their ejaculation, and their comments are included in the paper in some detail. In the questionnaire study[4,11] discussed above, 40% of the respondents reported experiencing ejaculation.

Anecdotal and interview-generated reports such as those noted above are far from adequate to show that the ejaculated fluid is anything other than urine. Such evidence would be provided by chemical analysis of the ejaculated fluid. Addiego et al[2] were the first to perform such a chemical analysis. They obtained samples of urine and ejaculate from 1 female subject. They reported a higher level of prostatic acid phosphatase in the ejaculate than in the urine. Prostatic acid phosphatase is found in high levels in male ejaculate and originates in the prostate which, of course, produces components of the male ejaculate. This evidence could be taken, indirectly, as support for a "female prostate" and, more indirectly, for the G-spot. However, Belzer[12] later noted that the test used was "not entirely specific for acid phosphatase," citing a review to this effect by Stolorow, Hauncher, and Stuver.[13] In another study[6] of the chemical nature of female ejaculate, 11 subjects were studied. All produced preorgasmic urine samples. All then engaged in "some form of non-coital activity resulting in orgasm" and 6 collected some resulting ejaculate. The urine and ejaculate samples did not differ in levels.

Anatomic Considerations

Other researchers have taken a more anatomic approach to the issue of prostate-like components in female ejaculate. If women ejaculate a fluid that is not urine, or has non-urine constituents, it must be coming from someplace other than the bladder. Following Severly and Bennett,[15] Tepper et al[16] suggested that any non-urine female ejaculate would likely come from the female paraurethral glands, also known as Skene's glands or ducts. On anatomic grounds, these glands were considered analogous with the male prostate by Huffman[17] who also provided a detailed anatomic description and notes on the history of anatomic thought on the nature of these glands. If these glands are analogous to the male prostate, it might be expected that their secretions would be similar to those of the prostate. It was this hypothesis that Tepper et al[16] tested.

Eighteen autopsy specimens and 1 surgical specimen were obtained. These were sectioned and examined for immunologic reactions to prostate-specific acid phosphatase and prostate-specific antigen by using a peroxidase-antiperoxidase method. The results showed that "eighty-three percent ($15/18$) of the specimens had glands that stained with antibody to prostate-specific antigen and 67% ($12/18$) with PSAcPh (prostate-specific acid phosphatase)."[16] The authors concluded that "we have clearly demonstrated... that cells of the female paraurethral glands and adjacent urethral mucosa contain antigenic substances identical to those found in the prostate." Heath,[18] commenting separately on this finding, stated that the "homology between male and female prostate was shown."

More recent studies[14] have come to similar conclusions and have confirmed the presence of prostate-specific antigen reactivity in the paraurethral tissues. These studies, using immunohistochemical techniques to look for prostate-specific antigen expression, found the market in the "superficial layer of the female secretory (luminal) cells of the female prostatic glands and membranes of secretory and basal cells and membranes of cells of pseudostratified columnar epithelium of ducts."[14] On the basis of these findings, Zaviacic and Ablin[14] argued for dropping the term *Skene's glands* and replacing it with *female prostate*. Whatever term one favors, these results are in line with a view of female ejaculate in which "evacuation of the female prostate induced by orgasmic contractions of the muscles surrounding the female urethra may account for the increased PSA (prostate-specific antigen) values in urine after orgasm."[14]

It was the results of the study by Pepper et al[16] that led Crooks and Baur,[4] in their aforementioned college sexuality text, to confuse the concept of glands that release something with a sensitive area that would have to have a large number of nerve endings to support the reported heightened sensitivity. Specifically, Crooks and Baur stated that the G-spot consists of a "system of glands (Skene's glands) and ducts that surround the urethra."

If the G-spot does exit, it will certainly be more than a "system of glands and ducts." If an area of tissue is highly sensitive, that sensitivity must be mediated by nerve endings, not ducts. One can ask whether, on embryologic grounds, one would expect to find tissue with nerve endings inside the vagina. Heath[18] seems to have been the first to discuss this issue in light of the topics considered in this article. He criticized Kinsey, Pomeroy, and Martin[19] for stating that the entire vagina originates from the mesoderm, which is "poorly supplied with end organs of touch." Rather, Heath[18] cites Koff's[20] work, which is said to show that the upper 80% of the vagina is of mesodermal origin, but the lower 20% is of ectodermal origin, the ectoderm also giving rise to the skin.

A more modern view of the embryology of the vagina is that the vestibulum, bladder, and urethra are of endodermal origin, whereas the rest of the vagina, and the vulva, are of ectodermal origin.[21] This view leaves open at least the possibility that tissue with nerve endings sufficient for the function of a G-spot could be present in the lower portion of the anterior vaginal wall, where the G-spot is said to be.

There have, of course, been histologic studies of the vagina and surrounding tissue. In 1958, Krantz[22] reviewed the early literature, starting with Tiedman's 1822[23] treatise, and then reported the results of his own microscopic analysis. The various studies Krantz reviewed are difficult to evaluate in terms of the issue at hand because they used various methods and many different species. Krantz himself examined only human tissue. In the vagina itself, what he termed "ganglion cells" were found "along the lateral walls of the vagina adjacent to the vascular supply" that were thought to be "parasympathetic terminal neurons." Regarding the types of nerve cell endings that mediate sensations of touch, pressure, and pain in cutaneous tissue, "no corpuscles were observed in the muscularis tunica propria and epithelial areas" although "a very small number/of fibers/were found to penetrate the tunica propria and occasionally terminate in the epithelium as free nerve endings." As would be expected from their well-known high levels of sensitivity, tissues of the external genitals were rich in the various disks, corpuscles, and nerve endings found in other highly sensitive cutaneous tissue.

No further work on the innervation of the vagina seems to have been done after Krantz[22] until 1995 when Hilliges et al[24] published their results. Anatomic techniques had obviously advanced between 1958 and 1995 and these latter authors used immunohistochemical techniques to search for nerve cells in the vagina. Twenty-four vaginal biopsy specimens, 4 from each of 6 women undergoing operation for "benign gynecological disorders not including the vagina," were obtained. The 4 locations from which biopsy specimens were obtained were the "anterior and posterior fornices, the anterior vaginal wall at the bladder neck level, and the introitus vagina region."

Results generally showed a greater degree of innervation than previously reported by Krantz.[22] There was innervation of the introitus vaginae, with this are showing free nerve endings and a few structures that resembled Merkel's disk. The anterior vaginal wall showed more innervation than the posterior wall, but this was subepithelial, and there was "no evidence for intra-epithelial innervation of this part of the vagina." Such innervation would be expected if a sensitive G-spot existed in the area.

The failure of Hilliges et al[24] to find a richly innervated area on the anterior vaginal wall does not prove that the G-spot does not exist there. The authors did not specifically set out to search for the G-spot and did not sample the entire anterior vaginal wall. Thus, they might have simply missed it. Nonetheless, the existence of such a spot would presume a plexus of nerve fibers, and no trace of such appeared in the results.

Finally, it should be pointed out that the issue of the existence of the G-spot is not just a point of minor anatomic interest. As noted, the G-spot seems to be widely accepted as being real, at least within a sample of American and

Canadian women.[4,11] If the G-spot does not exist, then many women have been seriously misinformed about their bodies and their sexuality. Women who fail to "find" their G-spot, because they fail to respond to stimulation as the G-spot myth suggests that they should, may end up feeling inadequate or abnormal.

Two conclusions emerge from this review. First, the widespread acceptance of the reality of the G-spot goes well beyond the available evidence. It is astonishing that examinations of only 12 women, of whom only 5 "had" G-spots, form the basis for the claim that this anatomic structure exists. Second, on the basis of the existing anatomic studies reviewed above, it seems unlikely that a richly innervated patch of tissue would have gone unnoticed for all these years. Until a thorough and careful histologic investigation of the relevant tissue is undertaken, the G-spot will remain a sort of gynecologic UFO: much searched for, much discussed, but unverified by objective means.

References

1. Ladas AK, Whipple B, Perry JD. *The G spot and other discoveries about human sexuality.* New York: Holt, Rinehart, and Winston; 1982.

2. Addiego F, Belzer EG, Comolli J, Moger W, Perry JD, Whipple B. Female ejaculation: a case study. *J Sex Res 1981;* 17: 1–13.

3. Grafenberg E. The role of the urethra in female orgasm. *Int J Sexology* 1950; 3: 145–8.

4. Davidson JK, Darling CA, Conway-Welch C. The role of the Grafenberg spot and female ejaculation in the female orgasmic response: an empirical analysis. *J Sex Marital Ther 1989;* 15: 102–20.

5. Crooks R, Baur K. *Our sexuality.* 7th ed. Pacific Grove (Calif): Brooks/Cole; 1999.

6. Goldberg DC, Whipple B, Fishkin RE, Waxman H, Fink PJ, Weisberg M. The Grafenberg spot and female ejaculation: a review of initial hypotheses. *J Sex Marital Ther 1983;* 9: 27–37.

7. Alzate H, Londono M. Vaginal erotic sensitivity. *J Sex Marital Ther 1984;* 14: 529–37.

8. Hardenbergh EW. Psychology of the feminine sex experience. *Int J Sexology 1949;* 2: 224–8.

9. Belzer EG. Orgasmic expulsion of females: a review and heuristic inquiry. *J Sex Res 1981;* 17: 1–12.

10. Darling CA, Davidson JK, Conway-Welch G. Female ejaculation: perceived origins, the Grafenberg spot/area, and sexual responsiveness. *Arch Sex Behav 1990;* 19: 29–47.

11. Belzer EG. A review of female ejaculation and the Grafenberg spot. *Women's Health 1984;* 9: 5–16.

12. Stolorow MD, Hauncher JD, Stuver WC. Identification of human seminal acid phosphatase by electrophoresis. *J Assoc Off Anal Chem 1976;* 59: 1352–6.

13. Zaviacic M, Ablin RJ. The female prostate and prostate-specific antigen. Immunohistochemical localization, implications for this prostate marker in women, and reasons for using the term "prostate" in the human female. *Histol Histopathol 2000;* 15: 131–42.

14. Severly JL, Bennett JW. Concerning female ejaculation and the female prostate. *J Sex Res 1978;* 14: 1–20.

15. Tepper SL, Jagirdar J, Heath D, Geller SA. Homology between the female paraurethral (Skene's) glands and the prostate. *Arch Pathol Lab Med 1984;* 108: 423–5.

16. Huffman JW. The detailed anatomy of the paraurethral ducts in the adult human female. *Am J Obstet Gynecol 1948;* 55: 86–101.

17. Heath D. An investigation into the origins of a copious vaginal discharge during intercourse: "enough to wet the bed"—that "is not urine." *J Sex Res 1984;* 108: 423–5.

18. Kinsey AC, Pomeroy WB, Martin CE. *Sexual behavior in the human female.* Philadelphia: WB Saunders; 1948.

19. Koff AK. Development of the vagina in the human fetus. *Contrib Embryol 1933;* 24: 59–90.

20. Westrom LV, Willen R. Vestibular nerve fiber proliferation in vulvar vestibulitis syndrome. *Obstet Gynecol 1998;* 91: 572–6.

21. Krantz K. Innervation of the human vulva and vagina. *Obstet Gynecol 1959;* 12: 382–96. 2fs

22. Tiedman F. *Tabula nervorum utera.* Heidelberg; 1822.

23. Hilliges M, Falconer C, Ekman-Ordeberg G, Johansson O. Innervation of the human vaginal mucosa as revealed by PGP 9.5 immunohistochemistry. *Acta Anat 1995;* 153: 119–26.

POSTSCRIPT

Does the G-Spot Really Exist?

Hines concludes his selection by calling the G-spot a "gynecologic UFO" —something that is much searched for and much discussed but unverified by objective means. What do you think about his assessment? Were you impressed by the apparent lack of empirical evidence? What do you make of two decades worth of sexologists acknowledging the existence of the G-spot, as identified anecdotally in their patients and research subjects and as identified in their practice? Schubach's doctoral research seems to indicate a difference in the chemical composition between urine and female ejaculatory fluid, "deurinized fluid," as he calls it. What is the significance of this finding, and why might women who ejaculate and researchers who study female ejaculation find this important?

Both authors comment on our understanding of the G-spot and female ejaculation as it relates to women's self-esteem. Schubach fears that mislabeling female ejaculation as being related to urination will lead to women feeling shameful in a culture that holds negative views of urine. Furthermore, ignoring the G-spot deprives women of pleasure that is as natural as the rest of their bodies. Hines is equally concerned about women's self-esteem. He believes that a community of sexologists that insists on the existence of the G-spot, despite inconclusive evidence, may result in women feeling badly about their bodies when they *cannot* find the G-spot.

What do you think of Schubach's recommendation to rename the G-spot the "G-crest?" What merits does this recommendation have? How would such a change impact on the current debate or on the women who say that they experience G-spot sensations and ejaculation?

Suggested Readings

- E. Grafenberg, "The Role of the Urethra in Female Orgasm," *International Journal of Sexology* (vol. 3, 1950).

- D. Heath, "An Investigation Into the Origins of a Copious Vaginal Discharge During Intercourse: 'Enough to Wet the Bed,'—That Is 'Not Urine,' " *Journal of Sex Research* (vol. 20, 1984).

- S. Reinberg, "The G-Spot: A Gynecological UFO?" *Reuters Health* (August 29, 2001).

- B. Whipple B. and B. Komisaruk, "The G-Spot, Orgasm, and Female Ejaculation: Are They Related?" *The First International Conference on Orgasm Presentation* (February 1991).

ISSUE 4

Should All Female Circumcision Be Banned?

YES: Loretta M. Kopelman, from "Female Circumcision/Genital Mutilation and Ethical Relativism," *Second Opinion* (October 1994)

NO: P. Masila Mutisya, from "A Symbolic Form of Female Circumcision Should Be Allowed for Those Who Want It," An Original Essay Written for This Volume (November 1997)

ISSUE SUMMARY

YES: Loretta M. Kopelman, a professor of medical humanities, argues that certain moral absolutes apply to all cultures and that these, combined with the many serious health and cultural consequences of female circumcision, require that all forms of female genital mutilation be eliminated.

NO: P. Masila Mutisya, a professor of multicultural education, contends that we should allow the simplest form of female circumcision, nicking the clitoral hood to draw a couple of drops of blood, as part of the rich heritage of rite of passage for newborn and pubertal girls in those cultures with this tradition.

Each year in central and northern Africa and southern Arabia, 4–5 million girls have parts of their external genitals surgically removed in ceremonies intended to honor and welcome the girls into their communities or into womanhood. About 80 million living women had this surgery performed sometime between infancy and puberty in ancient rituals said to promote chastity, religion, group identity, cleanliness, health, family values, and marriage goals. Female circumcision (FC) is deeply embedded in the cultures of many countries, including Ethiopia, Sudan, Somalia, Sierra Leone, Kenya, Tanzania, Chad, Gambia, Liberia, Mali, Senegal, Eritrea, Ivory Coast, Upper Volta, Mauritania, Nigeria, and Egypt.

Opponents of FC call it female genital mutilation (FGM) because the usual ways of performing FC frequently cause serious health problems, such as hemorrhaging, urinary and pelvic infection, painful intercourse (for both partners), infertility, delivery complications, and even death. Besides denying women orgasm, the health consequences of FC also strain the overburdened, limited health care systems in the developing nations in which it is practiced.

In Type 1 FC, the simplest form, the clitoral hood is pricked or removed. Type 1 FC should not preclude orgasms in later life, but it can when performed on the tiny genitals of infants with the pins, scissors, and knives that traditional practitioners commonly use. In Type 2 (intermediate) FC, the clitoris and most or all of the minor labia are removed. In Type 3 FC, known as pharonic circumcision, or infibulation, the clitoris, minor labia, and parts of the major labia are removed. The vulval wound is stitched closed, leaving only a small opening for passage of urine and menstrual flow. Traditional practitioners often use sharpened or hot stones or unsterilized razors or knives, frequently without anesthesia or antibiotics. Thorns are sometimes used to stitch up the wound, and a twig is often inserted to keep the passage open. Healing can take a month or more. In southern Arabia, Sudan, Somalia, Ethiopia, and other African nations, more than three-quarters of the girls undergo Type 2 or 3 FC.

Impassioned cultural clashes erupt when families migrate from countries where FC is customary to North America and Europe. In their new homes immigrant parents use traditional practitioners or ask local health professionals to perform FC. Some doctors and nurses perform FC for large fees; others do it because they are concerned about the unhygienic techniques of traditional practitioners. In the United Kingdom about 2,000 girls undergo FC each year, even though it is legally considered child abuse. Many international agencies, such as UNICEF, the International Federation of Gynecology and Obstetrics, and the World Health Organization (WHO), openly condemn and try to stop FC. France, Canada, and the United Kingdom have banned FC; the American Medical Association has denounced it; and the U.S. Congress has made all FC illegal.

The question discussed here is whether or not the traditional pluralism and openness of American culture can make some accommodation that would allow thousands of immigrants to maintain the essence of their ancient, traditional rites of passage for young girls in some symbolic way. Some commentators argue that we should prohibit Types 2 and 3 circumcision for health reasons but allow some symbolic ritual nicking of the clitoral hood as a major element in the extensive ceremonies and educational rites of passage that surround a girl's birth into her family and community or her passage to womanhood in these African and Arabic cultures. In the following selections, Loretta M. Kopelman advocates a ban on all female circumcision. P. Masila Mutisya advocates allowing a symbolic female circumcision, similar to the removal of the male foreskin (prepuce), with modern medical safeguards.

Loretta M. Kopelman

Female Circumcision/Genital Mutilation and Ethical Relativism

Reasons Given for Female Circumcision/Genital Mutilation

According to four independent series of studies conducted by investigators from countries where female circumcision is widely practiced (El Dareer 1982; Ntiri 1993; Koso-Thomas 1987; Abdalla 1982), the primary reasons given for performing this ritual surgery are that it (1) meets a religious requirement, (2) preserves group identity, (3) helps to maintain cleanliness and health, (4) preserves virginity and family honor and prevents immorality, and (5) furthers marriage goals including greater sexual pleasure for men.

El Dareer conducted her studies in the Sudan, Dr. Olayinka Koso-Thomas in and around Sierra Leone, and Raquiya Haji Dualeh Abdalla and Daphne Williams Ntiri in Somalia. They argue that the reasons for continuing this practice in their respective countries float on a sea of false beliefs, beliefs that thrive because of a lack of education and open discussion about reproduction and sexuality. Insofar as intercultural methods for evaluating factual and logical statements exist, people from other cultures should at least be able to understand these inconsistencies or mistaken factual beliefs and use them as basis for making some judgments having intercultural *moral* authority.

First, according to these studies the main reason given for performing female circumcision/genital mutilation is that it is regarded as a religious requirement. Most of the people practicing this ritual are Muslims, but it is not a practice required by the Koran (El Dareer 1982; Ntiri 1993). El Dareer writes: "Circumcision of women is not explicitly enjoined in the Koran, but there are two implicit sayings of the Prophet Mohammed: 'Circumcision is an ordinance in men and an embellishment in women' and, reportedly Mohammed said to Om Attiya, a woman who circumcised girls in El Medina, 'Do not go deep. It is more illuminating to the face and more enjoyable to the husband.' Another version says, 'Reduce but do not destroy. This is enjoyable to the woman and preferable to the man.' But there is nothing in the Koran to suggest that the Prophet commanded that women be circumcised. He advised that it was

From Loretta M. Kopelman, "Female Circumcision/Genital Mutilation and Ethical Relativism," *Second Opinion,* vol. 20, no. 2 (October 1994). Copyright © 1994 by The Park Ridge Center for the Study of Health, Faith, and Ethics, 211 East Ontario, Suite 800, Chicago, IL 60611. Reprinted by permission. Notes and references omitted.

important to both sexes that very little should be taken" (1992:72). Female circumcision/genital mutilation, moreover, is not practiced in the spiritual center of Islam, Saudi Arabia (Calder et al. 1993). Another reason for questioning this as a Muslim practice is that clitoridectomy and infibulation predate Islam, going back to the time of the pharaohs (Abdalla 1982; El Dareer 1992).

Second, many argue that the practice helps to preserve group identity. When Christian colonialists in Kenya introduced laws opposing the practice of female circumcision in the 1930s, African leader Kenyatta expressed a view still popular today: "This operation is still regarded as the very essence of an institution which has enormous educational, social, moral and religious implications, quite apart from the operation itself. For the present, it is impossible for a member of the [Kikuyu] tribe to imagine an initiation without clitoridectomy... the abolition of IRUA [the ritual operation] will destroy the tribal symbol which identifies the age group and prevent the Kikuyu from perpetuating that spirit of collectivism and national solidarity which they have been able to maintain from time immemorial" (Scheper-Hughes 1991:27). In addition, the practice is of social and economic importance to older women who are paid for performing the rituals (El Dareer 1982; Koso-Thomas 1987; Abdalla 1982; Ginsberg 1991).

Drs. Koso-Thomas, El Dareer, and Abdalla agree that people in these countries support female circumcision as a good practice, but only because they do not understand that it is a leading cause of sickness or even death for girls, mothers, and infants, and a major cause of infertility, infection, and maternal-fetal and marital complications. They conclude that these facts are not confronted because these societies do not speak openly of such matters. Abdalla writes, "There is no longer any reason, given the present state of progress in science, to tolerate confusion and ignorance about reproduction and women's sexuality" (1982:2). Female circumcision/genital mutilation is intended to honor women as male circumcision honors men, and members of cultures where the surgery is practiced are shocked by the analogy of clitoridectomy to removal of the penis (El Dareer 1982).

Third, the belief that the practice advances health and hygiene is incompatible with stable data from surveys done in these cultures, where female circumcision/genital mutilation has been linked to mortality or morbidity such as shock, infertility, infections, incontinence, maternal-fetal complications, and protracted labor. The tiny hole generally left for blood and urine to pass is a constant source of infection (El Dareer 1982; Koso-Thomas 1987; Abdalla 1982; Calder et al. 1993; Ntiri 1993). Koso-Thomas writes, "As for cleanliness, the presence of these scars prevents urine and menstrual flow escaping by the normal channels. This may lead to acute retention of urine and menstrual flow, and to a condition known as *hematocolpos*, which is highly detrimental to the health of the girl or woman concerned and causes odors more offensive than any that can occur through the natural secretions" (Koso-Thomas 1987:10). Investigators completing a recent study wrote: "The risk of medical complications after female circumcision is very high as revealed by the present study [of 290 Somali women, conducted in the capital of Mogadishu]. Complications which cause the death of the young girls must be a common occurrence especially in the rural areas.... Dribbling urine incontinence, painful menstruations, haematocolpos and painful intercourse are facts that Somali women have to live with—facts that strongly motivate attempts to change the practice of female circumcision" (Dirie and Lindmark 1992:482).

Fourth, investigators found that circumcision is thought necessary in these cultures to preserve virginity and family honor and to prevent immorality. Type 3 circumcision [in which the clitoris and most or all of the labia minora are removed] is used to keep women from having sexual intercourse before marriage and conceiving illegitimate children. In addition, many believe that Types 2 [in which the clitoris, the labia minora, and parts of the labia majora are removed] and 3 circumcision must be done because uncircumcised women have excessive and uncontrollable sexual drives. El Dareer, however, believes that this view is not consistently held—that women in the Sudan are respected and that Sudanese men would be shocked to apply this sometimes-held cultural view to members of their own families. This reason also seems incompatible with the general view, which investigators found was held by both men and women in these cultures, that sex cannot be pleasant for women (El Dareer 1982; Koso-Thomas 1987; Abdalla 1982). In addition, female circumcision/genital mutilation offers no foolproof way to promote chastity and can even lead to promiscuity because it does not diminish desire or libido even where it makes orgasms impossible (El Dareer 1982). Some women continually seek experiences with new sexual partners because they are left unsatisfied in their sexual encounters (Koso-Thomas 1987). Moreover, some pretend to be virgins by getting stitched up tightly again (El Dareer 1982).

Fifth, interviewers found that people practicing female circumcision/ genital mutilation believe that it furthers marriage goals, including greater sexual pleasure for men. To survive economically, women in these cultures must marry, and they will not be acceptable marriage partners unless they have undergone this ritual surgery (Abdalla 1982; Ntiri 1993). It is a curse, for example, to say that someone is the child of an uncircumcised woman (Koso-Thomas 1987). The widely held belief that infibulation enhances women's beauty and men's sexual pleasure makes it difficult for women who wish to marry to resist this practice (Koso-Thomas 1987; El Dareer 1992). Some men from these cultures, however, report that they enjoy sex more with uncircumcised women (Koso-Thomas 1987). Furthermore, female circumcision/genital mutilation is inconsistent with the established goals of some of these cultures because it is a leading cause of disability and contributes to the high mortality rate among mothers, fetuses, and children. Far from promoting the goals of marriage, it causes difficulty in consummating marriage, infertility, prolonged and obstructed labor, and morbidity and mortality.

Criticisms of Ethical Relativism

Examination of the debate concerning female circumcision suggests several conclusions about the extent to which people from outside a culture can understand or contribute to moral debates within it in a way that has moral force. First, the fact that a culture's moral and religious views are often intertwined with beliefs that are open to rational and empirical evaluation can be a basis of cross-cultural examination and intercultural moral criticism (Bambrough 1979). Defenders of female circumcision/genital mutilation do not claim that this practice is a moral or religious requirement and end the discussion; they are willing to give and defend reasons for their views. For example, advocates of female circumcision/genital mutilation claim that it benefits women's health and well-being. Such claims are open to cross-cultural examination because information is available to determine whether the practice promotes health or cause morbidity or mortality. Beliefs that the practice enhances fertility and promotes health, that women cannot have orgasms, and that allowing the baby's head to touch the clitoris during delivery causes death to the baby are incompatible with stable medical data (Koso-Thomas 1987). Thus an opening is allowed for genuine cross-cultural discussion or criticism of the practice.

Some claims about female circumcision/genital mutilation, however, are not as easily open to cross-cultural understanding. For example, cultures practicing the Type 3 surgery, infibulation, believe that it makes women more beautiful. For those who are not from these cultures, this belief is difficult to understand, especially when surveys show that many women in these cultures, when interviewed, attributed to infibulation their keloid scars, urine retention, pelvic infections, puerperal sepsis, and obstetrical problems (Ntiri 1993; Abdalla 1982). Koso-Thomas writes: "None of the reasons put forward in favor of circumcision have any real scientific or logical basis. It is surprising that aesthetics and the maintenance of cleanliness are advanced as grounds for female circumcision. The scars could hardly be thought of as contributing to beauty. The hardened scar and stump usually seen where the clitoris should be, or in the case of the infibulated vulva, taut skin with an ugly long scar down the middle, present a horrifying picture" (Koso-Thomas 1987:10). Thus not everyone in these cultures believes that these rituals enhance beauty; some find such claims difficult to understand.

Second, the debate over female circumcision/genital mutilation illustrates another difficulty for defenders of this version of ethical relativism concerning the problem of differentiating cultures. People who brought the practice of female circumcision/genital mutilation with them when they moved to another nation still claim to be a distinct cultural group. Some who moved to Britain, for example, resent the interference in their culture represented by laws that condemn the practice as child abuse (Thompson 1989). If ethical relativists are to appeal to cultural approval in making the final determination of what is good or bad, right or wrong, they must tell us how to distinguish one culture from another.

How exactly do we count or separate cultures? A society is not a nation-state, because some social groups have distinctive identities within nations. If we do not define societies as nations, however, how do we distinguish among cultural groups, for example, well enough to say that an action is child abuse in one culture but not in another? Subcultures in nations typically overlap and have many variations. Even if we could count cultural groups well enough to say exactly how to distinguish one culture from another, how and when would this be relevant? How big or old or vital must a culture, subculture, group, or cult be in order to be recognized as a society whose moral distinctions are self-contained and self-justifying?

A related problem is that there can be passionate disagreement, ambivalence, or rapid changes within a culture or group over what is approved or disapproved. According to ethical relativism, where there is significant disagreement within a culture there is no way to determine what is right or wrong. But what disagreement is significant? As we saw, some people in these cultures, often those with higher education, strongly disapprove of female circumcision/genital mutilation and work to stop it (El Dareer 1982; Koso-Thomas 1987; Ntiri 1993; Dirie and Lindmark 1992; Abdalla 1982). Are they in the same culture as their friends and relatives who approve of these rituals? It seems more accurate to say that people may belong to various groups that overlap and have many variations. This description, however, makes it difficult for ethical relativism to be regarded as a helpful theory for determining what is right or wrong. To say that something is right when it has cultural approval is useless if we cannot identify the relevant culture. Moreover, even where people agree about the rightness of certain practices, such as these rituals, they can sometimes be inconsistent. For example, in reviewing reasons given within cultures where female circumcision/genital mutilation is practiced, we saw that there was some inconsistency concerning whether women needed this surgery to control their sexual appetites, to make them more beautiful, or to prevent morbidity or mortality. Ethical relativists thus have extraordinary problems offering a useful account of what counts as a culture and establishes cultural approval or disapproval.

Third, despite some clear disagreement such as that over the rightness of female circumcision/genital mutilation, people from different parts of the world share common goals like the desirability of promoting people's health, happiness, opportunities, and cooperation, and the wisdom of stopping war, pollution, oppression, torture, and exploitation. These common goals make us a world community, and using shared methods of reasoning and evaluation, we can discuss how well they are understood or how well they are implemented in different parts of our world community. We can use shared goals to assess whether female circumcision/genital mutilation is more like respect or oppression, more like enhancement or diminishment of opportunities, or more like pleasure or torture. While there are, of course, genuine differences between citizens of the world, it is difficult to comprehend how they could be identified unless we could pick them out against a background of our similarities. Highlighting our differences, however useful for some purposes, should not eclipse the truth that we share many goals and values and are similar enough that we can assess each other's views as rational beings in a way that has moral force. Another way to express this is to say that we should recognize universal human rights or be respectful of each other as persons capable of reasoned discourse.

Fourth, this version of ethical relativism, if consistently held, leads to the abhorrent conclusion that we cannot make intercultural judgments with moral force about societies that start wars, practice torture, or exploit and oppress other groups; as long as these activities are approved in the society that does them, they are allegedly right. Yet the world community believed that it was making a cross-cultural judgment with moral force when it criticized the Communist Chinese government for crushing a pro-democracy student protest rally, the South Africans for upholding apartheid, the Soviets for using psychiatry to suppress dissent, and the Bosnian Serbs for carrying out the siege of Sarajevo. And the judgment was expressed without anyone's ascertaining whether the respective actions had widespread approval in those countries. In each case, representatives from the criticized society usually said something like, "You don't understand why this is morally justified in our culture even if it would not be in your society." If ethical relativism were convincing, these responses ought to be as well.

Relativists who want to defend sound social cross-cultural and moral judgments about the value of freedom and human rights in other cultures seem to have two choices. On the one hand, if they agree that some cross-cultural norms have moral authority, they should also agree that some intercultural judgments about female circumcision/genital mutilation may have moral authority. Some relativists take this route (see, for example, Sherwin 1992), thereby abandoning the version of ethical relativism being criticized herein. On the other hand, if they defend this version of ethical relativism yet make cross-cultural moral judgments about the importance of values like tolerance, group benefit, and the survival of cultures, they will have to admit to an inconsistency in their arguments. For example, anthropologist Scheper-Hughes (1991) advocates tolerance of other cultural value systems; she fails to see that she is saying that tolerance between cultures is *right* and that this is a cross-cultural moral judgment using a moral norm (tolerance). Similarly, relativists who say it is wrong to eliminate rituals that give meaning to other cultures are also inconsistent in making a judgment that presumes to have genuine cross-cultural moral authority. Even the sayings sometimes used by defenders of ethical relativism—such as "When in Rome do as the Romans" (Scheper-Hughes 1991)—mean it is *morally permissible* to adopt all the cultural norms in operation wherever one finds oneself. Thus it is not consistent for defenders of this version of ethical relativism to make intercultural moral judgments about tolerance, group benefit, intersocietal respect, or cultural diversity.

The burden of proof, then, is upon defenders of this version of ethical relativism to show why we cannot do something we think we sometimes do very well, namely, engage in intercultural moral discussion, cooperation, or criticism and give support to people whose welfare or rights are in jeopardy in other cultures. In addition, defenders of ethical relativism need to explain how we can justify the actions of international professional societies that take moral stands in adopting policy. For example, international groups may take moral stands that advocate fighting pandemics, stopping wars, halting oppression, promoting health education, or eliminating poverty, and they seem to have moral authority in some cases. Some might respond that our professional groups are themselves cultures of a sort. But this response raises the . . . problem of how to individuate a culture or society. . . .

Comment

We have sufficient reason, therefore, to conclude that these rituals of female circumcision/genital mutilation are wrong. For me to say they are wrong does not mean that they are disapproved by most people in my culture but wrong for reasons similar to those given by activists within these cultures who are working to stop these practices. They are wrong because the usual forms of the surgery deny women orgasms and because they cause medical complications and even death. It is one thing to say that these practices are wrong and that activists should be supported in their efforts to stop them; it is another matter to determine how to do this effectively. All agree that education may be the most important means to stop these practices. Some activists in these cultures want an immediate ban (Abdalla 1982). Other activists in these cultures encourage Type 1 circumcision (pricking or removing the clitoral hood) in order to "wean" people away from Types 2 and 3 by substitution. Type 1 has the least association with morbidity or mortality and, if there are no complications, does not preclude sexual orgasms in later life. The chance of success through this tactic is more promising and realistic, they hold, than what an outright ban would achieve; and people could continue many of their traditions and rituals of welcome without causing so much harm (El Dareer 1982). Other activists in these countries, such as Raquiya Abdalla, object to equating Type 1 circumcision in the female with male circumcision: "To me and to many others, the aim and results of any form of circumcision of women are quite different from those applying to the circumcision of men" (1982:8). Because of the hazards of even Type 1 circumcision, especially for infants, I agree with the World Health Organization and the American Medical Association that it would be best to stop all forms of ritual genital surgery on women. Bans have proven ineffective: this still-popular practice has been illegal in most countries for many years (Rushwan 1990; Ntiri 1993; El Dareer 1982). Other proposals by activists focus on education, fines, and carefully crafted legislation (El Dareer 1982; Abdalla 1982; Ozumba 1992; Dirie and Lindmark 1992; WHO 1992).

The critique of the reasons given to support female circumcision/genital mutilation in cultures where it is practiced shows us how to enter discussions, disputes, or assessments in ways that can have moral authority. We share common needs, goals, and methods of reasoning and evaluation. Together they enable us to evaluate many claims across cultures and sometimes to regard ourselves as part of a world community with interests in promoting people's health, happiness, empathy, and opportunities as well as desires to stop war, torture, pandemics, pollution, oppression, and injustice. Thus, ethical relativism—the view that to say something is right means it has cultural approval and to say it is wrong means it has cultural disapproval—is implausible as a useful theory, definition, or account of the meaning of moral judgments. The burden of proof therefore falls upon upholders of this version of ethical relativism to show why criticisms of other cultures always lack moral authority. Although many values are culturally determined and we should not impose moral judgments across cultures hastily, we sometimes know enough to condemn practices approved in other cultures. For example, we can understand enough of the debate about female circumcision/genital mutilation to draw some conclusions: it is wrong, oppressive, and not a voluntary practice in the sense that the people doing it comprehend information relevant to their decision. Moreover, it is a ritual, however well-meant, that violates justifiable and universal human rights or values supported in the human community, and we should promote international moral support for advocates working to stop the practice wherever it is carried out.

 **NO**

A Symbolic Form of Female Circumcision Should Be Allowed for Those Who Want It

In recent years, the issue of female circumcision has provoked heated discussion here in the United States and far from its cultural origins in Africa. As controversial as it is, the issue of female circumcision raises a very important point that needs attention across the board when we are dealing with cultural behaviors, traditions, and practices that are brought by immigrants into a foreign culture. Whether we are dealing with a sexual practice like female circumcision, parentally arranged marriages, child marriages, or a non-sexual custom, we must deal clearly with the implications of cross-cultural, intercultural and multicultural education. This need for cross-cultural sensitivity and understanding is fairly obvious from the blanket condemnations of all forms of female circumcision as a brutalization of women, and the parallel silence about its cultural meaning as an important rite of passage for women. There is certainly a lot of ignorance about African cultures among Americans, both in the general population with its vocal feminist advocacy groups as well as among our legislators and health care professionals. There is a real need for better understanding of these rich cultural traditions.

The issue here is not one of cultural relativism, or the lack of it. What I am concerned about is that it is all too easy to misinterpret the symbolism and meaning of a traditional cultural rite. Unless we understand the various forms of female circumcision and its cultural importance as part of a girl's rite of passage to womanhood we run the serious risk of doing more harm than good. Lack of understanding of the values of one culture leads to the imposition of the views and interpretations of the cultural majority on new minorities within a nation. This has often been the case in the United States with the miseducation and misinterpretation of many aspects of African cultures, as well as other cultures in this nation. This in turn leads to conflicts in social and psychological awareness that affect the identities of different people in our multicultural society. People of African descent seem to be more affected by this than others.

Loretta Kopelman's call for the abolition of all forms of female circumcision is a clear example of this cultural imperialism. This misunderstanding is also evident in ongoing discussions of female circumcision on the internet and in various journals.

In her discussion of female circumcision, Kopelman, a professor of medical humanities, attacks the cultural relativism theory. She argues that certain moral absolutes apply across the board to all cultures and that these principles clearly dictate that all forms of female circumcision should be banned regardless of its particular form and its symbolic role as a rite of passage in some African cultures. She maintains that the reasons given to explain why these rituals exist have no validity or value. For her, female circumcision falls in the same category as murder of the innocent and therefore should be totally banned.

I speak as an educator who understands the symbolism of the African rites of passage very well because I am part of one African culture in which this educational rite of passage is practiced. I find no evidence in Kopelman's arguments to indicate that she has any understanding of or appreciation for objective cross-cultural, intercultural, and multicultural interpretations. Her arguments are a classic example of how most westerners, rooted in the cultures of Europe and North America, so easily assume the role of dictating and imposing their morality on non-westerners without offering any viable alternative or accommodation. I think this is a way of saying that the people who have practiced these and other rituals for thousands of years before and after coming in contact with westerners, must abolish their culture and be assimilated into the dominant western Euro-American value and moral system, even though—and this is one of my major arguments—the western Euro-American culture which she seeks to impose on all others has very few if any educational culturally-based rites of passage for their youth. Barring marriage and death rituals, it is practically devoid of all rites of passage.

Most of the traditional education of African boys and girls for adulthood is informal. However, initiation rites, such as female circumcision, can be considered formal because they occur in a public community setting with specific symbolic activities and ceremonies, which differ according to the individual society. In those cultures where female circumcision is practiced, this community-based ritual is a formal recognition that the girl has successfully completed her preparation for womanhood and is ready for marriage. (The examples I cite below are mostly from the Kamba and Gikuyu people and Bantu ethnic groups.)

An African child's education for adulthood is matched with its cognitive development and readiness, and may begin anywhere between ages 4 and 12. Young girls are taught the skills of a woman, learning to cook, manage a home and handle other chores related to their domestic responsibilities. They are also taught the social importance of these responsibilities in terms of women's role as the pillars of society. They learn respect for their elders and their lineage, how to communicate without being offensive, an appreciation of their tribal or clan laws and their ethnic identity. An African child's education for adult responsibilities includes learning about their sexuality and the taboos of their culture related to sexual relationships. Such taboos include sexual abstinence until marriage and ways of dealing with temptations. Girls learn who they should and should not marry, how to make love to a man while enjoying themselves, how to avoid pregnancy because there are terrible consequences if one becomes pregnant before marriage, and also how to avoid divorce for irresponsible reasons. In our cultures, grandparents and aunts are usually responsible for educating girls for womanhood. Boys are given similar gender appropriate education in their youthful years.

Depending on the particular tribal culture, completion of this educational process is certified by a formal ritual such as female circumcision. Both the educational process and the formal ritual are essential because together they prepare the boy or girl for marriage. Without this education and a declaration of adulthood provided by a formal ritual capping the education, one is not eligible for marriage and is still considered a child.

I strongly disagree with Kopelman's position that *all* forms of female circumcision should be banned. I do agree, however, with her call for a ban on any mutilation and/or infibulation that involves cutting or severing of any part of a female genitalia for whatever reasons given, when this is known to result in any health or fertility complication or disorder whether minor or major.

My proposed solution stems from an understanding of the symbolic function female circumcision plays in the passage of an African girl into womanhood, and the reinforcement this ritual cutting plays in affirming the responsibilities of the African male. Kopelman's argument is based on a total distortion of the vital function female circumcision plays in the education girls from some African traditions need in their transition to womanhood. The reasons Kopelman cites are widely accepted by non-Africans (and some Africans) who do not truly understand or appreciate the depths of African rites of passage. I have provided details on this distortion elsewhere, in an article published in the *Journal of Black Studies* on "Demythologization and Demystification of African Initiation Rites: A Positive and Meaningful Education Aspect Heading for Extinction." In that article I pointed out the stereotypes critics of the African rites of passage use in misinterpreting this practice. Most of the stereotyped arguments do not acknowledge the considerable education that precedes the circumcision ceremony. This education provides an essential base of knowledge for the young woman to make the transition from childhood to adulthood. This education incorporates sex education, discipline, moral foundation, and gender awareness, a rare aspect in the socialization of today's youth in the United States of America.

My argument is that the education that precedes female circumcision enhances the psychological and social aspects that help shape the identity of African womanhood. This will be lost if the ritual is discontinued. These rites of passage provide a foundation of one's entire life which involves the awareness of the rules of the society and philosophy that guides such rules. This foundation provides young women—and men—with the essence of who they are and the framework of what they aspire to be. It provides the young person with confidence, efficacy and self-respect, which enhances the capacity to respect and value others as human beings. After this lesson, it is hard for the young person to take someone else's life or his/her own, a common occurrence in western societies. It is also establishes ownership of property, beginning with the gifts the initiates receive. This leads to developing responsible management skills needed to survive throughout a woman's life. The initiation and the knowledge achieved before and after circumcision give a young woman (or man) a sense of belonging or permanence. Consequently, one is very unlikely to find a young initiate feeling alienated from her or his society as we see in today's societies where children and teens find their identity in joining gangs or cults. Even in Africa today teenage pregnancies and youth violence, which were unheard of in precolonial times, are on the rise. Unfortunately these pregnancies are mostly caused by older men with teenage girls. Before the colonial powers began their campaign against African rites of passage, teen pregnancies were rare because both the teenagers and the older men knew that it was taboo to have sex before marriage and to have children one is not going to be responsible for.

Stereotypical Reasons Given by Kopelman and Others

Kopelman begins her argument for banning all female circumcision by citing several studies conducted by people who come from places where female infibulation and genital mutilation are widely practiced. Using these studies, she lists five reasons she attributes to those seeking to justify this practice: (1) This ritual satisfies a religious requirement, (2) It preserves group identity, (3) It helps maintain cleanliness, (4) It preserves virginity and family honor and prevents immorality, and (5) It furthers marriage goals, including greater sexual pleasure. Invalid as these reasons may be in supporting the morality and acceptability of female circumcision, the problem is that they are common "straw men" arguments set up by opponents of all female circumcision because they are easily refuted. In focusing on these stereotyped and culturally biased reasons, Kopelman and other critics totally ignore and fail to deal with the main purpose of why the circumcision ritual is performed by most Africans.

Of course, anyone who is presented with these five superficial arguments and is not informed about the true core meaning of female circumcision would be easily convinced that the ritual is barbarous and should be stopped immediately. Kopelman fails to point out why this ritual has prevailed for such a long time. Instead, she focuses on the most brutal and inhumane aspects (infibulation and mutilation), which are practiced by just a few African groups. She refers to these groups as Islamic-influenced peoples, even though she admits that among the few people who practice the extreme version, their practice predates the Islamic era. Nor does she explain which particular group of people or pharonic era first practiced these extremes. This careless reference leads people to forget that there are many other forms of the ritual which have the same symbolic meaning but do not involve the extremes of infibulation or clitoridectomy. These practices are performed safely. Some do not even involve circumcision but scarification for the purpose of shedding a little blood, a symbol of courage that is a universal component of male adolescent rites of passage. It is easy for someone like Kopelman not too see the importance of this symbolism, especially when she does not have any similar positive educational experience with which to compare it. Her argument therefore paints with a broad brush on the diversity within the African continent, and her position takes away the very essence of being of most Africans. Also, like other insensitive commentators on African cultures, she fails to point out how the influence of chastity and preservation of virginity for "man's pleasure" has been introduced in both cultural and religious perspectives from outside black Africa. European missionaries and colonialists, preceded by Arabs, followed the same pattern she adopts. Such attitudes have resulted in many Africans abandoning their traditional ways of life. This has created the many identity crises that Africans experience today.

As Africans have adopted attitudes alien to their culture when they interact with the non-Africans who reject and penalize their practice of traditional rites of passage, identity crises have gripped African societies. Examples of such crises are the increase of violence, teen pregnancies, and genocide, which were rare when the rites of passage were in effect. These crises have culminated in the destruction of the base foundation that guides Africans in conceptualizing who they are as human beings. This destruction of traditional cultures and their rites of passage has also resulted in Africans being viewed as objects of exploitation marginal to European culture, and becoming subjects to be acted upon rather than actors of their own way of life, for example, defining who they are as opposed to being defined by others. Kopelman adds wounds to the deep destruction of African cultures that has been imposed on them through miseducation. Like the colonialists before her, she is driven by hegemony in her value system and judgments of other cultures.

A Culturally Sensitive Alternative

In calling for the total abolition of all forms of female circumcision, Kopelman fails to offer any alternative that might be culturally accepted by both African immigrants and those adhering to the dominant Euro-American values of the United States. Instead of suggesting a substitute ritual that would fulfill the main purpose of female circumcision, Kopelman describes all forms of this varied cultural practice, even the most simple and symbolic, as a brutal ritual. She obviously does not think the people who practice this ritual are capable of making adjustments to end the atrocities and sometimes deadly consequences that frequently accompany this rite when practiced in lands where the majority of people have little or no knowledge of sterile techniques or access to modern medical care. She ignores the possibility that an alternative ritual might be accepted by peoples who have practiced female circumcision for centuries.

Let me cite an example of what I mean by a mutually acceptable form of female circumcision that would respect the ancient traditions of some African immigrants and at the same time avoid all the negative consequences of genital mutilation and infibulation. This simple but elegant alternative emerged from discussions between the staff at one American hospital and a group of Somali and other African refugees who have recently settled in Seattle, Washington, clinging to their traditions and insisting that their daughters undergo the ritual of genital cutting.

The staff at Seattle's Harborview Medical Center faced this problem when refugee mothers were asked before delivery if they wanted their baby circumcised if it was a boy. Some mothers responded, "Yes, and also if it is a girl." The hospital, which has a long history of sensitivity to diverse cultures and customs, convened a committee of doctors to discuss what to do about the requests. The hospital staff proposed a compromise, a simple, symbolic cut in the clitoral hood to draw a couple of drops of blood, which could be used in the ritual to bond the girl with the earth, her family and clan. Despite the sensationalized publicity given to the more brutal forms of genital mutilation and infibulation, this symbolic nicking of the clitoral hood to shed a few drops of blood is in fact what most Africans outside Somalia, the Sudan, and Ethiopia do in their female circumcisions.

However, when this suggested alternative became public knowledge, it threw the liberal city of Seattle into turmoil.

Mazurka Ramsey, an Ethiopian immigrant whose San Jose–based group, Forward USA, seeks to eliminate the ritual completely, asked: "How dare it even cross their mind? What the Somali, what the immigrants like me need is an education, not sensitivity to culture." Unlike Ramsey, who is eager to cast off her cultural heritage and adopt American values, other refugee parents continue to press to have their daughters circumcised, even though the Seattle Somali community has essentially agreed that the practice should be ended.

"You cannot take away the rights of families and women," Hersi Mohamed, a Somali elder, said. "As leaders and elders of the community we cannot force a mother to accept the general idea of the community. She can say, 'I want my girl to have letting of blood.'"

Though this is an issue physicians and hospitals across the country are facing with increasing regularity, Harborview is the only hospital so far to discuss the problem openly as a public health issue, rather than treating it simply as an outdated barbaric rite that should be wiped out and totally banned.

A new federal law, in effect since April 1997, sets a prison sentence of up to 5 years for anyone who "circumcises, excises, or infibulates" the genitals of girls under age 18. With some 150,000 females of African origin in the United States having already been cut or facing the possibility of being cut, the compromise suggested by Harborview Hospital makes good sense as an attempt to save girls from the most drastic forms of this ritual.

As the *Chicago Tribune* reported:

> "It would be a small cut to the prepuce, the hood above the clitoris, with no tissue excised, and this would be conducted under local anesthetic for children old enough to understand the procedure and give consent in combination with informed consent of the parents," said Harborview spokeswoman Tina Mankowski.
>
> "We are trying to provide a relatively safe procedure to a population of young women who traditionally have had some horrendous things done to them," she said, but added, "We are not now doing female circumcisions at Harborview, nor are we considering doing female circumcisions."
>
> Whether the proposal would be prohibited by the new law is one of the legal questions being reviewed by the Washington state attorney general.

The hospital's medical director will make no final decision on the proposal until the legal review is completed and a community-wide discussion is held, Mankowski said.

The Seattle area is home to about 3,500 members of a fast-growing Somali community. Some Somali and other African immigrants here have made it clear how deeply ingrained the practice is in their cultural and religious views.

Somali men and women told *The Seattle Times* their daughters would be shamed, dishonored and unmarriageable if they were not cut, an act they believe shows their purity.

They also said that if they could not get it done in the U.S. they would pay the $1,500 fare to fly their daughters to their homeland, where they face the extreme version of the cutting ritual. Some, but not all, of them said a symbolic cut on their daughters would be enough.

Unfortunately, the compromise collapsed when a group of feminists threatened to file a lawsuit charging the hospital staff with violation of the new federal law.

Instead of being creative and flexible like the staff at Harborview Hospital, Kopelman takes a dogmatic culturally-biased stance and calls on us to get rid of a cultural practice that predates European cultures, a custom that provides a foundation for many Africans' cultural identity. In essence, she suggests that Africans should abandon their way of life and become culture-less or ritual-less societies just as American society is. When a culture has no meaningful rites of passage for its youth, the young grow up without a sense of belonging, continuity and permanence, an experience of many youth and adults in both contemporary Africa and present American societies. As a result, psychologists and other mental health professionals are needed to provide a substitute ritual and rite of passage for many youth and adults looking for their identity. This search was unnecessary and rare in traditional African societies because they had meaningful rites of passage. Without a good foundation of identity development based on meaningful traditional rites of passage, many recent young immigrants from Africa try to cope or compensate with facial reconstructions, liposuctions, changing of skin color or bleaching (melanin) destruction, self-hate, bulimia, obesity, suicides and other types of self-abuse. Without rituals to confirm their respect for women, immigrant African males may come to treat women as objects as opposed to equal human beings.

The alternative I propose is a careful interpretation of the meaning of other peoples' cultures and examining them from their own perspective before jumping to judgments. Failure to take this approach only makes the situation worse. I therefore propose an alternative of just nicking the clitoris enough to perform the symbolic rituals. This would be preceded by the most important part, the education of a girl for the responsibilities of womanhood and a full explanation of the importance of the practice. This nicking would of course be done in a sanitized condition by a licensed physician. A careful analysis, as free of cultural bias as possible, should allow the continuation of many rites of passage that are an ancient part of immigrant cultures.

I also suggest that before we make sweeping generalizations about cultural practices, we should try to look into the perspective of the people we are trying to critique. Some practices may be a little difficult to understand, but with a careful, sensitive approach, it may be simpler than one might think. A great way to attempt to understand others is to learn their language as an avenue to a better understanding of the values and philosophical perspective. This is close to "walking in someone else's shoes," the best practice in cross-cultural and inter-cultural awareness.

POSTSCRIPT

Should All Female Circumcision Be Banned?

Sociologists and cultural anthropologists talk about "enculturation" as the process whereby people from one society and culture migrate from their homeland to another place where they have to adjust to a new culture with different values, attitudes, and behaviors.

Enculturation is a two-sided process. The obvious side involves the adjustments that the immigrants must make as they become acquainted with and part of the new society. The immigrants slowly, sometimes painfully, adjust their attitudes, behaviors, and values to accommodate the dominant majority society in which they are one of perhaps many minorities. They also gradually adopt some of the majority values and behaviors, even as they modify their own traditions. Sometimes, to avoid conflict, they may conceal from outsiders some of their more "unusual" attitudes and behaviors—"unusual" meaning unfamiliar to the majority—to avoid being singled out and discriminated against.

The less obvious side of enculturation is the inevitable adjustments that occur among people in the majority culture as they encounter and interact with minority immigrants who are in the process of moving into the mainstream and becoming part of the general culture. The issue of female genital cutting is typical of this process.

In late 1997 a report from Kenya illustrated the advantages of cultural sensitivity and the need to avoid imposing our values on other cultures. This report was published by Maendeleo ya Wanawake, the Kenyan national women's organization, and the Seattle, Washington–based Program for Appropriate Technology in Health, a nonprofit international organization for women's and children's health. They reported that a growing number of rural Kenyan families are turning to a new ritual called *Ntanira na Mugambo,* or "Circumcision Through Words." Developed by several Kenyan and international nongovernmental agencies working together for six years, "Circumcision Through Words" brings young girls together for a week of seclusion during which they learn traditional teachings about their coming roles as women, parents, and adults in the community, as well as more modern messages about personal health, reproductive issues, hygiene, communications skills, self-esteem, and dealing with peer pressure. A community celebration of song, dance, and feasting affirms the girls and their new place in the community.

As more and more immigrants enter the United States and become part of its ethnic and cultural diversity, the challenges of enculturation are likely to become more complex and demanding. Hence the importance of understanding the current debate over female circumcision. Most articles on the subject denounce the practice and call for a complete ban on any form of female circumcision. This side has now been canonized by enactment of the federal ban. As of late 1997 only P. Masila Mutisya has dared to raise the possibility of some kind of accommodation. What do you think of this seemingly one-sided debate?

Suggested Readings

R. Abcaria, "Rite or Wrong: Female Circumcisions Are Still Performed on African Continent," *Fayetteville Observer Times* (June 14, 1993).

A. M. A'Haleem, "Claiming Our Bodies and Our Rights: Exploring Female Circumcision as an Act of Violence," in M. Schuler, ed., *Freedom From Violence: Women's Strategies From Around the World* (Widbooks, 1992).

M. B. Assad, "Female Circumcision in Egypt: Social Implications, Current Research, and Prospects for Change," *Studies in Family Planning* (January 1980).

T. Brune, "Compromise Plan on Circumcision of Girls Gets Little Support," *Chicago Tribune* (October 28, 1996).

E. Dorkenoo, *Cutting the Rose: Female Genital Mutilation—The Practice and Its Prevention* (Minority Rights Group, 1994).

O. Koso-Thomas, *The Circumcision of Women: A Strategy for Eradication* (Zed Books, 1992).

M. Mutisya, "Demythologization and Demystification of African Initiation Rites: A Positive and Meaningful Educational Aspect Heading for Extinction," *Journal of Black Studies* (September 1996).

C. M. Nangoli, *No More Lies About Africa: Here Is the Truth From an African* (African Heritage Publishers, 1986).

Should Health Insurers Be Required to Pay for Infertility Treatments?

YES: Diane D. Aronson, from "Should Health Insurers Be Forced to Pay for Infertility Treatments? Yes," *Insight on the News* (February 8, 1999)

NO: Merrill Matthews, Jr., from "Should Health Insurers Be Forced to Pay for Infertility Treatments? No," *Insight on the News* (February 8, 1999)

ISSUE SUMMARY

YES: Diane D. Aronson, executive director of RESOLVE, the National Infertility Association's consumer-advocacy and patient-support organization, argues that infertility is a disease of the reproductive system that strikes people in all walks of life. She concludes that requiring insurance companies to pay for proven medical treatments for infertility is the right thing to do in a country that places great value on healthy families.

NO: Merrill Matthews, Jr., a medical ethicist and vice president of domestic policy at the National Center for Policy Analysis, maintains that requiring all health insurance plans to pay for infertility treatments could significantly increase insurance costs for everyone.

In 1978, the birth of Louise Joy Brown, the world's first test-tube baby, marked the dawn of high-tech infertility treatments. Only a decade or two ago, reproductive "miracles" made front-page headlines. As we enter the twenty-first century, women are having seven, even eight, babies in one delivery. Infertile couples are paying several thousand dollars for egg donors. A single sperm is microinjected into an egg, which is then implanted in a surrogate mother's uterus. Sisters, mothers, and mothers-in-law serve as surrogates for women who cannot carry a full-term pregnancy. Eggs and sperm, or fertilized eggs, are harvested and inserted in the fallopian tubes of infertile women. Japanese scientists are currently experimenting with an artificial uterus. The possibilities appear unlimited in this brave new world of having babies.

Remedies for infertility can come at a steep price. About 85 percent of infertile couples can eventually have a baby with low-tech treatments that cost under $2,000. For couples under age 35, the average high-tech cost is about $25,000; for older couples, over age 35, the cost rises to an average of $45,000. Achieving a pregnancy with donor sperm can cost about $8,000; donor eggs, $30,000; a surrogate mother, $60,000; and a surrogate mother impregnated with donor eggs, about $90,000. The neonatal costs of the Chukwu octuplets born in Houston, Texas, on December 20, 1998, have been estimated at $2 million. One can add to this base another very conservative $1.6 million in costs to raise these eight infants to age 18.

Compare these costs with a basic fee of $8,000 for adoption, without legal, court, and certificate costs. There is also a waiting period of about a year and a half for adoption. Adopting a child from another country can run about $15,000 for basic costs.

At the same time, the number of reproductive age couples in the United States with infertility problems has been rising, from 8 percent in 1983 to a current 10 percent. One in four couples over age 35 is infertile. These figures are important for this controversial issue. If voters force the states or federal government to require insurance companies to provide coverage for some or all infertility treatments, the average citizen will have to pick up the additional cost. Projecting today's costs ahead five or ten years can be risky for two reasons. First, the number of couples in the high-infertility-rate group, over age 35, is growing rapidly as more and more women and men delay starting a family while they develop their careers and attend college and graduate school. Second, as medical knowledge and skills in treating infertility increase, the success rate increases. Better success rates encourage more couples to try both the low- and high-tech solutions. Better success rates also encourage more physicians to train in this financially rewarding specialization. In the past 20 years, the number of board-certified endocrinologists—one of the specializations in infertility technology—has increased from 100 to 500. Hospitals and clinics update their facilities and pass the costs onto their patients and to the taxpayers.

In the following selections, Diane D. Aronson argues that couples who need medical assistance for infertility should not be denied the opportunity to become pregnant and have children. She observes that legislators and employers are beginning to recognize that helping couples who are struggling to build a much-wanted family is the "right thing to do." Merrill Matthews, Jr., does not object to insurance companies paying for modern medical interventions, which is what most infertile couples need. However, he does object to the costs. He is concerned about the rare but multimillion-dollar cost of high profile cases of multiple births, which whet the appetite for more reproductive technology; the complications that come with different state and federal mandates; and the fairness of applying such mandates.

Diane D. Aronson  **YES**

Should Health Insurers Be Forced to Pay for Infertility Treatments? Yes

W hat is the most important concern in your life? For many people, the answer would be family. If you are a couple with a vision of building a family, the condition of infertility can interrupt this basic human desire. Infertility is a life-changing crisis that affects more than 10 percent of the reproductive-age population in the United States. Having children and raising a family, which comes easily to many couples, can be a heartbreaking challenge for those afflicted with infertility.

Infertility is a disease of the reproductive system which affects both men and women; it is not elective or selective. It strikes people in all walks of life, and it crosses racial, ethnic, religious and socioeconomic boundaries. Couples who experience infertility most often have to pay out of pocket for their diagnoses and treatments. Health-insurance coverage usually either is nonexistent or minimal.

For many couples, only medical treatment can enable them to become pregnant and have children. While adoption is an option for many, the costs can reach $30,000, and there are not enough babies available in the United States to meet the need. Proven medical treatments are available, and insurance coverage should be provided as it is for other diseases. Insurance covers the maternal and neonatal costs for fertile couples who are able to have children. Individuals with infertility pay into the insurance plans that cover those costs, even though they often cannot access care to bear children. Couples who need medical assistance should not be denied the opportunity to become pregnant and have children.

In any given month, a normally fertile couple has a 22 percent chance of becoming pregnant. Nearly two-thirds of couples receiving infertility treatments have successful pregnancies. Most who successfully obtain medical assistance for infertility are able to do so through relatively low-cost ($500 to $2,000) and noninvasive treatments such as medication or intrauterine insemination.

Approximately 5 percent of couples who seek treatment undergo assisted reproductive technology, or ART, such as in vitro fertilization, which costs approximately $12,000 per attempt. When the woman has blocked fallopian tubes or the man has a low sperm count, ART treatment may be the only method by which a couple can become pregnant. Another treatment option is surgery, which usually costs more than ART but often is covered by insurance plans. Because of this coverage, couples may undergo multiple surgical procedures, even if ART would be the best and most cost-effective option. Such partial coverage encourages inefficiency and, at times, incorrect treatment choices. Insurance coverage of the range of treatments would allow for better management of care, as physicians and patients could then better determine the most effective treatment path.

Infertility insurance coverage also would help to manage the rate of multiple births that result from some treatments. The multiple-birth rate among those who obtain infertility treatments is higher than among the general population. The neonatal costs following multiple births are high, as are the health risks to the mother and the babies. (The neonatal costs of the Chukwu octuplet births in Houston on Dec. 20, 1998, are estimated to be more than $2 million.)

When couples are struggling to have a child and do not have insurance coverage, they may be more willing to take risks in treatment that increase their chances of having a pregnancy but also could increase the chances of having a multiple birth. When paying out of pocket, knowing that they will not be able to afford more than a certain number of treatments affects their decisions and their willingness to take risks. Insurance coverage would remove that incentive. Further, insurance coverage would bring about additional oversight and management of care from the insurance company, which could in turn reduce the rate of multiple births. A 1998 study, led by physician David Frankfurter of Beth Israel Deaconess Medical Center in Boston, found that in states with mandated infertility-insurance coverage the average number of embryos transferred in an in vitro fertilization attempt was lower and the multiple-birth rate per attempt was lower than in states without mandates. The study's authors concluded that this lower rate of multiple births may be a result of less pressure from patients to maximize the chance of pregnancy and increased pressure from insurers to minimize the likelihood of multiple births.

Couples who experience infertility ride an emotional roller coaster—from diagnosis through treatment—a very difficult experience. The physical and emotional struggles are further exacerbated when couples face financial hurdles because of a lack of insurance coverage. Alice D. Domar of the Mind/Body Institute at Beth Israel Deaconess Medical Center led a study of women with chronic diseases which found that the psychological effect of experiencing infertility was similar to that of cancer and heart disease. Compounding the emotional distress is the stigma of infertility and the difficulty that many couples have in telling their family and friends.

What is fair when it comes to insurance coverage? The Supreme Court strengthened the arguments in favor of infertility-insurance coverage when it issued a ruling in June 1998 that demonstrated the importance of reproduction and the ability to have children. In *Bragdon vs. Abbott* the high court ruled that reproduction is a major life activity under the Americans with Disabilities Act, or ADA. According to the ADA, an individual is disabled if he or she has a mental or physical impairment that substantially limits one or more major life activities. Therefore, those who are impaired in their ability to reproduce may qualify for protection from discrimination based on that disability. This ruling allows those experiencing infertility to make claims of discrimination when employers specifically exclude infertility treatment from insurance plans. A number of lawsuits have arisen in the wake of that decision.

While Bragdon was not a case involving infertility (the plaintiff was an HIV-positive woman who was denied dental care), lower courts have ruled in cases specific to infertility that it qualifies as a disability under the ADA. In *Bielicki vs. The City of Chicago,* police officers Anita and Vince Bielicki sued the city of Chicago for excluding infertility treatment from their health plans. After the U.S. District Court for the Northern District of Illinois ruled that reproduction is a major life activity and that the Bielickis' lawsuit could go forward, the city decided to settle. Most infertility-treatment costs incurred by employees in the previous 10 years were reimbursed, and city health-insurance plans now include infertility coverage. The precedents set by this case and the Supreme Court ruling, and the prospect of further lawsuits, have brought infertility-insurance coverage to the attention of a growing number of employers and legislators.

William M. Mercer, a benefits consulting firm, published a report in 1997 which disclosed that approximately 25 percent of employers provide some infertility insurance coverage. Another consulting firm, the Segal Co., issued an August 1998 report which found that only 7 percent of employer plans cover infertility treatment, and about 14 percent of plans cover the costs of infertility diagnosis. Most of those plans that cover treatment do not cover all infertility services.

The costs of including infertility coverage in an insurance plan are low. Studies cited by the Mercer report found that the cost of in vitro fertilization coverage is approximately $2.50 per member per year. Another study, by Martha Griffin and William F Panak, published in the July 1998 issue of *Fertility and Sterility,* found that the cost of comprehensive infertility coverage is $1.71 per family plan per month. Isn't it worth the cost of a monthly cup of coffee to ensure that couples who are struggling to build much-wanted families are afforded the option?

Several state legislatures have responded to the needs of their constituents and recognized the importance of supporting couples who are striving to build their families. Thirteen states enacted infertility insurance laws after they determined that such financial assistance is in the best interest of their residents. The mandates are quite different in scope and substance. Ten states have a mandate to provide some level of infertility insurance. Three states have a mandate to offer under which insurance companies must have infertility insurance available for purchase, but employers do not have to choose to provide that coverage to their employees.

A number of state legislatures considered infertility-insurance laws in the 1997–98 legislative session, and new legislation is being drafted for introduction in 1999. Mandates may be introduced in Florida, Indiana, Michigan, Nevada, New Hampshire, New Jersey, New York, Pennsylvania, Tennessee and Texas. Infertility patients, providers and others who understand the need for insurance coverage are working to gather support for mandates, and a number of legislators have committed to assist.

The existing infertility-insurance mandates have allowed many couples to obtain needed medical treatments and to build their families. However, even in states with mandates, many employees still do not have insurance coverage because of the Employee Retirement Income Security Act, or ERISA. Employers who self-insure are exempt from any state health-insurance mandates, including infertility mandates. In some states, more than 50 percent of employees work for exempted employers. Self-insured employers sometimes do choose to follow the state's policy lead and provide infertility coverage to their employees. A federal infertility insurance mandate, a long-term goal of infertility community, would cover all employers and make coverage consistent across states.

Legislators and employers are beginning to recognize that helping couples who are struggling to build much-wanted families is the right thing to do. In a country that places great value in family, it is salutary that insurance coverage for couples with infertility is just around the corner.

 **NO**

Should Health Insurers Be Forced to Pay for Infertility Treatments? No

When miracles happen on a regular basis, they no longer are miracles—and they may even be seen as problems. That's what has happened with the miracle of multiple births.

Geraldine Brodrick, 29, of Sydney, Australia, performed a miracle in 1971 when she gave birth to nine babies. All died. But 30 years of advances in infertility treatments and neonatology have made multiple births almost common and fairly safe. Bobbi McCaughey of Carlisle, Iowa, also 29, gave birth to septuplets in 1997, all of whom survived. And now Nkem Chukwu of Houston has given birth to octuplets, one of whom died. There also are nonscientific reasons for the increase in the frequency of multiple births. One is that health insurers often are willing or required to pay for infertility treatments. As a result, an increasing number of infertile couples seeks counseling and medical help in having a baby.

According to the Centers for Disease Control and Prevention, 1.2 million women (about 2 percent) of reproductive age visited a medical professional about infertility in 1995. And 9.3 million women (15 percent) had used some kind of fertility service at one time in their lives, compared with 6.8 million (12 percent) who had done so in 1988.

Most women who pursue treatment need only moderate medical intervention, such as counseling or drug therapy. Others need more aggressive or invasive care, such as surgery or assisted reproductive technology, or ART. ART includes such procedures as in vitro fertilization, in which eggs and sperm are taken from the couple, fertilized outside the womb and then implanted in the uterus.

While moderate medical intervention for infertility can be relatively affordable for most couples—$500 to $2,000—more aggressive therapy can cost as much as $12,000. And in vitro fertilization can be expensive—$10,000 to $15,000 per attempt. It often takes several attempts before a prospective mother is successfully impregnated—which can drive up the cost significantly.

According to a 1994 *New England Journal of Medicine* study by Peter J. Neumann et al., the estimated cost per live delivery for in vitro fertilization ranged between $66,667 in the first cycle to $114,286 by the sixth cycle. A July 1998 study by Martha Griffin and William F. Panak, published in *Fertility and Sterility*, found the cost of ART per live delivery in 1993 was $59,484.

Because some infertility treatments can be prohibitively expensive for middle- and lower-income families, advocacy groups have lobbied legislators to require insurance to cover the treatments—and many have listened. For years state legislatures have passed laws—"mandates"—that require insurers to cover providers such as chiropractors and podiatrists or for services such as drug and alcohol-abuse treatments. In 1965 there were only eight mandates nationwide. Today there are more than 1,000. And one mandate that has been gaining popularity—especially among politicians who want to be perceived as sympathetic to women's needs —requires health insurers to cover infertility treatments.

While these mandates make insurance coverage more comprehensive, they also make it more expensive because people use insurance for services they previously paid for out of pocket. For example, consider a patient who was spending $50 a month out of pocket to visit a chiropractor. If the government requires insurers to cover 80 percent of his cost, the patient then is out only $10 a month. If he believes he benefits from the chiropractic care, he may double the frequency of his visits and still spend less than he spent before the mandate was passed. While the patient's personal health-care costs have gone down, total costs to the system have doubled—from $50 to $100 a month. If many patients do the same, insurers eventually will have to increase their rates to make up for the additional costs.

So while it may be true that chiropractors charge less per service than medical doctors and may in certain circumstances provide better care, the additional utilization increases overall health-care costs. Of course, special interests who push for insurance coverage of their particular specialty may believe that such action will improve the quality of care. But they also know that providers will get more visits and therefore more money. That's one of the reasons they work so hard to get legislators to mandate coverage of their specialty. And that's also why they search for data and justifications that will "prove" their assertions.

For example, Griffin, a doctoral candidate in the College of Nursing at the University of Rhode Island, and Panak, a psychologist at the University of Northern Iowa, believe that insurance should cover infertility treatments and produced a study to justify their beliefs. Their examination of the Massachusetts infertility mandate led them to claim that "limiting the number of ART attempts could motivate clinics to maintain policies of transferring numerous embryos as a way of increasing success rates for couples who cannot afford numerous ART attempts. Thus, limits on ART cycles inadvertently could maintain high rates of multiple births and the associated medical complications and economic costs of these births."

In other words, if cost were not a factor, infertility clinics and patients might be less aggressive in their attempts to ensure pregnancy on the first attempt by implanting numerous embryos. If true, that could decrease the number of multiple births and costs would go down.

The problem is that mandates also increase total utilization of health care. If insurance is required to cover infertility treatments, more women will get the treatments. The attempt to remove or destroy some of the fertilized embryos, a process known as selective reduction, is seen by many couples as abortion, a broader social issue that many people oppose. Chukwu was offered selective reduction and declined for religious reasons. Indeed, because some women are reluctant to have embryos removed, there is a debate within the medical community about whether such women should even be offered fertility drugs. Thus, multiple births will not go down as the authors suggest.

Proponents of infertility mandates also assert that the cost of adding the coverage is minimal and would have little impact on premiums. In support, they cite various studies that project a premium increase of between $0.40 and $2.50 per family per month.

There are several problems with these projections. First, they seldom take into consideration other factors. For example, Chukwu's medical bills for her octuplets will reach an estimated $2 million. She is covered by insurance, so the family will not have to bear most of the cost; the insurer will. But insurance is just a pass-through mechanism. That is, insurers pass expenses on to all the people who pay the premiums. Thus policyholders pay higher premiums for the infertility treatments of others and eventually bear the costs of postnatal care.

Actuaries take these collateral effects into consideration when calculating the costs of mandates. For example, when Milliman & Robertson, one of the leading actuarial firms in the country, did a cost analysis of a typical infertility mandate adopted by state legislatures, it estimated the mandate would increase the cost of a health-insurance policy 3 to 5 percent per year, or $105 to $175 a year for a basic health-insurance policy that had no other mandates included.

Which brings us to a second problem. Even if proponents of insurance coverage for infertility were correct in asserting that a mandate would be relatively inexpensive, the larger problem is the total number of mandates. Most states have adopted 30 to 40 health-insurance mandates. While the Milliman & Robertson study makes it clear that most of these mandates are inexpensive— adding less than 1 percent to the cost of a policy—the sum of their costs can make a health-insurance policy prohibitively expensive, boosting premiums by 40 percent to 50 percent in most states.

A third problem is fairness. Thirteen states have adopted some form of infertility mandate. In some cases the legislation requires insurers to cover infertility treatments; in other cases it requires only that coverage be offered. Some states limit how much money insurers are required to spend on treatments (say, to $15,000), while other states exempt very small employers (those with, say, fewer than 25 employees).

However, state-insurance laws primarily affect only small employers and individuals such as the self-employed who purchase private insurance for themselves and their families. That's because most large employers self-insure under the Employee Retirement Income Security Act, or ERISA, a federal law that supersedes state laws. Companies that insure their employees under ERISA avoid state mandates completely.

Thus state mandates affect only a small segment of those with private insurance, and the costs of those mandates fall on a relatively small number of people. As a result, premium increases in the small group and individual health-insurance markets grow much faster than in the large group market. Ironically, it is in the small group and individual markets where people are least able to afford the premium increases.

Of course, many large companies that self-insure voluntarily cover infertility treatments. But that's a choice the companies have made, not one imposed by government. It's those governmental impositions that can lead a business or a family to decide to cancel coverage. Which leads us to the real question: Do we want to put an increasing number of low-income families at risk of lacking basic health insurance so that infertile couples can have their treatments paid for by somebody else?

At a time when health-insurance premiums are projected to increase significantly during the next few years and demographers are worried about world population growth, it simply makes no sense for the government to force insurers to subsidize infertility treatments. Those who have the income to pay for the treatments or who are disciplined enough to save the money to pay for them should have that option. But since it is their choice, it should be their responsibility, not a financial burden that others must bear.

POSTSCRIPT

Should Health Insurers Be Required to Pay for Infertility Treatments?

The controversy about whether or not insurance companies should be required to pay for infertility treatments available now or in the future raises two questions. The first question is, How do we view infertility? Is it a disease, a disability, or an emotionally draining, psychologically devastating disappointment for some men and women? Unlike a disease, infertility is certainly not life threatening. So where does infertility fit into the priorities of the health care budget? Consider that many insurance companies will not pay for the contraceptive pill for women seeking to avoid unwanted pregnancies, and many will not pay for regular mammograms for women at risk for breast cancer.

The second question is international in scope. Around the world, the fertility rate is dropping. European countries and Japan are well below replacement level, with 1.3 to 1.5 children per fertile woman. Despite the fact that the United States has a total fertility rate slightly above replacement level, America's population is expected to rise from the current 276 million to 338 million in 2025 and over 400 million in 2050. In the same 50 years the world's population is expected to rise from its current 6 billion to almost 8 billion in 2025 and over 10 billion in 2050.

In the early 1960s, America and the world saw the birth of reproductive technologies, which for the first time in human history separated sexual intercourse and intimacy from the baby-making process. Also, for the first time, sex and reproduction became separate issues, each with their own ethic to be worked out within changing social values. On the side of sexual values, many feel that "the pill" and women's liberation have led to a widespread acceptance of premarital sex. On the reproductive side, we are still wrestling with the values we want to hold to in this sometimes frightening new era of test-tube babies, frozen embryos, embryo transplants, surrogate mothers, three mothers and two fathers for a single baby, and future possibilities such as the genetically engineered "designer child."

Suggested Readings

Anonymous, "Baby Business," *The Colorado Business Journal* (February 19, 1999).

L. M. Silver, *Remaking Eden: Cloning and Beyond in a Brave New World* (Avon Books, 1997).

On the Internet . . .

American Counseling Association

The article on this Web site maintained by the American Counseling Association addresses the complex boundary issues that can result from relationships
between counselors and clients as well as between professors and students.

http://www.counseling.org/enews/volume_2/0206b.htm

The Kinsey Institute for Research

The Kinsey Institute for Research is a private, not-for-profit corporation affiliated
with Indiana University. The Kinsey Institute promotes interdisciplinary research
and scholarship in the fields of human sexuality, gender, and reproduction.

http://www.indiana.edu/~kinsey

National Marriage Project

The mission of the National Marriage Project is to strengthen the institution of
marriage by providing research and analysis that informs public policy, edu-
cates the American public, and focuses attention on the decline of marriage as
an institution.

http://marriage.rutgers.edu

Alternatives to Marriage Project

The Alternatives to Marriage Project is a national nonprofit organization for
unmarried people, including people who choose not to marry, cannot marry, or
are among the majority of people who live together before marriage.

http://www.unmarried.org

PART 2

Social Issues

*C*ompeting philosophical forces drive concerns about human sexuality on a societal level. Some are primarily focused on the well-being of individuals (or groups of individuals) and their right to individual expression versus their protection from harm; others are mainly concerned with either maintaining or questioning established social norms; still others are engaged by the question of whether or not tax dollars should be used to fund programs and research not endorsed by all. This section examines nine such questions that affect our social understanding of sexuality.

- Do Schools Perpetuate a Gender Bias?

- Should Public Libraries Provide Sexuality Information?

- Is Pornography Harmful to Women?

- Should Sexual Relationships Between Professors and Students Be Banned?

- Does Recent Pedophilia Research Threaten Accepted Moral Standards?

- Should Federal Funding of Stem Cell Research Be Restricted?

- Should States Fund Sexuality Research?

- Is Cohabitation Before Marriage a Bad Idea?

- Is the Model of Normal and Vandalized Gendermaps/Lovemaps Biased?

ISSUE 6

Do Schools Perpetuate a Gender Bias?

YES: Janice Weinman, from "Girls Still Face Barriers in Schools That Prevent Them From Reaching Their Full Potential," *Insight on the News* (December 14, 1998)

NO: Judith Kleinfeld, from "In Fact, the Public Schools Are Biased Against Boys, Particularly Minority Males," *Insight on the News* (December 14, 1998)

ISSUE SUMMARY

YES: Janice Weinman, executive director of the American Association of University Women (AAUW), states that, while there has been some progress since the AAUW published its study entitled *How Schools Shortchange Girls* in 1991, its 1998 review of 1,000 research studies entitled *Gender Gaps: Where Schools Still Fail Our Children* found that girls still face a gender gap in math, science, and computer science.

NO: Psychologist and author Judith Kleinfeld argues that despite appearances, girls still have an advantage over boys in terms of their future plans, teachers' expectations, and everyday school experiences. Furthermore, minority males in particular are at a disadvantage educationally.

In every country there are more male architects than female architects. Why is this so? Why do females outnumber males in other careers? Are these gender differences due to teachers paying more attention to male students than to female students, taking more questions from males than females, and/or guiding males into certain courses and academic tracks and females into less challenging ones? Do female teachers favor female students over male students? Do male teachers tend not to refer male students for counseling or remedial courses when they really need this extra help? Are the gender differences we see in post-school career paths due to a social bias?

   In 1970 women accounted for only 8 percent of all medical degrees, 5 percent of law degrees, and 1 percent of dental degrees. In 1990, women earned 36 percent of medical degrees, 40 percent of law degrees, and 32 percent of dental degrees. In 1999 more women than men attended college. The women also earned higher grades and graduated more often.

In an article entitled "Sex Differences in the Brain," *Scientific American* (September 1992), Doreen Kimura, a professor of psychology and neural research, probes beneath the surface of possible gender biases in American schools. She describes a wide range of differences in the way males and females learn and states that these differences are a reflection of differing hormonal influences on fetal brain development. Kimura maintains that this helps to explain differences in occupational interests and overall capabilities between the sexes.

On the other hand, social psychologist Carol Tavris concludes in *The Mismeasure of Women* (Peter Smith Publishers, 1998), that scientific efforts conducted over the past century have yielded enough conflicting views and distorted findings to invalidate the idea that gender differences are rooted in the brain. She maintains that although biology is not irrelevant to human behavior, it is not fully responsible. The notion of gender difference, in her opinion, has consistently been used to define women as fundamentally different from and inferior to men in body, psyche, and brain.

The question of whether women and men are essentially similar or different is often drowned in emotional responses, unspoken assumptions, and activist politics. This sometimes results in patriarchal biases that dogmatically stress gender differences as justification for "natural gender roles" and can lead to sex discrimination. But similar emotional responses, unspoken assumptions, and activist politics are just as likely to result in a different bias that dogmatically maintains that the only significant difference between men and women is in their sexual anatomy.

For 3,000 years many Western thinkers have viewed human development as the result to two separate, parallel, noninteracting influences. *Nature*—genes and hormones—was believed to be dominant before birth and irrelevant after birth. *Nurture*—the learning and social environment—was believed to be irrelevant during the nine months of pregnancy, but would dominate after birth.

As you read these two selections, see if you can detect any traces or undercurrents of the *Nature vs. Nurture* debate. If you find these undercurrents, do they influence your own appraisal of the arguments presented?

In the following selections, Janice Weinman cites an AAUW report in order to support her conviction that both the quantity and quality of education for females falls short of that for males. Judith Kleinfeld counters that males, particularly minority males, are at a disadvantage when it comes to educational opportunities. She asserts that the AAUW report is merely "junk science."

Janice Weinman  **YES**

Girls Still Face Barriers in Schools That Prevent Them From Reaching Their Full Potential

The American Association of University Women, or AAUW, has been a non-profit, nonpartisan advocate for equal opportunities for women and girls for more than a century. Specifically, we work to improve education for girls.

The need for this is clear. AAUW's 1992 report, *How Schools Shortchange Girls*, reviewed more than 1,300 studies and documented disturbing evidence that girls receive an inequitable education, both in quality and quantity, in America's classrooms. In particular, we found girls faced a gender gap in math and science.

In October, the AAUW Educational Foundation released *Gender Gaps: Where Schools Still Fail Our Children*. Synthesizing 1,000 research studies, *Gender Gaps* measures schools' progress in providing a fair and equitable education since 1992. While girls have improved in some areas, such as math and science, they face an alarming new gap in technology that threatens to make women bystanders in the 21st-century economy.

Gender Gaps found that girls make up only a small percentage of students in computer-science classes. While boys are more likely to enroll in advanced computer-applications and graphics courses, girls take data-entry and clerical classes, the 1990s version of typing. Boys enter the classroom with more prior experience with computers and other technology than girls. Girls consistently rate themselves significantly lower than boys on computer ability, and boys exhibit higher self-confidence and a more positive attitude about computers than do girls.

Critics such as Professor Judith Kleinfeld have questioned why research should focus on the educational experiences of girls. They contend that girls are in fact doing quite well in school. The attention AAUW brings to girls and gender equity, they argue, leads to the neglect of boys.

AAUW believes that all students deserve a good education. To make sure that all students are performing to high academic standards, educators must address the learning needs of different groups of students—boys and girls, African-Americans and Hispanics, rich and poor. AAUW agrees that boys, like girls, face academic challenges. In fact, *Gender Gaps* clearly highlights the fact that boys still lag behind in communications skills. These gaps must be addressed by schools so that all children, boys and girls, have equal opportunity to develop to their full potential.

AAUW's work to eliminate gender bias in the classroom and address gender gaps in education benefits both boys and girls. Rather than pit one group against another, we believe this is a win-win scenario for all students. However, since Kleinfeld does make some specific charges against AAUW's research, allow me to address her claims.

First, Kleinfeld's report—commissioned by the conservative Women's Freedom Network—uses 1998 figures, which show girls improving in math and science, to critique our 1992 finding that there was a gender gap in math and science. That's like using today's lower crime rates to say a 6-year-old study on increasing crime rates created a false alarm. AAUW recognizes and applauds the gains girls have made during the last six years. In fact, *Gender Gaps* documents the improvements girls have made in math and science since AAUW brought national attention to the problem in1992.

Even if you look at the most recent data, the way Kleinfeld does, there still are significant gender differences in schools that must be addressed, including grades and test scores, health and development risks and career development.

As both *How Schools Shortchange Girls* and *Gender Gaps* reported, girls earn better grades than boys. Despite this fact, boys continue to score higher than girls on high-stakes tests—the Preliminary Scholastic Assessment Tests, or PSAT, the Scholastic Assessment Tests, or SAT, the American College Test, or ACT—that determine college admissions and scholarship opportunities. Boys score higher on both the math and verbal sections on these exams, with the gender gaps being the widest for high-scoring students.

As both *Gender Gaps* and Kleinfeld point out, girls' enrollment in advanced placement, or AP, or honors courses is comparable to those of boys, except in AP physics and AP computer science. In fact, more girls take AP English, foreign language and biology. However, girls do not score as well as boys on the AP exams that can earn college credit, even in subjects such as English where girls earn top grades.

Girls' academic success also is affected by the tough issues facing students—pregnancy, violence and harassment—that rarely are discussed in school. AAUW believes that schools can play a key role in developing healthy and well-balanced students.

Although Kleinfeld tries to discredit AAUW's work by pointing to the large number of boys in special education, our 1992 report paid careful attention to the fact that boys outnumbered girls in these programs by startling percentages. It also cited studies on learning disabilities and attention-deficit disorders that indicated that they occurred almost equally in boys and girls.

Girls continue to be more vulnerable to some risks than boys. As *Gender Gaps* reports, one in five girls has been sexually or physically abused, one in four shows signs of depression and one in four doesn't get health care when she needs it. Schools limit gender equity when they fail to confront or discuss risk factors for students.

AAUW also is well-known for our research on self-esteem. In 1991, AAUW commissioned the first national scientific survey on self-esteem, *Shortchanging Girls, Shortchanging America.* This survey was stratified by region, included an unprecedented number of children (3,000 children ages 9 to 15), and rigorously was reviewed by a team of academic advisers. The 1991 survey offered solid evidence of differences in self-esteem between girls and boys.

Although girls who were surveyed for *Shortchanging Girls, Shortchanging America* self-reported that teachers called on and gave more attention to girls, their self-esteem nevertheless declined. Despite girls' perceptions, the 1992 report, which looked at many other studies in addition to the AAUW survey, found that girls received significantly less attention than boys in the classroom. Contrary to what Kleinfeld asserts, neither AAUW's 1991 survey nor 1992 report drew a causal relationship between self-esteem and academic achievement. AAUW's research on self-esteem looked at multiple patterns across multiple indicators—including general self-esteem, family importance, academic self-esteem, isolation, voice, acceptance, friends and attention in classrooms—and used multiple methodologies. The repeated conclusion our research revealed is that girls face a dramatic drop in self-esteem as they get older that has devastating consequences on their aspirations and their futures. Kleinfeld's work looks at only two questions from our survey to draw her own conclusions.

Beyond K–12 public schools, Kleinfeld looks at college degrees to declare that women have achieved parity in the professional world. Although more women than men enter college, entry into higher education doesn't guarantee equitable conditions. That's why AAUW has worked to include key provisions in the reauthorization of the Higher Education Act to make sure women's needs are addressed on campus. For example, although women are three times as likely as men to be single parents while in college, campus-based child care still is hard to find and afford.

And women still are underrepresented in nontraditional fields such as math and science that lead to greater earning power upon graduation. There are disparities at the undergraduate, master's and doctorate levels in these fields, which have a profound effect on careers.

You only need to look outside of the classroom and into the boardroom to see that women are still a long way from equality. Women earn only 76 cents for every dollar that a man earns. In 1995, women represented 70 percent of all adults with incomes below the poverty level, and two out of three minimum-age earners are women. Out of the entire Fortune 500, there are only two female CEOs and a total of seven in the Fortune 1,000. And women only make up 11 percent of Congress.

No one wins in Kleinfeld's who's-worse-off debate. AAUW's work to eliminate gender bias in the classroom and address gender gaps in education benefits both boys and girls. Our research has resonated with parents, teachers and policymakers who have used our research as a catalyst for positive change in their public schools. Our 1,500 branches across the country conduct programs to empower and encourage young girls. Our fellowships help women succeed in school and advance into fields that historically have been off limits.

AAUW believes that all students deserve a good education and the opportunity to develop to their full potential. And we know from experience that we can help girls close the gender gap—we've seen them improve in math and science. Now we must do the same for technology to make sure all students have the technological skills to compete in the 21st century.

Judith Kleinfeld

 **NO**

In Fact, the Public Schools Are Biased Against Boys, Particularly Minority Males

T hink back to your own school days. Who got into more trouble in school—the boys or the girls? Who got the best grades—the boys or the girls? Who was the valedictorian in your high school—a boy or a girl?

Yes, school is just the same as you remember it.

Feminist-advocacy groups such as the American Association of University Women, or AAUW, have promoted a big lie: the idea that schools shortchange girls. The AAUW studies are advocacy research—junk science. In fact, their latest study is going to give me lots of examples for my research-methods class on how to lie with statistics. It's all there—graphs drawn to make a little gap look like a big one, percentages calculated with the wrong numerical base to show that girls score lower than boys on advanced placement, or AP, tests in English when the girls actually score higher. Such a gold mine of tricks!

Why the deception? The short answer is money. The long answer is money and career advancement. The idea that females are victims garners millions of dollars in federal and foundation funding for feminist-advocacy groups to launch special programs for girls. This idea also helps well-educated women gain special preferences in their battle for elite jobs at the top.

Who are the real victims? The losers are the students the schools really do shortchange—mostly minority males. Women's-advocacy groups have hijacked the moral capital of the civil-rights movement to promote the special interests of well-off, well-connected women. Along the way they have scared many parents, who are worrying about their daughters in the schools when they should be worrying about their sons.

When I told my own university students that the AAUW had just discovered a new gender gap—a computer gap—a great groan arose from the class. Puzzled and surprised, I asked each student how he or she used computers. Are women really going to be bystanders in the technological 21st century, as the AAUW would have us believe?

The students' answers laid bare the fallacy in the AAUW's latest headline-grabber. The women in the class, no less than the men, could use spreadsheets, databases and word-processing programs. The women could search the Internet. The women learned the computer programs they needed to use.

So what's all the hysteria about the computer gap? If you read the 1998 AAUW report, you will be in for a surprise. All this uproar comes down to a difference of 5 percent in the proportion of male high-school students (30 percent) compared to female high-school students (25 percent) who sign up for computer-science courses. These are the kinds of courses that teach computer-programming skills for students interested in computer-science careers.

Males indeed are more likely than females to choose computer science as a career. So what? Women aren't as interested as men in turning into Dilberts-in-a-cubicle. According to a report on women in mathematics and science from the National Center for Education Statistics, twice as many female college students (20 percent) compared to male college students (less than 10 percent) now seek prestigious professional careers.

The truth is that males and females have somewhat different interests and somewhat different areas of intellectual strength and weakness, and these differences show up in schools. Here are the facts:

Grades: Females are ahead.   If the schools were biased against girls, such bias should be easy to detect. After all, the schools give clear and measurable rewards: grades, class rank and honors. These rewards are valuable in getting into an elite college or getting a good job.

Every study, even the AAUW's own 1998 report, concedes that girls consistently earn higher grades than boys throughout their schooling. Girls get higher class rank and more academic honors in every field except mathematics and science (I'll discuss this difference later). Girls, not boys, are more apt to be chosen for gifted and talented programs, the gateway into a far higher-quality education. Girls drop out of school less often than boys and less often repeat a grade. Wherever the schools hand out the prizes, girls get more than their share.

Standardized achievement tests: Females do better in some subjects; males do better in others.   Even though girls get better grades, the schools still might be short-changing girls if they actually aren't learning as much as boys. Grades, after all, have a lot to do with whether students are willing to play along with the school's demands for neatness and conformity.

On standardized tests, females surpass males by a mile on tests of writing ability. Females also surpass males in reading achievement and in study skills. Males surpass females on tests of science, mathematics and a few areas of social studies.

The gender gap in mathematics and science is closing, as the AAUW 1998 report admits. The gender-equity police take credit for it, but the real cause is higher graduation requirements in high school. Girls now take just as many high-school science and mathematics courses as boys do, with the exception of a small difference in physics.

In a nutshell, boys end up with lower grades than girls even in subjects where standardized tests show boys know more. So against which sex are schools biased?

High-stakes tests: What's really going on.   The AAUW makes much of the fact that males surpass females on high-stakes tests, such as the Scholastic Assessment Tests, or SAT. Here's what they don't tell you. More than 75,500 additional females take the SAT than males, and these "additional" females are less likely to have taken rigorous academic courses than other students, points out a 1998 College Board study on sex and the SAT.

Here is the way the trick works. Let's say you are comparing the top-10 male basketball players with the top 10 female players in the same high school. Assume that the males and the females have the same shooting ability. But then add to the female group five girls who try hard but aren't as good. Of course, the female shooting average will be lower than the males'.

The AAUW pulls a similar trick in comparing scores on AP tests, tough tests taken by the most advanced high-school students. The AAUW report admits that girls take AP tests in greater number than boys but pulls a fast one by saying that these girls earn lower scores even in areas of historic strength, such as English.

Take a look at the actual facts in the federal report, *The Condition of Education 1998*. Almost twice as many girls as boys took the AP English test. Among the girls, 46 per 1,000 12th-graders got a score of 3 or higher, qualifying them for college credit. Among the boys, 27 per 1,000 12th-graders got such a high score. What's the truth? Girls earn far higher scores than boys on the AP English test, the opposite of what the AAUW claims.

Males fall at the extremes—flaming failures and academic stars.   More boys do show up at the top in fields such as mathematics and science. But then more boys also show up at the bottom. Boys are twice as likely to be placed in special-education classes for the learning-disabled. Boys outnumber girls by 4–1 in neurological impairments such as autism or dyslexia.

This has less to do with bias than with biology. On many human characteristics, including intellectual abilities, males are just more variable than females. More males show up at the high end of the bell curve and more males show up at the low end of the bell curve. From the standpoint of natural selection, males are the more expendable sex. Nature takes more chances with males, producing more oddities of every kind, whether genius or insanity.

Women's advocacy groups push programs to equalize male and females in mathematics and science. Social engineering cannot make real differences go away, nor should it.

College success: Females now surpass males.   Many people don't realize that women have become the majority of college students. In 1996, women earned 55 percent of bachelor's degrees and 55 percent of all master's degrees, and African-American females are much further ahead.

Insofar as self-esteem is concerned, both girls and boys have rather high opinions of themselves. The best research, now accepted even by feminist-advocacy groups, shows no difference between teenage boys and girls in self-esteem. The latest AAUW report on gender gaps is strangely silent about the self-esteem gap they trumpeted a few years ago.

On the issue of whether girls get less class participation than boys, it is clear that teachers do not silence girls. Everyone agrees that teachers give boys more attention of the negative, disciplinary kind. Who gets more academic attention? This research is a confusing mess, with no clear patterns.

So, who are the public schools biased against? The right answer is boys. Many studies show that American schools, far from shortchanging girls, are biased against boys. In fact, the AAUW found the same thing but buried these results in unpublished tables. I had to badger the AAUW office for weeks to get a 1990 Greenberg-Lake survey and pay close to $100 for the photocopying. But you can see that the AAUW had good reason to hide these findings. According to the AAUW's hidden study, both boys and girls agree, sometimes by overwhelming margins, that teachers think girls are smarter, compliment girls more often and like to be around girls more.

The media doesn't often report studies which contradict the feminist party line. A good example is the 1997 report on gender issues published by the Met-Life Foundation, an organization with no political ax to grind. This study concludes:

1. Contrary to the commonly held view that boys are at an advantage over girls in school, girls appear to have an advantage over boys in terms of their future plans, teachers' expectations, everyday experiences at schools and interactions in the classroom;
2. Minority girls hold the most optimistic views of the future and are the group most likely to focus on education goals;
3. Minority boys are the most likely to feel discouraged about the future and the least interested in getting a good education; and
4. Teachers nationwide view girls as higher achievers and more likely to succeed than boys.

If anyone needs help in school, it is minority boys. They are the victims of the AAUW's junk science.

Do Schools Perpetuate a Gender Bias?

Jerome Kagan, a major researcher in the development of personality, asserts that many prefer to downplay nature and emphasize nurture when discussing the origin of phychological differences in males and females. This tendency, he says, owes much to the prevailing commitment Americans have to egalitarianism. If differences between individuals, between the genders, or between gender orientations are innate and biologically based, there is little that can be done about them. If, however, differences are due to inequities in the social environment, there may be a lot that can be done to reduce or eliminate these differences. But there is a third option. This option has three essential components. First is the belief that male and female brains and personalities are gender differentiated by hormones and genes as a fetus is developing in the womb and after birth. Second is the observation that parents, teachers, and society engage in biased gender scripting. Third is the conclusion that innate biological differences in the brain interact with gender-biased scripting at critical periods throughout our lives.

Alice Rossi, in her 1983 Presidential Address to the American Sociological Association, pointed out that attempts to explain human behavior and therapies that seek to change behavior "carry a high risk of eventual irrelevance [if they] neglect the fundamental biological and neural differences between the sexes [and] the mounting evidence of sexual dimorphism from the biological and neural sciences." Although Rossi seems to favor the belief that male and female brains are wired differently, she offers an important distinction. She carefully states that gender "diversity is a biological fact, while [gender] equality is a political, ethical, and social precept."

If the biological and neuropsychological evidence supports the existence of significant differences in male and female brains, then we have to be careful to view these differences as part of human diversity and not in terms of superior versus inferior or good versus bad. Human diversity does not necessarily deny or obstruct human equality, because human equality is a political, moral, and social issue. Too often human diversity is used to support the superiority of one group over another group.

On the other hand, educators of all grades may need to carefully examine the ways in which boys and girls are treated differently in their classrooms. Some researchers have observed a tendency for educators of preschool students to compliment boys on their *performance* (e.g., "Billy, you're such a good runner!") and girls on their *appearance* (e.g., "Karen, you look so pretty today!"). Furthermore, when an educator gives a simple instruction like, "I need a few strong boys to help me move some chairs," she or he may be completely unaware that the directions exclude girls from the possibility of helping. Educators who begin to recognize that the key skill needed for such an activity is *strength* and not *being a boy* will help their students make empowering strides toward life's opportunities.

Suggested Readings

N. Angier, "How Biology Affects Behavior and Vice Versa," *The New York Times* (May 30, 1995).

A. Fausto-Sterling, *Myths of Gender: Biological Theories About Women and Men,* 2d ed. (Basic Books, 1992).

C. Gorman, "Sizing Up the Sexes," *Time* (January 20, 1992).

D. Kimura, "Sex Differences in the Brain," *Scientific American* (September 1992).

R. Pool, *Eve's Rib: Searching for the Biological Roots of Sex Differences* (Crown Publishers, 1994).

C. Tavris, *The Mismeasure of Woman: Why Women Are Not the Better Sex, the Inferior Sex, or the Opposite Sex* (Simon & Schuster, 1992).

L. Wright, "Double Mystery," *The New Yorker* (August 7, 1995).

ISSUE 7

Should Public Libraries Provide Sexuality Information?

YES: Martha Cornog, from "Is Sex Safe in Your Library? How to Fight Censorship," *Library Journal* (August 1993)

NO: James L. Sauer, from "In Defense of Censorship," *The Christian Librarian* (February 1993)

ISSUE SUMMARY

YES: Martha Cornog, editor of *Libraries, Erotica, and Pornography*, maintains that public libraries have a responsibility to preserve all literature that is part of our cultural heritage for patrons and future generations. Public libraries that preserve and make available materials, including controversial sexuality materials, facilitate and promote debate, which is essential in the democratic process.

NO: James L. Sauer, a librarian at Eastern College in Phoenixville, Pennsylvania, states that free speech is not unlimited—it is governed by and must serve the moral order. Thus, it is proper for libraries to use their censorship power to curb unfettered expression that violates or attacks the moral values of society.

Gershon Legman, writing in "The Lure of the Forbidden," in Martha Cornog, ed., *Libraries, Erotica, and Pornography* (Oryx Press, 1991), makes this statement:

> The libraries' censorship, except at the provincial lending level . . . has paradoxically had the opposite effect: that of preserving, in many cases, the very books that would otherwise have been destroyed. . . . For essentially, the libraries' effort is to protect the books for and sometimes against the readers, and not to protect the readers from the books.

The role of the library in deciding what materials should and should not be made available to the public—or even if libraries have the right to refrain from providing certain material—is the focus of this issue. Censorship in any form has always raised controversy in countries in which freedom of speech is a valued right. The issue becomes even more complicated when the speech in question is sexual in nature, as the following examples illustrate.

In 1985 Congressman Chalmers P. Wylie (R-Ohio) added an amendment to the Library of Congress appropriations bill that would have reduced the library's budget by the exact amount it would cost to have *Playboy* magazine put into Braille and made available through the National Library Service for the Blind and Physically Handicapped. After the Librarian of Congress withdrew *Playboy* from the list of magazines to be put into Braille, Playboy Enterprises, several blind individuals and advocacy organizations, and the American Library Association sued successfully for full funding.

In 1993 libraries across the nation had to decide whether or not to purchase pop singer Madonna's sexually explicit picture book *Sex*. Some libraries faced massive demonstrations, letter and phone campaigns, and interventions by civic leaders. Nearly all retained the book despite the protests. The anti-*Sex* contingent cited as reasons for not carrying the book its lack of enduring value, poor binding, high price, and self-promotional ballyhoo. The pro-*Sex* contingent denounced censorship and cited as reasons for carrying the book its ranking as a best-seller, public interest, the author's popularity, and a desire to spare patrons the cost of satisfying their curiosity.

Since 1992 the Fairfax County, Virginia, Public Library Board of Trustees has been locked in a disagreement with the Fairfax County Board of Supervisors. At issue is the policy of having free copies of the *Washington Blade,* a gay newspaper, available along with other free information in library lobbies. Responding to complaints from patrons and conservative Christian activists, county supervisors have pressured the library to remove the *Blade* or to restrict access to it. The library board twice voted to retain the newspaper, which, in the interim, moved its sexually explicit personal ads to a separate section not included with library copies. County supervisors threatened to abolish the library board but lacked the authority to do so. More recently, one supervisor proposed prohibiting county employees from participating in any activity that might encourage violation of the state's rarely enforced antisodomy law, which would make those who put the *Blade* in the lobbies subject to being fired. Other efforts focused on encouraging the selection of antigay board members.

Meanwhile, the Fairfax library system purchased 11 titles suggested by Christian activists to balance the over 100 gay books in its collection. These titles offer the conservative Christian perspective that homosexuality can be "cured" or "reformed" through counseling and changes in lifestyle. The Fairfax Lesbian and Gay Citizens Association responded by donating 78 titles to counter the antigay books.

The tensions public libraries face in these and similar debates over the censorship of sexuality materials are likely to increase as the gap grows between religious conservatives who favor censorship to preserve moral values and liberals who favor free speech and open debate.

In the following selections, Martha Cornog criticizes the censors and argues that public libraries have a responsibility to make available informative, if controversial, sexuality materials. James L. Sauer defends censorship as a valuable process through which the morals of society may be preserved.

Martha Cornog  **YES**

Is Sex Safe in Your Library?
How to Fight Censorship

When most of us think of free libraries, we think of free books, even books that have been described as *improper, questionable, controversial, objectionable,* or as exotic, erotic literature—all euphemisms for books about sex. Of the three historical arenas for censorship—sex, religion, and politics—only sex has maintained enough widespread power to evoke the censor as we enter the 21st century. We have laws against sexual expression but not against religious or political expression. Thus, librarians cannot avoid censorship battles about sex, especially at a time when sexual issues saturate the media and sexual problems beset patrons who desperately need information about sexual harassment, AIDS, sex education, abortion, or homosexuality.

Yet library censorship, especially of sexuality materials, has proliferated in the last 25 years. Where is censorship headed? What does it mean for libraries?

Censorship of sexuality and other controversial materials has increased partly because there is so much more to censor. The most visible tension currently centers on gay and lesbian materials. One freedom to read expert who requested anonymity suggested, "homosexuality has replaced communism as the scapegoat for the right of center." Conservative groups are working to pass laws against governmental "promoting" of homosexuality, and librarians in both Colorado and Oregon have reported increased challenges to gay materials even though Colorado's Amendment 2 did pass and Oregon's Measure 9 did not.

However, sharp rises in the incidence of homosexuality-based censorship are not endemic to Colorado and Oregon. Gay books now make up as much as one-third of sex-related library challenges nationwide.

The percentage of libraries reporting challenges on *all* material has more than doubled since 1980—when library surveys indicated 20 percent of those surveyed reporting challenges—to between 40 and 50 percent reporting challenges today. Still, the American Library Association's Office for Intellectual Freedom estimates only *15 percent* of censorship attempts ever reach tabulation.

Access by children and young adults represents a large percentage of the challenges to sexuality materials. This author's analysis of such challenges in

From Martha Cornog, "Is Sex Safe in Your Library? How to Fight Censorship," *Library Journal* (August 1993). Copyright © 1993 by Reed Elsevier, Inc. Reprinted by permission.

both school and public libraries from 1991 to 1993 shows that 70–90 percent of sex-related challenges involved access by younger people. Censorship attempts relating to sex and to "objectionable language" appear to differ in one important way from other attempts: they are more likely to result in removal of books, whether in school or public libraries.

Getting Worse Before It Gets Better

Controversy over sex books will get worse before it gets better. "If you can't deal with the fact that these groups are here, then you're in the wrong job," said Dennis Day, director of the Salt Lake City Public Library. To make matters more complex, groups that traditionally support censorship are at odds. At a recent conference of the Association of Christian Librarians, Craighton Hippenhammer reported results of an intellectual freedom survey of Christian college and Bible college librarians. There was, he said, a divergence of opinion, with some supporting censorship and others dead set against it. Though feminists are against sexism, they do not agree on whether censorship is an acceptable means to that end. Two feminist groups, Feminists for Free Expression and Women Against Pornography, oppose each other over censorship of sexuality materials. With many censors, each opposing one another, no consensus emerges, resulting in a lot of confusion and little clear dialog.

For some librarians, censorship cases are, at best, irritants, distractions—annoyances best ignored, pacified, and dealt with quickly and quietly, even in advance with self-imposed censorship—to make way for the "real business" of librarianship. "[Censorship] is not as important as the meat and potatoes of our profession, which is getting people to read," said James Casey, director of the Oak Lawn Public Library, IL. But censors intrinsically oppose the major goal of librarianship by impeding reading and therefore must be taken very seriously. No longer sedate, passive temples, libraries can be vital and exciting places to learn about all sides of controversial issues. Librarians can capitalize on censorship attempts by transforming their libraries into major players in the community, a place of importance in the public mind, a resource for democracy.

Potent PR

Moreover, controversy can be potent public relations. When the right to read is threatened, supporters come out of the woodwork. Patrons, too. Officials at the Fort Vancouver Public Library, WA, reported that after they added Madonna's *Sex* in reference, more than 900 people came to see the controversial book for themselves. Many expressed appreciation at being able to see what young people are exposed to.

Most censorship incidents, however, do not elicit the spectacular and daunting tactics used recently by groups to attack *Sex* and *Daddy's Roommate* and the libraries that carry them: massive telephone campaigns, bomb threats, and media blitzes. Many complaints can be settled with active listening and civil discussion. Yet the range of tactics and scenarios for which librarians must be prepared has certainly expanded:

- The Downers Grove Public Library, IL, and the Austin Public Library, TX, received notice from their respective state attorney's offices that Madonna's *Sex* might violate laws prohibiting distribution of pornography to minors, and the Casa Grande PL, AZ, received a similar notice from the police about *Truly Tasteless Jokes.* All three libraries immediately restricted the books to those age 18 and over.
- A lobbyist-attorney, retained by the Arizona State Library Association to assist in passing a library exemption to state anti-obscenity laws, faced daily harassment from a local minister who set up a stand outside state buildings and loudly trumpeted the names of all who were expected to vote for the exemption. The exemption bill did not pass.
- In three California high school libraries, vice principals removed *Annie on My Mind* and *All American Boys,* donated by a gay group, and did not return them to the shelves despite repeated requests from librarians.
- In Florida, members of the American Family Association mobilized an extensive campaign against a gay and lesbian film festival held by the Leon County PL, with appeals to the library board, radio exhortations, threatening and obscene telephone calls, and disruptive protesters. The festival had been approved by three separate library board votes.

Ain't Seen Nothin' Yet

Still, in the estimation of one anonymous censorship veteran, librarians haven't seen anything yet. "I believe we'll see in the next few years the same type of tactics used against libraries that were used against abortion clinics." But statistics show that the extremists may be beating their heads against the wall. This author's analysis of 222 sexual censorship cases from 1991 to 1993 in school and public libraries suggests that more extreme tactics do not necessarily result in the removal of books.

While libraries use a variety of formal and informal reconsideration procedures, what *is* associated with removal of books is avoidance of established process—decisions made unilaterally by a library director or administrator. Conversely, retention of sexuality materials seems to be associated with use of a formal process, particularly a "two-tiered" system: review by a reconsideration committee of some type, followed by final decision by an administrator or board.

By smartening up and becoming wiser to the ways of their opponents as well as more media-savvy, libraries across the country are confronting the controversy surrounding censorship issues head on—and winning:

- Downers Grove PL, which had restricted Madonna's *Sex* after notice from the State Attorney's office, later requested a written opinion from that office as to whether or not giving the book to minors violated the state's Harmful Material Act. When the library found out it was within the law, it made *Sex* available to all patrons but added an option to its circulation policy allowing parents to restrict their own children's borrowing privileges.

- In Oak Lawn, another public library successfully fought two censorship attempts in two years to keep Gershon Legman's bawdy classic *The Limerick* off its shelves—the first attempt from a school principal, the second from a Catholic organization. The library jump-started its public relations program, hiring a full-time staff member who edited a semimonthly newsletter, wrote columns and press releases for local newspapers, and planned numerous adult and youth programs. Since the newsletter began, library circulation and program participation has risen dramatically.

- The Fort Vancouver PL responded proactively to the Madonna book with an open letter to patrons, explaining reasons for purchase and the freedom to read. Similarly, Carolyn Anthony, director of the Skokie PL, IL, sent a memo to staff providing background information on the book, why it was ordered, and how to defend it against complaints. Both libraries have retained the title....

Controversy a Healthy Sign

Librarians must be willing to see controversy about sexuality materials as part of the democratic process and as an opportunity to enlarge the library's role in that process. Rather than looking at censorship as confusion among noisy and conflicting demands, the best course may be to view the controversy as a healthy sign of debate and involvement in which the library can provide materials on all sides of the issue. Controversy can be used to facilitate the mission of the library.

So when the library announces loudly that, yes, we have *Sex,* and *Daddy's Roommate,* and dictionaries with dirty words, and *Playboy,* and *Changing Bodies, Changing Lives*—and books about sex from religious, feminist, and minority viewpoints as well—then patrons and readers can only increase, because people need to become informed about sexuality to make their own decisions about sexual issues. Libraries can use censorship to encourage people to read, and they must take the risks that come with the controversy. If they do not, the library dwindles in books and in influence, to a small, sanitized, and quite trivial retreat from reality.

James L. Sauer  **NO**

In Defense of Censorship

The "great debate" of civil life is really about control of various "pulpits." Parenthood is a pulpit, as is a Newspaper. Schools are pulpits. The church is an obvious pulpit. A public library is a pulpit. Television is an ubiquitous pulpit. And the Presidency is a bully pulpit.

The current conflict is really about who shall control these "pulpits." It is a battle of power and control over the soul of society. The issue has two facets. First, who shall be included on a given pulpit—who shall have the right to rule in the family; to pontificate in the schools; to choose books in the public library. It is the power of the pulpit committee; it is the function of selection. And second, who shall be excluded from speaking. This power deals with the limitation of debate. It exercises suppressive powers, and is best known by the label of censorship. The selective and censorial functions in our society are under the power of the knowledge professions: teachers, librarians, media powers, psychologists, and talk show hosts. Ideas and actions are advocated; other world views are denigrated. It is a commonplace notion of modern life that censorship is an evil. As Joel Belz has pointed out, "Our society fervently rejects censorship as a bad thing. No one doing a word search of the last 1,000 uses of 'censorship' in the major media is likely to find a single case where reference is positive. We just tend to assume that censorship is wrong."

I do not make that assumption. Censorship is a natural part of the communication process by which we include and exclude information from life's great debate. To act is to select; to choose is to censor. Only certain modes of censorship are inherently wrong; those modes which attempt to control the pulpits of others by deceit and force—which cross governmental lines and abrogate the order of God's creation for family, society, and state. Selection has its proper role, censorship its rightful limit.

As the devouring statism of our century grows in power and control, we seem to be losing any sense of when selection and censorship are just or unjust. Censorship is attacked in order to advance vice; and selection rights are asserted in order to repress virtue. We have lost Edmund Burke's notion of a "liberty connected with order: that not only exists along with order and virtue, but which cannot exist at all without them."

It may startle practitioners of professional information services to know that librarians, editors, publishers, news men, and teachers, are the chief censors of our society. They select ideas—they funnel and shape the terms of contemporary life. Not only do they select what shall be discussed and censor what shall not be seen, but they do so, usually, without the consent of the communities they serve. The citizen's group which boycotts a movie theatre showing the Last Temptation of Christ is far less of a censor than the librarian who excludes popular religious titles from the public library collection. The citizen's group is expressing a consumer's choice; the librarian is ignoring a community's values.

Defining the C Word

Perhaps the first thing we must do is to eliminate the largely negative view we hold of the word "censorship." We approach this label in a biased manner. Censorship has had a number of emotionally neutral meanings throughout history which we might well remember.

In Roman society, the censor was one who acted as an inspector of public morals. The censor was a protector of civil, social, and religious order. The censors were also census takers and property assessors. They also had the power to tax, which as we know in our day, is the power to destroy.

In modern life, a censor is any official who examines publications for objectionable material. For example, an editor or library book reviewer is such a figure; as is a policeman on the vice squad. It is a secondary question as to what they are finding objectionable.

A censor also monitors forbidden communication. Such censorship was a common task during the last two world wars when the correspondence of soldiers was monitored to preserve security. Such censorship is practiced in totalitarian lands during times of peace.

Finally, self censorship is a psychological mechanism that represses unacceptable notions before they reach fruition. Before we dismiss this psychological notion, it is wise to realize that such censorship is practiced by every human mind. It is an absolute necessity. We cannot survive psychologically without repressing anti-social thoughts and acts. And by analogy, if we must suppress violence and a wanton libido in our own minds and actions, does it not give some credence to the notion of suppressing such evils in the body politic.

Where Do Our Rights Come From?

It is a common presupposition of the information masters that we have an absolute right to full self-expression and unfettered freedom of speech and press, and that no one has the right to restrict this. Though professing relativistic ignorance of all other moral values, the modernist is absolutely sure of one thing: censorship is wrong.

But where does this absolute right of expression come from? There are in fact only three possible sources: God, nature, or society.

First, if God is the author of our rights, and specifically, our right to self-expression then it should be revealed in Scripture and Christian tradition. But in fact it is not so revealed. Instead, we find two opposite principles: the suppression of evil and the encouragement of virtue. Suppression of evil ideas, words, and actions is a central focus of Scripture. From the Ten Commandments to the holy prophets, to Christ's extension of morality to our thought life, you have in the Biblical worldview full liberty to do good, but you do not have a concomitant right to sin.

Second, it is futile to look to nature as the source of rights. Nature can be viewed in two ways: as an expression of a divine will (Providence) or as a unwilled expression of chance relationships (evolution). If we look to providential nature (the nature's God of our founding fathers), we are turned back to the Judeo-Christian tradition. Natural law and reason are seen in service to a revealed order; a gentlemen's religion, a kind of moralistic deism. If we look to evolutionary nature we wind up with rights in process, not fixed rights at all. Instead, we find notions of efficiency, power, and biological fitness. One does not have rights in nature, one merely survives.

Third, if society grants us our rights by the social contract, then those rights exist in two patterns. First, we find legal rights in a static pattern as expressed, for instance, in our Constitution. This pattern involves relatively fixed, nonarbitrary law structures, and can only be altered by changing the law. Without a moral order behind these constitutional rights, we find that such rights have no absolute nature. Amendments can be made to add to or take away from our rights. This makes such rights in actuality privileges. When we speak of rights, we mean provisional rights; when we speak of unalienable rights, we mean God-given rights.

The second pattern is through evolutionary, sociological law. This pattern suggests that our rights evolve, that science, public opinion, and changing mores alter the meaning of law. Hence, the so called "right of privacy" discovered by our Supreme Court in 1973. Rights can appear and disappear almost overnight using "sociological law." The notion of an evolving synthetic law system is present in the Marxist worldview. A right defined in such a society changes colors with the seasons.

A right to free speech, therefore, in so far as it exists, must have its foundation in the Judeo-Christian tradition. It cannot be separated from that tradition's view of moral order. Separate from that tradition, it is but an idea which evolves with nature and society.

Censorship in Society

If we do not have a right to full self-expression—since such a right can only spring absolutely from God—then by what criteria can self-expression and freedom of speech be reasonably curtailed? Up until the last century in the West, the following restrictions on the right of free speech were considered natural and self-evident.

1. The Suppression of Evil, especially pornography. Every good society will desire to repress anti-social acts which demean life and human sexuality. The censorship of pornography is necessary not because we are repelled by it, but because we are overwhelmingly attracted to it. Pornography is anti-woman and anti-child. Destructive to familial happiness, it feeds a fantasy world of mechanical sex and abusive domination. No one who truly understands masculine psychology or who has read the terrible acts described in a book like *Pornography's Victims* can believe that pornography is harmless.
2. Suppression of Slander and Libel. No just society willingly condones lies, especially harmful lies told about its citizens.
3. Suppression of Acts of Symbolic Desecration. No one should have a right to paint swastikas on synagogues, to defecate on the Bible, or to burn a flag.
4. Suppression of Anti-Social Acts. It is a general truism accepted by most human beings that your neighbor does not have the right to shout at the top of his lungs into your ear. It is a cliche of law that no one has the right to scream fire in a crowded theatre. Flashers do not have the right to "express" themselves in public.
5. Suppression of National Secrets. Certainly, this last area is liable to abuse. We can all imagine a Pentagon official classifying laundry lists as top secret; or a politician hiding his crimes behind national security. Nevertheless, any society which wishes to preserve itself from its enemies must censor information needed for its existence.

Who Should Censor?

All the spheres of life are governed. Without these governments civil life could not function. Proper censorship involves the suppressive function at its appropriate level. Where then does censorship begin and who should act as censor?

1. Censorship begins with the individual. Self censorship is the psychological repression of interior evil and the resisting of exterior temptation. Turning off the television, for instance, is an act of self censorship. Some older people have the habit of turning down their hearing aids—one of the benefits of old age.
2. Family censorship involves repressing evils in this fundamental institution. For example, you might not merely turn the TV off, you might actually throw the one-eyed god out. Familial censorship is also illustrated in parental control of children's reading. One of the contributing factors in the dissolution of the modern family has been our inability to control the invasion of destructive values into our homes.
3. Specific communities also exercise censorship in their own narrow areas of control. For instance, we have churches defining the doctrinal material found in their church libraries. Organizations, businesses, and civic groups set guidelines for the values expressed in their publications. The local peace group logically offers only pacifist materials from

its book table. Academic libraries define for themselves what is and what is not scholarly material.

4. Censorship takes place in the general community. Public libraries develop their own ordering and discarding policies. Such policies may be set by local governments, library boards, librarians, or citizens. What librarians often deplore as censorship is when someone besides the "professionals" want to have a say in establishing selection policies. It is a battle for control of the "pulpit committee."

5. State officials sometimes censor by setting guidelines and restrictions on the use of tax money. As a purchaser and provider of services, shouldn't the elected officials of a state have a say in how the tax dollars are to be used? If they say that "x" dollars can be used for purchasing a certain type of material, and "y" dollars cannot be used to further a particular partisan worldview, is this not a just use of state money, which is to say, taxpayer's money?

6. The federal government's situation is exactly like that of the state's. It is perfectly proper for the federal government to use its censorship power by determining the nature of the art it is going to purchase. Most citizens do not believe that a crucifix submerged in urine is creativity worthy of civic support. Mr. Maplethorpe, and other so called artists, can take any number of pictures of men with objects thrust into their anal cavities but that is no reason why the people should be forced to pay for these unique acts of "self expression." Censorship and selection, like the freedom of speech itself, have their natural limits. The citizen properly uses his suppressive powers through his exercise of speech, freedom of press, letter writing, and voting. He acts in community through petitions, pickets, and boycotts. And he acts collectively in the state through the ultimate sanctions of fines, the seizing of materials, and arrests. All is done according to the moral framework of Western society and by the rule of law.

Just Censorship

When the *Information Class Tribune* of the ACLU hysterically tells us that "If we let them ban *Teen Slut* today, they'll be burning the Mona Lisa tomorrow," we can be assured that we are not dealing with reason but with an absolutist ideology. Our society banned pornography until the last 40 years; and the people produced in those earlier decades were more virtuous, more chaste, more honest, more cultured, and more literate than the current masses. It was a Catholic culture that produced the Mona Lisa. It was a Reformed Protestant culture that produced the Miltonic defense of free speech found in the Areopagitica. Only a society which censors *Teen Slut* will preserve a world in which the Mona Lisa is valued; only a nation which suppresses evil will conserve a world in which the Miltonic freedom of thought can have any meaning. In a sense, the censorship issue bears a close resemblance to the just war theory debate. Just as militarists believe that war is always good and pacifists believe that war is always bad, so we find similar extremes in the censorship controversy. The totalitarian believes that everything should come under the scrutiny of the new order; the anti-censorship activist believes that nothing—no matter how vile, destructive or crude—should be suppressed. And just as the just war theory seeks to develop some rational and accepted moral framework to limit the evils of war, so a just censorship view attempts to curb the evils of unfettered expression and totalitarian thought control by defining the limits of liberty. The object sought is the golden mean. The aim is freedom in a civil, social, and humane society. As the writer of Ecclesiastes says, "There is a time to be silent, and a time to speak." Proper selection allows each of us to speak in his sphere. Proper censorship defines when it is time to be silent.

POSTSCRIPT

Should Public Libraries Provide Sexuality Information?

The role of the library as a repository for sexuality materials dates back to the early 1880s and the "Enfer" or "Hell" collection of the National Library in Paris. This library was unique in listing its erotic holdings in its printed catalog. Among English-speaking countries, the earliest erotic collection is the "Private Case" in the British Museum Library. The catalog of books in this collection was tightly guarded. Censorship, restricted circulation, and book burning served the Victorian notion that silence was the best way to deal with sexuality. American public libraries commonly took their role as guardians of social morals quite seriously, refusing to put certain books on their shelves.

In 1910 a growing concern in the United States about good health prompted the American Medical Association and the Society of Sanitary and Moral Prophylaxis to support libraries' circulating a few approved books on sexual education and health. While most libraries did buy books of "physiological information," they usually restricted the books' circulation.

When sexologist Alfred Kinsey and his colleagues published *Sexual Behavior in the Human Male* in 1948 and *Sexual Behavior in the Human Female* in 1953, many libraries restricted their circulation to physicians and psychologists. In 1966, circulation of William Masters and Virginia Johnson's best seller *Human Sexual Reponse* was also initially limited to physicians and health care professionals.

From the birth of public libraries to the present, sexuality materials have posed a problem. In the past, the emphasis on censorship favored the library's role as guardian of society's morality. More recently this has shifted to favoring the individual's right to read whatever he or she chooses, as expressed in the American Library Association's *Intellectual Freedom Manual*.

Suggested Readings

American Library Association, *Intellectual Freedom Manual,* 4th ed. (American Library Association, 1992).

S. C. Brubaker, "In Praise of Censorship," *The Public Interest* (Winter 1994).

M. Cornog, ed., *Libraries, Erotica, and Pornography* (Oryx Press, 1991).

M. Cornog and T. Perper, *For Sex Education, See Librarian: A Guide to Issues and Resources* (Greenwood Press, 1996).

D. F. Ring, "Defending the Intended Mission," *Public Libraries* (July–August 1994).

L. Schlessinger, "Is Your Library Friend or Foe?" *Dr. Laura Perspective* (July 1999).

M. Stover, "Libraries, Censorship, and Social Protest," *American Libraries* (November 1994).

ISSUE 8

Is Pornography Harmful to Women?

YES: Elizabeth Cramer et al., from "Violent Pornography and Abuse of Women: Theory to Practice," *Violence and Victims* (vol. 13, no. 4, 1998)

NO: Nadine Strossen, from "The Perils of Pornophobia," *The Humanist* (May/June 1995)

ISSUE SUMMARY

YES: Researchers Elizabeth Cramer et al. state that their study of abused women shows that the use of pornography by males is directly linked with the physical and sexual abuse of women.

NO: Professor of law Nadine Strossen argues that misguided assaults on pornography have resulted in the naive belief that pornography is a major weapon that men use to degrade and dominate women.

Although the First Amendment to the U.S. Constitution protects freedom of speech, Americans have always had restraints on what they can say and write in public. Over 70 years ago, Chief Justice Oliver Wendell Holmes ruled that the First Amendment does not give someone the right to shout "Fire!" in a crowded theater because of the harm such an act could cause. This court ruling supports the efforts of some anti-pornography feminists, who contend that the violence and degrading portrayals of women found in pornography can lead to the abuse of women in real life. Feminists Andrea Dworkin and Catharine MacKinnon call for banning not only "traditional" pornography but also publications, acts, and verbalizations that can be construed as offensive and demeaning to women. Dworkin and MacKinnon define pornography as the major weapon in a cultural war between females and males that permeates every aspect of American lives and society.

At the root of the debate is how we define pornography. Feminist Pat Califia points out that some feminists, as well as the organization Women Against Violence in Pornography and the Media (WAVPM), have adopted a very broad definition. Califia states that according to their definition, "Pornography can include a picture of a woman whose body is smeared with honey, a woman stabbing a man in the back, or a woman dressed in leather towering over two men, as well as films showing various sex acts. This vague definition allowed them to support their contention that pornography objectifies and demeans women, since any image that is objectifying and demeaning is called pornographic." This definition also allows some to maintain that they are fighting against sexist stereotypes of women and not trying to censor sexually explicit material. In their view, misogyny (the hatred of women) is more prevalent and pernicious in pornography than in any other type of media.

Some counter that the focus and efforts of those who oppose pornography are an example of elitist white females worrying about themselves and their "sensitivities" while they ignore the very real physical violence that inner-city residents, women and men alike, face daily. Instead of trying to work out an agreement on what is pornographic, some maintain that the focus should be on gaining greater political and economic equality for women.

As you read the selections, try to develop a classification of different types of pornography. How should the new feminist-produced soft-core pornography, some of which appears in magazines like *Cosmopolitan,* that portrays women as persons who enjoy sexual pleasure as much as men do be viewed? How should pornography produced by gays and lesbians for gay and lesbian readers be viewed? What about erotic romantic novels? Decide which types you might want to make illegal, if any. Do you believe society would benefit from restricting or banning some types of sexually explicit material? For instance, should soft-core pornography, which involves nudity and genital depictions, be treated the same as hard-core pornography, which involves graphic presentation of sexual play, intercourse, and oral sex? What about pornography that includes anal sex, light and/or heavy bondage, bestiality, or other fetishistic behavior? What about topless dancers at bars, strippers on stage or at parties, or live sex acts on stage? How should suggestive advertisements, telephone sex, or "cybersex" on the Internet be viewed?

You may also want to think about what role pornography plays in American society. Why does so much pornography depict violent sex, and the degradation and victimization of women? Is pornography a symptom of a psychologically unhealthy society, or a healthy safety valve in a society that is basically uncomfortable with sexuality? If we were more accepting and had a positive view of sex that allowed it a natural place in our daily lives, would hard-core pornography continue to sell as well as it does today?

In the following selections, Elizabeth Cramer et al. present the results of a study to demonstrate the correlation between the abuse of women and the use of pornography by the abuser. Nadine Strossen argues that the condemnation of pornography can be carried too far and that universal censorship is not the solution to end violence against women.

Elizabeth Cramer et al.  **YES**

Violent Pornography and Abuse of Women: Theory to Practice

The charge has been made that pornography is the theory and rape is the practice (Kramarae & Treechler, 1985). The final report of the Attorney General's Commission on Pornography (1986), also known as the Meese Commission, stated that there was indeed a connection between persons' use of violent pornography and their use of violence in intimate relationships. The Meese Commission defined pornography as "material predominantly sexually specific and intended for the purpose of sexual arousal" (p. 228–29). They further divided pornography into two subcategories: (1) erotica, which features nudity and explicit consensual sex, and (2) pornography, which contains both nonviolent materials depicting domination and humiliation, and sexually explicit material containing violence. Only the latter category was used to define pornography in the present study. Degrading and violent sexual materials have been identified as potentially the most damaging of all types of erotica to the formation of egalitarian, mutually satisfying relationships (Linz, Donerstein, & Penrod, 1988).

Theory to Practice

Does the theory of pornography (that using pornographic materials actually teaches the user that women are there for the gratification of men, and that women enjoy the sexual "liberation" that violence brings) become the practice of pornography? Social learning theory states that we learn about how to act in social situations by observing society around us (Bandura, 1977). Cowan, Lee, Levy, and Smyer (1988) did a content analysis of 45 adult only, x-rated films randomly selected from a list of 121 adult movie titles readily available from a family videocassette store. They found that 60% of the video time was devoted to explicit portrayals of sexual acts. Of these depictions, 78% were coded as dominant and 82% as exploitive, with men doing almost 80% of the dominating/exploiting. Where women were shown as dominating/exploiting, their targets were most frequently other women. A woman's rape was shown in over half of the films, and 90% of the rapists were men. Physically aggressive acts

From Elizabeth Cramer, Judith McFarlane, Barbara Parker, Karen Soeken, Concepcion Silva, and Sally Reel, "Violent Pornography and Abuse of Women: Theory to Practice," *Violence and Victims*, vol. 13, no. 4 (1998). Copyright © 1998 by Springer Publishing Company, Inc. Reprinted by permission of Springer Publishing Company, Inc., New York 10012. References omitted.

appeared in 73% of the movies. Status inequities were shown with the men portrayed as professionals, and the women as secretaries, homemakers, students.... The authors state that "the message that men receive from these videos ... is a distorted characterization of both male and female sexuality that is particularly degrading to women" (p. 309)....

There is also a racist component in portrayals of pornographic sex. In an examination of the covers of 60 pornographic magazines and a content analysis of 7 pornographic books, Mayall and Russell (1993) found that African American women were "portrayed in a variety of derogatory and stereotypic ways —as animalistic, incapable of self-control, sexually depraved, impulsive, unclean...." Jewish women were also identified as a separate class, with these women being spoken of as "Jewish whores," "Yiddish swine," etc., and portrayed as submitting to, and enjoying, sexual degradation by Aryan "masters" (p. 176)....

Since more than 25% of all women will suffer from a sexual attack during their lifetime (Remer & Witten, 1988) and women's enjoyment of rape is a common theme in pornography (Cowan et al., 1988; Russell et al., 1993), the question of whether viewers of pornography have callous views of rape and/or are more likely to deny men's responsibility in cases of rape has been raised. Malamuth (1981) in a study of 271 male and female students found that exposure to sexually violent films increased men's acceptance of both rape myths ("women say no when they mean yes," "most women who have been raped were asking for it," "many women secretly want to be raped") and interpersonal violence against women. (Interestingly, women in the study were less accepting of rape myths and interpersonal violence after viewing sexually violent films.) Findings similar to these have been supported by Demare, Briere and Lips (1988), Garcia (1986), Linz, Donnerstein, and Penrod (1988), Malamuth and Check (1985). Linz, Donnerstein and Penrod (1984) found that exposure to one film juxtaposing sexual situations and violence per day for 5 days lowered the subjects' anxiety and depressive reactions to the violence in these films over the course of viewing. Subjects who rated the material as progressively less offensive or violent over the course of the series were also more likely to view the victim as responsible for her assault, judged her as offering less resistance to her abuser, and found her less sympathetic, less attractive and less worthy as an individual at the end of the series.

All of the studies mentioned above have taken place in a laboratory setting, and the criticism can be leveled at them that a laboratory is very different from real life. Does pornography relate to the abuse of women outside of the laboratory setting? The authors' previous study found a correlation between battering of women and pornography use by the abuser in a more naturalistic setting (Cramer & McFarlane, 1994). In this study, 87 women pressing charges of physical abuse against an intimate partner were asked if this partner used violent pornography. Forty percent of the women reported pornography use by the abuser. Of these, 35 women (53%) stated that they had been asked or forced to enact scenes they had been shown. Thirty-six (40%) of the subjects had been raped and of these, 74% stated that their partner had used pornography. Twenty-six percent of the women had been reminded of pornography during the abuse incidents. Sommers and Check (1987) also found that battered women experienced significantly more sexual aggression from their partners than the nonbattered control group and that 39% of these women (vs. 3% of the controls) answered yes to the question of whether their partner had ever tried to get them to act out pornographic scenes they had viewed. Russell and colleagues (1985) stated that 14% of a random selection of 930 women from the San Francisco area reported that they had been asked to pose for pornographic pictures, and 10% had been upset by a partner trying to enact scenes from the pornography that had been seen. In a study with current and former prostitutes in the San Francisco Bay area Silbert and Pines (1993) found that 24% of 193 women who had been raped mentioned allusions to pornographic material on the part of the rapist during the assault. This figure is even more significant when it is understood that these comments were spontaneously offered by correspondents during the course of interviews soliciting information about their sexual assault experiences, with no reference to the issues of pornography being made by the interviewer. . . .

Procedures

A prospective cohort design was followed. Approximately equal numbers of African American, non-Hispanic Anglo-American, and Hispanic women, who reported abuse in the year prior to or during pregnancy, were assessed for severity of abuse and their partners' use of pornography, and then assigned to an intervention or control group and followed until the baby was 12 months of age. . . .

Sample   This report is from 198 abused women of whom 35.4% ($n = 70$) are African American, 32.8% ($n = 65$) Hispanic (primarily Mexican and Mexican-American), and 31.8% ($n = 63$) are White American women. (Hispanic was defined as non-Anglo and non-African American and of Spanish speaking decent.)

The women were between the ages of 14 and 42, with a mean age of 23.2 years (standard deviation = 5.6); 29.6% were teenagers (i.e., 19 years or less). All women had incomes below the poverty level as defined using each state's criteria for Women, Infants, and Children (WIC) program eligibility.

Instruments

Abuse Screen

The Abuse Screen consists of five questions to determine abuse status and perpetrator within a defined period of time. (See Box). . . .

Index of Spouse Abuse (ISA)

The ISA is a 30-item, self-report scale designed to measure the severity or magnitude of physical (ISA-P) and nonphysical (ISA-NP) abuse inflicted on a woman by her male partner (Hudson & McIntosh, 1981). . . .

Danger Assessment Scale (DAS)

The DAS, consisting of 14 items with yes/no response format, is designed to assist abused women in determining their potential danger of homicide (Campbell, 1986). All items refer to risk factors that have been associated with homicides in situations involving battering. . . .

(CIRCLE <u>YES</u> OR <u>NO</u> FOR EACH QUESTION)

1. Have you **EVER** been emotionally or physically abused by your **partner or someone** important **to you?**   YES   NO
2. **IN THE YEAR BEFORE YOU WERE PREGNANT,** were you pushed, shoved, slapped, hit, kicked or otherwise physically hurt by someone?   YES   NO
    If YES, by whom?_____
3. **WHILE YOU WERE PREGNANT** were you pushed, shoved, slapped, hit, kicked or otherwise physically hurt by someone?   YES   NO
    If YES, by whom?_____
4. **IN THE YEAR BEFORE YOU WERE PREGNANT,** did anyone force you to have sexual activities?   YES   NO
    If YES, who?_____
5. **WHILE YOU WERE PREGNANT** did anyone force you to have sexual activities? YES   NO
    If YES, who?_____
6. Are you afraid of your partner or anyone you listed above?   YES   NO

Severity of Violence Against Women Scales (SVAWS)

The SVAWS is a 46-item questionnaire designed to measure two major dimensions: behaviors which threaten physical violence and actual physical violence (Marshall, 1992). Included are nine factors or subscales that have been demonstrated valid through factor analytic techniques: Symbolic Violence and Mild, Moderate, and Serious Threats (Threats of Violence Dimension), and Mild, Minor, Moderate, Serious, and Sexual Violence (Actual Violence Dimension). . . .

Relationship Inventory

The authors designed the Relationship Inventory to assess the status of the relationship including information about the abusers' use of pornography. The following introductory comment was read by the investigators to each woman. "The next questions are about pornography and abuse. We define pornography as sexually violent scenes where a woman is being hurt. For example, the woman is held or tied down." Four questions with a yes/no response option were asked: Does the man who abuses you EVER use pornographic magazines films, or videos? Does the man who abuses you EVER show you or make you look at pornographic scenes in magazines, films or videos? Does the man who abuses you EVER ask you or force you to act out the pornographic scenes he has looked at? Does the man who abuses you EVER ask you or force you to pose for pornographic pictures? ...

Discussion and Conclusions

The findings of this ethnically stratified cohort study of 198 abused women indicate that 40.9% of the women report use of pornographic material by the abuser with the proportion of pornographic use significantly higher for Whites compared to Blacks and Hispanics. Ethnic differences exist for all four pornographic questions, with a greater proportion of White women responding "yes" to all the pornographic questions. If one accepts social learning theory, this would tend to confirm findings of the 1970 Commission on Pornography and Obscenity which stated that White males use more pornography than other ethnic or racial groups, since most of the relationships in this study did not cross racial lines. These ethnic differences also agree with the authors' earlier study of abuse during pregnancy that found both frequency and severity of physical abuse significantly higher for White women compared to African American and Hispanic women (McFarlane, Parker, Soeken, & Bullock, 1992).

In this study, when three groups were formed according to the abuser's use of pornography and associated involvement of the woman in pornographic activities, violence scores were highest for women reporting the abuser asked or forced them to look at, act out or pose for pornographic scenes, pictures. Severity of violence was not related simply to whether the abuser used pornography.

... Stated differently, one out of four abusive men forced their partner to participate with them in their use of pornography. Using other measures of violence, this subsample of abusers was consistently the most violent.

Although some would argue that since forcing a woman to participate in a sexual act is violence, the relationship between these variables is tautological. However, the entire sample was of women currently in a relationship with a violent man and only one fourth of the women reported being forced to participate in pornographic activities. Additional research is needed to further describe the differences between these groups of abusive men.

In considering these findings, several points need to be emphasized. First, in collecting the data, we were careful to define pornography by saying "We are talking about when women are held down or hurt," thus making sure that the women were not reporting on simple nudity. Second, the entire sample was women who had been physically or sexually assaulted by their male partner in the previous 12 months. To summarize, in this sample of 198 women, 2 out of 5 reported that their husband or male partner had used pornographic materials that depicted women in sexually violent scenes. The rate was highest for White women, followed by Hispanic women, with Black women reporting the lowest rate. Of those who did report any use of pornography, approximately 55% of the men forced the women to participate. ...

Implications exist for both women and men. Requested or forced involvement of women in pornographic activities may indicate the likelihood for increased violence and associated trauma for women. This information can be offered to abused women as part of comprehensive counseling, advocacy, and education. Women provided with information on behaviors associated with increased violence can make informed decisions that protect not only their own safety, but that of their children. Equally important is to provide men with information regarding the degree to which pornography may influence their behavior toward women. Of particular concern is the degree to which pornography is used by men for sexual information. Certainly, to present sexual information to both males and females with an egalitarian relationship of mutual respect will contribute to decreasing violence toward women.

Nadine Strossen

The Perils of Pornophobia

In 1992, in response to a complaint, officials at Pennsylvania State University unceremoniously removed Francisco de Goya's masterpiece, *The Nude Maja*, from a classroom wall. The complaint had not been lodged by Jesse Helms or some irate member of the Christian Coalition. Instead, the complainant was a feminist English professor who protested that the eighteenth-century painting of a recumbent nude woman made her and her female students "uncomfortable."

This was not an isolated incident. At the University of Arizona at Tucson, feminist students physically attacked a graduate student's exhibit of photographic self-portraits. Why? The artist had photographed *herself* in her *underwear*. And at the University of Michigan Law School, feminist students who had organized a conference on "Prostitution: From Academia to Activism" removed a feminist-curated art exhibition held in conjunction with the conference. Their reason? Conference speakers had complained that a composite videotape containing interviews of working prostitutes was "pornographic" and therefore unacceptable.

What is wrong with this picture? Where have they come from—these feminists who behave like religious conservatives, who censor works of art because they deal with sexual themes? Have not feminists long known that censorship is a dangerous weapon which, if permitted, would inevitably be turned against them? Certainly that was the irrefutable lesson of the early women's rights movement, when Margaret Sanger, Mary Ware Dennett, and other activists were arrested, charged with "obscenity," and prosecuted for distributing educational pamphlets about sex and birth control. Theirs was a struggle for freedom of sexual expression and full gender equality, which they understood to be mutually reinforcing.

Theirs was also a lesson well understood by the second wave of feminism in the 1970s, when writers such as Germaine Greer, Betty Friedan, and Betty Dodson boldly asserted that women had the right to be free from discrimination not only in the workplace and in the classroom but in the bedroom as well. Freedom from limiting, conventional stereotypes concerning female sexuality was an essential aspect of what we then called "women's liberation." Women

From Nadine Strossen, "The Perils of Pornophobia," *The Humanist,* vol. 55, no. 3 (May/June 1995), pp. 7–9. Copyright © 1995 by Nadine Strossen. Reprinted by permission of the author.

should not be seen as victims in their sexual relations with men but as equally assertive partners, just as capable of experiencing sexual pleasure.

But it is a lesson that, alas, many feminists have now forgotten. Today, an increasingly influential feminist pro-censorship movement threatens to impair the very women's rights movement it professes to serve. Led by law professor Catharine MacKinnon and writer Andrea Dworkin, this faction of the feminist movement maintains that sexually oriented *expression*—not sex-segregated labor markets, sexist concepts of marriage and family, or pent-up rage—is the preeminent cause of discrimination and violence against women. Their solution is seemingly simple: suppress all "pornography."

Censorship, however, is never a simple matter. First, the offense must be described. And how does one define something so infinitely variable, so deeply personal, so uniquely individualized as the image, the word, and the fantasy that cause sexual arousal? For decades, the U.S. Supreme Court has engaged in a Sisyphean struggle to craft a definition of *obscenity* that the lower courts can apply with some fairness and consistency. Their dilemma was best summed up in former Justice Potter Stewart's now famous statement: "I shall not today attempt further to define [obscenity]: and perhaps I could never succeed in intelligibly doing so. But I know it when I see it."

The censorious feminists are not so modest as Justice Stewart. They have fashioned an elaborate definition of *pornography* that encompasses vastly more material than does the currently recognized law of *obscenity*. As set out in their model law (which has been considered in more than a dozen jurisdictions in the United States and overseas, and which has been substantially adopted in Canada), pornography is "the sexually explicit subordination of women through pictures and/or words." The model law lists eight different criteria that attempt to illustrate their concept of "subordination," such as depictions in which "women are presented in postures or positions of sexual submission, servility, or display" or "women are presented in scenarios of degradation, humiliation, injury, torture . . . in a context that makes these conditions sexual." This linguistic driftnet can ensnare anything from religious imagery and documentary footage about the mass rapes in the Balkans to self-help books about women's health. Indeed, the Boston Women's Health Book Collective, publisher of the now-classic book on women's health and sexuality, *Our Bodies, Ourselves,* actively campaigned against the MacKinnon-Dworkin model law when it was proposed in Cambridge, Massachusetts, in 1985, recognizing that the book's explicit text and pictures could be targeted as pornographic under the law.

Although the "MacDworkinite" approach to pornography has an intuitive appeal to many feminists, it is *itself* based on subordinating and demeaning stereotypes about women. Central to the pornophobic feminists—and to many traditional conservatives and right-wing fundamentalists, as well—is the notion that *sex* is inherently degrading to women (although not to men). Not just sexual expression but sex itself—even consensual, nonviolent sex—is an evil from which women, like children, must be protected.

MacKinnon puts it this way: "Compare victims' reports of rape with women's reports of sex. They look a lot alike. . . . The major distinction between intercourse (normal) and rape (abnormal) is that the normal happens so often that one cannot get anyone to see anything wrong with it." And from Dworkin: "Intercourse remains a means or the means of physiologically making a woman inferior." Given society's pervasive sexism, she believes, women cannot freely consent to sexual relations with men; those who do consent are, in Dworkin's words, "collaborators . . . experiencing pleasure in their own inferiority."

These ideas are hardly radical. Rather, they are a reincarnation of disempowering puritanical, Victorian notions that feminists have long tried to consign to the dustbin of history: woman as sexual victim; man as voracious satyr. The MacDworkinite approach to sexual expression is a throwback to the archaic stereotypes that formed the basis for nineteenth-century laws which prohibited "vulgar" or sexually suggestive language from being used in the presence of women and girls.

In those days, women were barred from practicing law and serving as jurors lest they be exposed to such language. Such "protective" laws have historically functioned to bar women from full legal equality. Paternalism always leads to exclusion, discrimination, and the loss of freedom and autonomy. And in its most extreme form, it leads to purdah, in which women are completely shrouded from public view.

⌒⊙⌒

The pro-censorship feminists are not fighting alone. Although they try to distance themselves from such traditional "family-values" conservatives as Jesse Helms, Phyllis Schlafly, and Donald Wildmon, who are less interested in protecting women than in preserving male dominance, a common hatred of sexual expression and fondness for censorship unite the two camps. For example, the Indianapolis City Council adopted the MacKinnon-Dworkin model law in 1984 thanks to the hard work of former council member Beulah Coughenour, a leader of the Indiana Stop ERA movement. (Federal courts later declared the law unconstitutional.) And when Phyllis Schlafly's Eagle Forum and Beverly LaHaye's Concerned Women for America launched their "Enough Is Enough" anti-pornography campaign, they trumpeted the words of Andrea Dworkin in promotional materials.

This mutually reinforcing relationship does a serious disservice to the fight for women's equality. It lends credibility to and strengthens the right wing and its anti-feminist, anti-choice, homophobic agenda. This is particularly damaging in light of the growing influence of the religious right in the Republican Party and the recent Republican sweep of both Congress and many state governments. If anyone doubts that the newly empowered GOP intends to forge ahead with anti-woman agendas, they need only read the party's "Contract with America" which, among other things, reintroduces the recently repealed "gag rule" forbidding government-funded family-planning clinics from even discussing abortion with their patients.

The pro-censorship feminists base their efforts on the largely unexamined assumption that ridding society of pornography would reduce sexism and violence against women. If there were any evidence that this were true, anti-censorship feminists—myself included—would be compelled at least to reexamine our opposition to censorship. But there is no such evidence to be found.

A causal connection between exposure to pornography and the commission of sexual violence has never been established. The National Research Council's Panel on Understanding and Preventing Violence concluded in a 1993 survey of laboratory studies that "demonstrated empirical links between pornography and sex crimes in general are weak or absent." Even according to another research literature survey that former U.S. Surgeon General C. Everett Koop conducted at the behest of the staunchly anti-pornography Meese Commission, only two reliable generalizations could be made about the impact of "degrading" sexual material on its viewers: it caused them to think that a variety of sexual practices was more common than they had previously believed, and to more accurately estimate the prevalence of varied sexual practices.

Correlational studies are similarly unsupportive of the pro-censorship cause. There are no consistent correlations between the availability of pornography in various communities, states and countries and their rates of sexual offenses. If anything, studies suggest an inverse relationship: a greater availability of sexually explicit material seems to correlate not with higher rates of sexual violence but, rather, with higher indices of gender equality. For example, Singapore, with its tight restrictions on pornography, has experienced a much greater increase in rape rates than has Sweden, with its liberalized obscenity laws.

There *is* mounting evidence, however, that MacDworkinite-type laws will be used against the very people they are supposed to protect—namely, women. In 1992, for example, the Canadian Supreme Court incorporated the MacKinnon-Dworkin concept of pornography into Canadian obscenity law. Since that ruling, in *Butler v. The Queen*—which MacKinnon enthusiastically hailed as "a stunning victory for women"—well over half of all feminist bookstores in Canada have had materials confiscated or detained by customs. According to the *Feminist Bookstore News,* a Canadian publication, "The *Butler* decision has been used . . . only to seize lesbian, gay, and feminist material."

Ironically but predictably, one of the victims of Canada's new law is Andrea Dworkin herself. Two of her books, *Pornography: Men Possessing Women* and *Women Hating,* were seized, custom officials said, because they "illegally eroticized pain and bondage." Like the MacKinnon-Dworkin model law, the *Butler* decision makes no exceptions for material that is part of a feminist critique of pornography or other feminist presentation. And this inevitably overbroad sweep is precisely why censorship is antithetical to the fight for women's rights.

The pornophobia that grips MacKinnon, Dworkin, and their followers has had further counterproductive impacts on the fight for women's rights. Censorship factionalism within the feminist movement has led to an enormously wasteful diversion of energy from the real cause of and solutions to the ongoing problems of discrimination and violence against women. Moreover, the "porn-made-me-do-it" defense, whereby convicted rapists cite MacKinnon and Dworkin in seeking to reduce their sentences, actually impedes the aggressive enforcement of criminal laws against sexual violence.

A return to the basic principles of women's liberation would put the feminist movement back on course. We women are entitled to freedom of expression—to read, think, speak, sing, write, paint, dance, photograph, film, and fantasize as we wish. We are also entitled to our dignity, autonomy, and equality. Fortunately, we can—and will—have both.

POSTSCRIPT

Is Pornography Harmful to Women?

The issue of pornography and its potential harms, particularly in reinforcing the subjugation and humiliation of females, is a perplexing one. Efforts to censor speech, writing, and pictorial material (including classical art) have been continuous throughout American history. The success of censorship efforts depends mainly on the dominating views in the particular era in which the efforts are being made, and on whether conservative or liberal views dominate during that period. In the conservative Victorian era, morals crusader Anthony Comstock persuaded Congress to adopt a broadly worded law banning "any book, painting, photograph, or other material design, adapted, or intended to explain human sexual functions, prevent conception, or produce abortion." That 1873 law was in effect for almost a hundred years, until the U.S. Supreme Court declared its last remnants unconstitutional by allowing the sale of contraceptives to married women in 1963 and to single women in 1972.

In 1986, a pornography commission headed by then–Attorney General Edwin Meese maintained that the "totality of evidence" clearly documented the social dangers of pornography and justified severe penalties and efforts to restrict and eliminate it. At the same time, then–Surgeon General C. Everett Koop arrived at conclusions that opposed those of the Meese commission. Koop stated that "Much research is still needed in order to demonstrate that the present knowledge [of laboratory studies] has significant real world implications for predicting [sexual] behavior."

Suggested Readings

K. Davies, "Voluntary Exposure to Pornography and Men's Attitudes Toward Feminism and Rape," *Journal of Sex Research* (1997).

A. Leuchtag, "The Culture of Pornography," *The Humanist* (May/June 1995).

E. Schlosser, "The Business of Pornography," *U.S. News & World Report* (February 10, 1997).

N. Strossen, *Defending Pornography: Free Speech, Sex, and the Fight for Women's Rights* (Scribner, 1995).

B. Thompson, *Soft Core: Moral Crusades Against Pornography in Britain and America* (Cassell, 1995).

ISSUE 9

Should Sexual Relationships Between Professors and Students Be Banned?

YES: Brian Martin, from "Staff-Student Sex: Abuse of Trust and Conflict of Interest," *The Australian* (October 23, 1991)

NO: Barry M. Dank and Joseph S. Fulda, from "Forbidden Love: Student-Professor Romances," *Sexuality and Culture* (vol. 1, 1997)

ISSUE SUMMARY

YES: Professor Brian Martin asserts that sexual relationships between professors and students are inappropriate and constitute an abuse of trust. He contends that universities need to establish clear and firm policies against such abuse.

NO: Professor of sociology Barry M. Dank and author Joseph S. Fulda counter that efforts to ban all romances between students and faculty on college campuses feed off unrelated notions of sexual harassment and pedophilia, treat female students as incompetent children incapable of giving informed consent, and are fueled by a resentment toward societal norms about older men dating and marrying younger women.

Romantic and sexual relationships between students and faculty or staff members have been part of college life since ancient times. One of the greatest romances in human history rocked the University of Paris in the twelfth century when Pierre Abelard, a professor of logic, and one of his students, Heloise, fell in love and secretly married. After being castrated by thugs hired by her uncle, Abelard became an abbot of a monastery and Heloise an abbess of a convent. Their subsequent correspondence, especially three letters written by Heloise, are among the world's greatest love letters.

Heloise was a rarity at the University of Paris 800 years ago, as were women in higher education before the 1950s. After World War II and the start of the women's rights movement, the number of female students attending colleges and universities exploded to the point where there are now more women than men in college. More female students means more opportunities for male faculty members and these students to be attracted to each other and develop a sexual relationship. Although there are no hard statistics, a background check of faculty and staff spouses on any large campus today would likely reveal a significant number of university employees and faculty who have married former students. Romances between students and faculty members may be less common in small colleges, especially those with a conservative religious atmosphere, and more common in large state and public universities with larger populations of older graduate students. When a romance between a student and a faculty member ends, the student may come to the conclusion that she or he was the victim of sexual harassment and pressured into an intimate relationship that was never really desired.

Recent public and legal awareness of sexual harassment have turned professor-student relationships into a major political and legal debate. Similar workplace relationships have resulted in litigation. Plaintiffs have been awarded millions of dollars in damages in cases when a consensual relationship turned sour between a manager and an employee and the employer did not take action to resolve repeated complaints of sexual harassment, which followed when the manager refused to accept the end of the relationship. To avoid this risk, some corporations have adopted policies that ban all amorous and sexual relationships between employees, regardless of their position in the company. In some companies, when two employees start a romantic relationship and one supervises or evaluates the other, they must immediately advise their supervisor so that one or the other can be given a lateral transfer to avoid any appearance of conflict of interest and reduce the risk of sexual harassment charges being made. In other companies, the ban covers all employees and requires that both employees be terminated unless one seeks employment elsewhere.

Do you think a strict ban on amorous or erotic relationships between faculty and students is necessary to avoid the potential of harm to students, or would such a ban create too much distance between professors and students? What kind of policy does your college have? What kind of policy do you think it should have?

In the following selections, Brian Martin maintains that sexual relationships between professors and students should be banned because this type of relationship is by nature unequal and may cause professors to abuse their position of authority. Barry M. Dank and Joseph S. Fulda counter that to ban sexual relationships between professors and students is to repress the freedom of consenting adults.

Brian Martin

 **YES**

Staff-Student Sex: Abuse of Trust and Conflict of Interest

In July 1990, the Vice-Chancellor of the University of Wollongong, Australia, made an important statement against sexual harassment. In it he also raised an even more sensitive topic: sexual relations between staff and students.

The Vice-Chancellor's statement included the following sentences: "Of particular concern in Universities are situations with students when positions of privilege are abused. For instance, normal social relationships among staff and students must never develop into closer individual relationships in which students may feel their academic progress depends upon compliance with the wishes of a staff member or members." This mild-sounding statement is dynamite in the university context.

No one knows the prevalence of sexual activity between faculty and students at universities, but it is undoubtedly higher than many would imagine. Take the case of the associate professor who has had a series of "serious" relationships with undergraduate women whom he met in his sophomore class. Each relationship lasts just one year, typically terminating in a terrible breakup, with devastating effects on the student.

Then there is the charming full professor who expects—and often achieves—some level of sexual intimacy with every new female Ph.D. student. Some refuse to be won over and worry about their scholarships and supervision; those who acquiesce may become afraid to protest about the professor's casual treatment of their feelings and unable to find a way to withdraw from the relationship.

Finally, there is the charismatic teacher who is always available to discuss issues with freshmen in informal settings—such as his house. Many young female students are attracted by his intelligence and sophistication and eager for a closer relationship. He is willing to oblige. He maintains sexual relationships with five or six of them at a time—at least for the first part of each year.

Let's be clear what's being discussed here. These cases represent something different from sexual harassment, which means forms of sexual behaviour which are unsolicited, unwelcome and unreciprocated. Sexual harassment can include sexual remarks or gestures, pinching, touching, kissing, sexual propositions, grabbing at women's bodies, rape and other sexual violence. Sexual harassment also includes propositions to women promising better marks in exchange for sexual favours ("an A for a lay"). Female workers as well as students are potential targets of sexual harassment. Only a tiny proportion of sexual harassment is directed against men.

Sexual harassment has been on the agenda in universities and other organisations for a number of years. There are policies against it and committees to hear grievances. The Vice-Chancellor's statement was primarily about sexual harassment. But it went further.

The women in the cases described above entered into sexual relationships with faculty without being forced. Yet, it can be argued, these relationships are most inappropriate.

University teachers hold positions of trust. They are expected to design teaching programmes and carry out their teaching duties to help their students develop as mature thinkers. This may involve close working relationships in tutorials or laboratories, individual meetings to discuss projects or essays, and more casual occasions for intellectual give and take. For impressionable young students, the boundaries between intellectual development and personal life may become blurred. In this situation, some academics easily move from intellectual to personal to sexual relationships.

In their book *The Lecherous Professor,* Billie Wright Dziech and Linda Weiner argue that "Few students are ever, in the strictest sense, consenting adults. A student can never be a genuine equal of a professor insofar as his professional position gives him power over her.... Whether the student consents to the involvement or whether the professor ever intends to use his power against her is not the point. The issue is that the power and the role disparity always exist" (p. 74).

As well as an abuse of trust, sexual relationships between teachers and students represent a serious conflict of interest. The possibility of favouritism in assessment is obvious, as is the possibility of harsh marking for those who have broken off relationships. But this is only the beginning of the problems. Even if academic evaluations are kept completely independent of personal involvements, it is likely that there will be an appearance of bias in the eyes of other students and staff.

Another real problem arises when an academic—especially a powerful academic—has a relationship with a student in a colleague's class. Pressure may be brought to bear on the colleague to give preferential treatment to the student, such as better marks, extensions on essays, or extra help. Even without pressure, preferential treatment may be provided to avoid risking the colleague's displeasure. When there are multiple relationships involving several staff and students, the possibilities for conflict of interest are mind-boggling.

Sometimes it is difficult to draw a firm line between acceptable and unacceptable behaviours. But a few things should be clear. Sexual relationships should not be permitted between a teacher and the students in his own class or under his supervision. If a relationship is anticipated, then mutually agreeable arrangements should be made to change teaching or assessment.

To some, this will sound like common sense, and they may argue that restrictions should go much further. Others may see such a prohibition as unduly restrictive. But it is no different from what is expected of doctors in relation to patients.

At some universities, any academic found to have sexual relations with a student is subject to dismissal. Such strong policies grow out of sexual harassment legislation: the courts have upheld the dismissal of a professor involved in an apparently consensual sexual relationship with a student.

A tough policy against staff-student sex, implemented over the past decade, would decimate the ranks of many university departments. Those affected could legitimately say that they "didn't think it was wrong."

That indeed is the problem. Abuse of trust and conflict of interest from staff-student sexual relationships are all too common because administrators have been too blind or unconcerned to take a stand against them. Universities need to develop clear and firm policies against sexual abuses so that no academic can make the excuse that he "didn't know."

NO

Barry M. Dank and Joseph S. Fulda

Forbidden Love: Student–Professor Romances

Introduction

A prominent concern—often overshadowing academics—of American universities during the past decade has been dealing with issues surrounding sexual harassment. Generally, universities have developed policies that sanction "unwanted sexual attention" and that prohibit working and, increasingly, learning environments which are held to be "hostile" to women. During this same period, a literature has emerged which has called on universities to expand the definition of sexual harassment to include a ban on intimate relationships between students and faculty. Such a proposal came to the forefront of university attention in 1993 when the Committee on Women's Concerns at the University of Virginia proposed a university-wide ban on all sexual fraternization between undergraduates and professors. This [selection] critiques the intellectual underpinnings of the banning movement and explores the underlying psychosocial dynamics which have propelled the movement forward.

The Lens of the Law

Central to the proscription of sexual harassment is the principle that women have the right to be protected from unwanted sexual attention in formal organizational settings. In 1986, the U.S. Supreme Court in *Meritor Savings Bank v. Vinson* noted that "The unwelcomeness standard has the benefit of allowing claimants to determine subjectively what constitutes offensive behavior.... Violators will be put on notice that their behavior constitutes harassment" (Hallinan, 1993, p. 452, emphasis added). *Meritor* in essence elevated "the reasonable woman" into the central position of deciding what constitutes harassment; it is her subjectivity that counts. That the male may not have intended to harass is irrelevant under *Meritor*. Along with a number of other Federal cases (Hallinan, 1993), *Meritor* not only put the woman in the position of defining unwanted sexual attention but also in the position of defining what is a "hostile" work environment—even when the woman was not a recipient of sexually harassing or directly hostile behavior. Thus, the U.S. District Court for the District of Columbia found in *Broderick v. Ruder* (1988) that Catherine Broderick could prevail in her claim of sexual harassment since her co-workers and their supervisors engaged in sexual behavior in such a manner as to lead her to conclude that such behaviors led to unfair promotions and raises, thereby creating a hostile work environment for her (Hallinan, 1993, p. 455).

American universities come under the jurisdiction of this case law via application of Title IX of the Education Amendments of 1972 which prohibits educational institutions from engaging in sex discrimination, which *Meritor* held to include sexual harassment. Federal courts have ruled that the " ... same standards developed to interpret Title VII of the Civil Rights Act of 1964 must be used to decide Title IX cases" (Wagner, 1993, p. B1). More recently, the Supreme Court ruled in *Franklin v. Gwinnet County Public Schools* (1992) that students who had been sexually harassed could sue educational institutions when such institutions were a party to the harassment (Wagner, 1993).

The Distorted Lens of the Feminist Banners

Given the above decisions, and their applicability to universities, it would appear safe to conclude that the concept of sexual harassment had been well-defined, and that any remaining work to be done in the university and workplace centered around education and application. Such, however, has not been the case. Starting in the 1980's, a feminist literature emerged calling for the banning of intimate, organizationally based, asymmetrical relationships and the subsumption of such relationships under the rubric of sexual harassment. Thus, when individuals in asymmetrical relationships engage in sexual behavior such a relationship is seen as sexual harassment with the person in the superordinate position viewed as the harasser and the person in the subordinate position as the victim. Louise Fitzgerald provides a representative statement of sexual asymmetry as sexual harassment when she states: "When a formal power differential exists, ALL sexist or sexual behavior is seen as harassment, since the woman is not considered to be in a position to object, resist, or give fully free consent; when no such differential exists, it is the recipient's experience and perception of the behavior as offensive that constitutes the defining factor" (Quoted in Paludi and Barickman, 1991a, p. 7). Or, as Paludi and Barickman put it: "Sexual harassment is an issue of organizational power. Since work (and academic) organizations are defined by vertical stratification and asymmetrical relations between supervisors and subordinates ... individuals can use the power of their position to extort sexual gratification from their subordinates" (Paludi and Barickman, 1991b, p. 151).

As indicated in these statements, the woman's perception of the situation is no longer central. What is central is her organizational position relative to the man. If her organizational position is subordinate and she is involved in an intimate relationship, she is seen as simply incapable of giving fully free consent. Given that consent is precluded in an asymmetric relationship, the banning of such relationships becomes appropriate. Indeed, if such a ban does not exist, the non-prohibiting organizations may become liable for the resulting "sexual harassment."

Although the principles which lead to the prohibition of intimate asymmetrical relationships are applicable to both the workplace and the university, concern has been predominantly within the university; and within the university, concern has overwhelmingly focused on student-faculty relationships. It is in the context of student-faculty relationships that the inapplicability of the concept of consent has been advocated with particular vigor. In 1984 the authors of *The Lecherous Professor* set the tone of the debate when they spoke of consent in student–faculty relationships as a myth. As they advocate: "Few students are ever, in the strictest sense, consenting adults. A student can never be a genuine equal of a professor insofar as his professional position gives him power over her" (Dziech and Weiner, 1984, p. 74). Or as Sandler succinctly puts it: "Another myth is that of the consenting adult. True consent can occur only between equals, and a relationship does not consist of equals when one party has power over the other" (1990, p. 8).

Given the belief that consent is a myth, it follows that a student in a relationship with a professor cannot meaningfully indicate to herself or others whether the professorial attention is welcome or unwelcome. As [Eileen] Wagner has indicated: "The usefulness of the argument that a student consented to a sexual relationship... lost significant ground when the Supreme Court set the Title VII standard of forbidden behavior at 'unwelcome'. How many coeds have endured the sexual advances of their teachers out of fear, fascination, or just plain naiveté, but found them 'unwelcome' nonetheless?" (1993, p. B1). And even when a student internally "feels" that the attention is wanted, consent still cannot be given, these writers argue. As student Lori Peters found as a result of her "consensual" relationship with a professor: "My experience with sexual harassment has led me to believe that in the context of power imbalance there is no such thing as consent. Where the power lies so lies the responsibility..." (1989, p. 21). Another way of putting it is that to the feminist banners, the subjective perceptions of the female student are neither a necessary nor a sufficient condition in determining whether sexual harassment has occurred. A professor may propose and a student may accept, but according to this emerging perspective, the professor is still guilty of harassment since the student is in an asymmetrical relationship and is simply incapable of consent. As Fitzgerald has indicated: "... perceptions alone (whether those of observers or victims) are not adequate for a valid definition. Women, after all, are socialized to accept many nonconsensual or even offensive sexual interactions as being nonremarkable" (1990, p. 37). The feminist perspective thus rejects the doctrine of *Meritor* lock, stock, and barrel. Sexual harassment is defined, not subjectively by the woman, but objectively by what feminists like to call "the power relations."

Contextual Versus Categorical Bans

Given the belief that consent is an impossibility in student–faculty relationships, the banning of such relationships becomes axiomatic. The issue then is whether the ban should be contextual, i.e., only in the context of a direct

supervisory relationship such as exists in the classroom or between dissertation adviser and doctoral candidate, or categorical, i.e., with absolutely no
fraternization between students and faculty.

Prior to the 1993 movement for categorical banning, there were a number
of universities that formally adopted the principle of asymmetry to discourage
or ban intimate relationships when the professor was in a direct supervisory
relationship with the student. For example, the policy at Indiana University is
representative of contextual banning: "All amorous or sexual relationships between faculty members and students are unacceptable when the faculty member has a professional responsibility for the student. Voluntary consent by the
student in such a relationship is suspect, given the fundamental asymmetric nature of the relationship." The Tufts University policy is similar: "It is a violation
of university policy if a faculty member... engages in an amorous dating or
sexual relationship with a student whom he/she instructs, evaluates, supervises,
advises. Voluntary consent by the student... is suspect."

The principle of asymmetry as a rationale for bans on student–faculty
relationships had been advocated in the early eighties as part of the Harvard
University policy on sexual harassment: "Relationships between officers and
students are always fundamentally asymmetric in nature." However, attempts
by universities during the eighties to formally adopt categorical bans generally
failed as reflected by the rejection of such policies by the university faculties
at UCLA and the University of Texas, Arlington in 1986 (Keller, 1990, p. 29).
It was Ann Lane, Professor of History and Director of Women's Studies and
a member of the Committee on Women's Concerns at the University of Virginia, who launched the University of Virginia's campaign for a categorical ban
on undergraduate–faculty fraternization and who quickly became the symbolic
leader of the movement for such bans at universities across the nation.

Professors as Sex Objects

For Ann Lane the boundary dividing students and professors was inviolate. And,
as for professors who crossed such boundaries, for Lane "... the common story
is the teacher who is a sickie" (Dateline NBC, May 25, 1993). It was cast as an
issue of "... teachers [who] should keep their hands off of students in or out
of the classroom. Freedom of speech, which is what the academy is committed
to is not the same as free sex" (Oprah Winfrey Transcripts, 1993, p. 12). Lane
viewed the implementation of such bans as all but inevitable "... coming in
the wake of Anita Hill, and Tailhook and priests molesting children. We are
now aware of layers of sexual abuse in a variety of places that we were not
willing to talk about years ago" (Dateline NBC, May 25, 1993).

Lane objectifies professors who are sexually involved with students as being intrinsically abusive. In fact, the entirety of the banning literature makes
professors out as sexually obsessed predators who prey on their female students
and treat them as sexual objects. Perhaps not surprisingly, while condemning
professional objectification of female students, feminist banners have no problem with sexually objectifying professors. Almost all of the banning literature
since the publication of *The Lecherous Professor* is simply an embellishment

on this theme. Illustrative of such objectification is that of Adrienne Rich: "Finally rape of the mind.... Most young women experience a profound mixture of humiliation and intellectual self-doubt over sexual gestures by men who have power to award grades, open doors to grants and graduate school.... Even if turned aside, such gestures constitute mental rape, destruction to a woman's ego. They are acts of domination, as despicable as the molestation of the daughter by the father" (1985, p. 26).

Given the powerful imagery of the predatory, sex-obsessed professor, it is also not surprising that such imagery also contains elements of pollution and poison, elements that often characterize the imagery of threatening outsiders (Dank, 1980; Douglas, 1970). As feminist scholar Catherine Stimpson notes: "Today the psychological and social pollution ... harassment spews forth is like air pollution. No one defends either one of them.... [B]elow the stratosphere, in classrooms and laboratories, sexual louts refuse to disappear, imposing themselves on a significant proportion of our students..." (Stimpson, 1989, p. 1). Some may view such rhetoric as simple hyperbole. Others, however, take it quite seriously, invoking it in the attempt to implement categorical bans. Thus, Robin Wilson, President of California State University, Chico invoked the following imagery in his advocacy of categorical bans: "A love affair between a faculty member and a student is poison" (Sacramento Bee, 1993, p. FO 4). The professor intimately involved with a student has thus been effectively dehumanized—deprived of individual motivations—not to mention feelings—and is seen entirely in categorical terms. English Professor Joan Blythe has poignantly responded to this objectification and dehumanization:

> Education is also a transformation of us by our students, allowing us to learn and be changed by our encounter in the classroom. This ban is a prophylactic to that kind of fertility because it presents me, the teacher, as rapacious, predatory, dangerous even before I walk into the classroom.... [I]n setting up a law you have immediately cast me as a potential raptor. You are emphasizing my role not as educator but as assailant. You define me in negative terms, stripping me of my ability to teach. (Harper's, 1993, p. 42)

The Student as Innocent Child

Just as the banning movement has objectified professors, it has also objectified female students. The literature has almost uniformly cast female students as gullible, innocent, helpless children or youths who must confront the all-powerful manipulative male professor. It is an imagery that reinforces the premise that female students cannot give consent. Since there is a social consensus that children cannot give sexual consent, and since the images of student and child are so often used interchangeably, the premise that female students cannot give sexual consent to their male professors since they are childlike, innocent, and powerless meets with social receptivity.

Illustrative of this construction of female students as innocents who need protection is the commentary by [Vita] Rabinowitz:

> They [female students] are at that developmental stage in which it is common to question values and standards of behavior and open themselves to new viewpoints and experiences.... Students look up to their professors with great admiration, and attribute to them such appealing characteristics as brilliance, sophistication, wisdom and maturity. (1990, p. 105)

Or as [Sue Rosenberg] Zalk has written:

> The bottom line in the relationship between faculty member and student is POWER. The faculty member has it and the student does not.... The student does not negotiate—indeed, has nothing to negotiate with. There are no exceptions to this. Knowledge and wisdom are power. While superior knowledge, and presumably greater wisdom, are often ascribed to faculty members by society at large, the students' adolescent idealism exaggerates its extent.... (1990, p. 145)

And Ann Lane has directly invoked the image of the innocent young girl in her advocacy of categorical banning. In responding to a question as to whether she made any differentiation between female students in or out of the professor's classroom, she stated:

> No.... An 18-year old woman, first time away from home, she's in this new environment. She changes her major... she might think she'll never take a chemistry class, because she can go out with the chemistry teacher. But... she suddenly decides she wants to be a vet and now she has to take chemistry, but the relationship has ended badly. We have situations where the woman can't even walk into the classroom or won't even walk into the building. (Oprah Winfrey Transcripts, 1993, p. 13)

Given the helpless-child imagery of female students, they are seen as needing protection from predatory male professors, protection in the form of prohibition. Such protection is necessary even if it is unwanted since female subjectivity is not of central concern. Others know what is best for them (Sipchen, 1994). Again, as Ann Lane has stated: "And the ban that we have at the University of Virginia is aimed at faculty, not at students, although the students are responding to it as if it were. But it really is aimed at faculty..." (Oprah Winfrey Transcripts, 1993, p. 16). The banners' reduction of female students to children places them into the traditional protected category of "women and children." It functions to disempower female students and empower (feminist) professors and administrators as their protectors. Ironically, it not only affirms an asymmetrical, not equalitarian, relationship between professors and students, it flies in the face of what many believe is the core of true feminism —the empowerment of all women. As Katie Roiphe has pointed out, campus feminists often do just the opposite: "Any value there may be in promoting this idea about female passivity and gullibility is eclipsed by its negative effects. Feminist educators should keep track of the images they project: women can't take care of themselves, they can't make their own decisions" (1993, p. 69). Anne Bailey, Student Council President at the University of Virginia, certainly did not play this passive and gullible role when she publicly stated her opposition to the ban proposed by Ann Lane. As Bailey characterized it: "It's an invasion of the private lives of consenting adults, and it reeks of paternalism. We're old enough to go to war and to have an abortion, so I think we're old enough to decide who to go to bed with" (Jacobs, 1993). Or as one Wellesley graduate succinctly stated to her former feminist professors: "We don't need Big Mommy to tell us what's going on" (Collison, 1993, p. A17).

The banners' emphasis on the youthfulness and childlike qualities of female students is also at odds with demographics of female students at American universities: 59% are 22 or older, 43% are 25 or older, and 30% are 30 or older (*Chronicle of Higher Education,* September 2, 1996, p. 17). In fact, the student population is aging rather significantly. The proportion of students entering college at the age of 25 or older was 28% in 1972; in 1986, it was 38%. Despite the demographics, banning advocates continue to see student-faculty romances through the child–adult lens. It serves well for their purposes because of the powerful taboos surrounding adult–child sexuality. Invoking this model functions powerfully as a device of social control, pornographizing student-faculty romances and reinforcing the professor-as-child-molester caricature. No wonder so few male professors are willing to come forward as involved or formerly involved in intimate relationships with students. Even those in ongoing marriages have generally chosen to remain insulated from the public throughout the debate....

The Real Issue: Age and Age-Disloyalty

Given that the professor and student categories are age-differentiated, it is to be expected that romantic liaisons between students and faculty members are almost always older man–younger woman. Skeen and Nielsen found an average age differential of 10 years. Of course, romantic relationships generally reflect the proclivity of women to be attracted to older men and of men to be attracted to younger women (Buss, 1994). With academic couples, the age differential tends to be significantly above that of non-academic couples: at times so great as to reflect a crossing of generational boundaries—middle-aged men paired with women in their twenties.

It is our observation that many women are deeply offended by older men dating and/or marrying much younger women. Why? Given the age and dating norms in American society, the eligible men for middle-aged single women are their cohorts—middle-aged men. The field of eligibles is further narrowed for middle-aged academic women because social norms dictate not dating and/or marrying "down." Thus, the female academic's field of eligible men is radically decreased by their academic accomplishments. Of course, the most eligible men for middle-aged academic women in terms of propinquity, age, and social status are academic middle-aged men. And it is these same men who are perhaps seen as deserting their female age cohorts to date much younger students. In fact, we would go so far as to suggest that many women—particularly academic women —resent the power that young women have to attract their eligibles. In fact, one can view the banning movement as reflecting a rather traditional generational conflict—an attempt by older women to control the dating/mating behavior of younger women. This attempt, of course, is disguised by the banners' construction of the lecherous-predatory-male-professor as exploiting younger women. But the banners undermine a key feminist principle, that "no" means "no," when they assert, at least in this context, that "yes" means "no," as well. Surely, if anything means "yes," "yes" means "yes"!

[Warren] Farrell (1993) captures the potentially traumatic nature of the situation when he makes the following comparison: "When a man is forced into early retirement, he is often being given up for the younger man. Being forced into early retirement can be to a man what being 'given up for a younger woman' is for a woman" (p. 174). Given this framework, it is only to be expected that many academic women would feel hostility toward student–faculty couples. Unfortunately, too many campus feminists have dealt with their problem by advocating policies that effectively disempower, infantilize, and patronize younger women. Such infantilization is evidenced by their inability to imagine a female student ever taking the initiative with a male professor consenting (Pichaske, 1995).

To be sure, few feminist academics have conceded such motivations. When there are such public avowals, it is usually by men coming to the defense of women. When the Provost of Tufts University, Sol Gittleman, was interviewed in *The New York Times* regarding his ban of student–faculty couples, he indicated that he based his decision in part on his being tired of seeing professors "dump" their wives for younger women (Gross, 1993).

Interestingly enough, some banners do back off when same-age relationships are invoked in student–faculty relationships. Susan Webb, author of *Step Forward: Sexual Harassment in the Workplace,* is supportive of categorical banning, but yet stated the following: " ... I think it'll be difficult to place a ban on any relationship between any student whatsoever. I'm 52 years old; the professor is 53, what's the big deal?" (Oprah Winfrey Transcripts, 1993, p. 18). Perusal of the feminist literature on age and ageism also suggests this dynamic in the campus banning movement. Lois Banner's writings certainly can be used as a rationale for such banning. In her book, *In Full Flower: Aging Women, Power and Sexuality,* she writes:

> I have argued that the privilege of aging men to form relationships with younger women lies at the heart of patriarchal inequalities between the sexes. (Banner, 1992, p. 5)

And:

> The phenomenon [older man, younger woman] had seemed to me a quintessential example of sexism, a final ironic proof of the unequal access to power between men and women. For, in addition, to all their other privileges, men as they aged were still regarded as virile and attractive, with bulging stomachs and balding heads. Young women are drawn to their power—whether monetary or personal—and deficiencies overlooked. (Banner, 1992, p. 4)

Concluding Remarks

Given the prevalent caricaturing of student–faculty romances, such relationships give the impression of professorial abuse thus presenting problems for university administrators concerned with public relations and "appearances." But such superficial concerns must not be used as a rationale of repression of the associative freedoms. The concept of informed consent between adults should be the guiding principle for intimate relations—on or off campus. This principle has been recognized by the U.S. Supreme Court in *Roberts v. United States Jaycees*. "Stating that intimate association, an intrinsic element of personal liberty, is secured generally by the Bill of Rights and the Fourteenth Amendment, the Court explained that 'choices to enter into and maintain certain intimate relationships must be secured against undue intrusion by the State'" (Keller, 1990, p. 30). It is the principles that are reflected in this decision, applicable in law only to public institutions, but appropriate ethically for all institutions, that best reflect the American tradition and that best protect everyone, students, professors, and others, alike. As Elisabeth Keller writes:

> The freedom to decline or resist intimate associations is inextricably bound up with the freedom to form desirable intimate associations. Upholding both of these freedoms simultaneously in the university may appear to engender inherent conflict. However, the right to form adult consensual intimate relationships is a fundamental personal freedom which must be protected. A strong and effective university policy against sexual harassment together with the recognition of the right to privacy of faculty members and students will serve the interests of both the university and the individual. (Keller, 1990, p. 32)

POSTSCRIPT

Should Sexual Relationships Between Professors and Students Be Banned?

Yale and other universities have adopted a policy that prohibits all amorous or sexually intimate consensual relationships between faculty members and students. On the other hand, colleges such as the University of Virginia have opted to revise and strengthen their conflict-of-interest policies and warn both faculty and students that the school will take whatever steps are necessary to remove any appearance of conflict of interest in the review and evaluation of student academic performance. They also advise faculty and students of the real risk that such relationships can and often do end in recrimination and accusations of harassment and coercion when a consensual relationship goes sour.

The American Association of University Professors (AAUP) has counseled hundreds of colleges and universities on their sexual harassment policies each year. AAUP warns about potential exploitation in such relationships but stops short of requiring a ban on consensual relationships. Instead, AAUP recommends "effective steps" to prevent student reviews, evaluations, and recommendations from being tainted by intimate friendships.

This controversy is part of a much broader and more complex debate about the right every citizen has to privacy and free association guaranteed by the U.S. Constitution. Similar ongoing and unresolved debates are raging over the propriety and ethics of romantic and sexual relationships between physicians, psychologists, clergy and ministers, therapists, counselors, and social workers and their clients.

With the work environment increasingly requiring continuing advanced education to keep up with the rapid pace of change, the average age of college students is rising. Three out of five college students today do not fit the traditional 18-to-22-year-old cohort. Fully one-third of America's college students are age 30 years and older. How does this shift affect this controversy? What arguments can be made in support of limiting the personal privacy of graduate students in their late twenties and older?

How can universities avoid "building a wall of fear around male faculty" as Dank and Fulda suggest is happening? What substance, if any, can you find in their assertion that supporters of a total ban on student-professor consensually intimate relationships are "pornographizing student-faculty romances and reinforcing the professor-as-child-molester caricature"?

Another interesting question in this controversy comes from the difficulty in defining *erotic, romantic,* and *sexual* when at least 10 percent of college students were born and raised in other cultures, where very different views of these terms prevail.

Suggested Readings

A. Bloom, "Love Is in the Air: Learn About the Bright Side of Workplace Romance," http://www.careerbuilder.com (January 2, 2001).

B. M. Dank and R. Refinetti, *Sexuality and Culture, vol. 1* (Transaction Publishers, 1997).

J. B. Dullard et al., "Close Relationships in Task Environments: Perceptions of Relational Types, Illicitness and Power," *Management Communication Quarterly* (vol. 7), pp. 227–255.

B. W. Dziech, "The Abuse of Power in Intimate Relationships," *The Chronicle of Higher Education* (March 20, 1998).

B. W. Dziech and L. Weiner, *The Lecherous Professor: Sexual Harassment on Campus* (Beacon Press, 1984).

B. W. Dziech and M. W. Hawkins, *Sexual Harassment in Higher Education* (Garland Press, 1998).

K. Hallinan, "Invasion of Privacy or Protection Against Sex Harassment: Co-Employee Dating and Employer Liability," *Columbia Journal of Law and Social Problems* (vol. 26), pp. 435–464.

M. Langelan, *Back Off! How to Confront and Stop Sexual Harassment and Harassers* (Simon & Schuster, 1993).

M. Paludi, ed., *Ivory Power: Sexual Harassment on Campus* (State University of New York Press, 1990).

P. Rutter, *Sex in the Forbidden Zone: When Men in Power—Therapists, Doctors, Clergy, Teachers and Others—Betray Women's Trust* (Unwin Paperbacks, 1990).

B. Sipchen, "A Lesson in Love? The Latest Campus Debate Is Whether Student-Professor Romances Are About Power or Passion," *Los Angeles Times* (September 16, 1994), pp. El, E6.

A. Tate, "Companies Firm Against Dating in Workplace," *Daily Herald* (January 23, 1998).

ISSUE 10

Does Recent Pedophilia Research Threaten Accepted Moral Standards?

YES: Laura Schlessinger, from "Evil Among Us," *Dr. Laura Perspective* (June 1999)

NO: Sharon Lamb, from "Psychology: Some Victims Don't Need Pity," *The Boston Globe* (August 1, 1999)

ISSUE SUMMARY

YES: Radio commentator Laura Schlessinger denounces a study, published by the American Psychological Association (APA), that reexamined the results and conclusions from 59 earlier studies of child sexual abuse (CSA) in more than 37,000 college students. Schlessinger views this study as a "pseudo-scientific" attempt to convince people to accept pedophilia as normal.

NO: Sharon Lamb, a *Boston Globe* commentator, argues that solid, scientific research on child sexual abuse should be accepted, even when it calls into question common assumptions about CSA and its consequences.

In the fall of 1998, *Psychological Bulletin,* the official publication of the American Psychological Association, contained a research report entitled "A Meta-Analytic Examination of Assumed Properties of Child Sexual Abuse Using College Samples." This report was written by three respected researchers with solid publication records, Bruce Rind (Temple University), Robert Bauserman (Maryland State Health Department), and Philip Tromovitch (University of Pennsylvania). It received some discussion and notice in the academic world, but nothing unusual.

However, a few people alerted Laura Schlessinger, conservative radio and television commentator. Schlessinger immediately launched a campaign to "rally the troops to fight the enemy at the barricades and save our nation" from being turned into a nation of pedophiles. Joined by The Family Research Council and the National Association for the Research and Therapy of Homosexuality (NARTH), Schlessinger enlisted the aid of a few conservative Washington lawmakers, who prepared a bill condemning the report. On July

12, 1999, Representative Matt Salmon (R-Arizona) called on members of the House of Representatives to condemn what has become known for brevity's sake as "the Rind research or report." The purpose of this study, Salmon maintained, was to make pedophilia normal and acceptable. The representatives unanimously voted to condemn the report. Only a handful of representatives abstained, questioning the wisdom of assuming that the editors of the *Psychological Bulletin* would publish a report endorsing and promoting pedophilia. These representatives were also concerned about the wisdom of condemning a scholarly publication that none of them had seen or read in its full form.

Some believe that the conclusions of the Rind research is great news for some sexual abuse victims. If it is true that many [or even a few] victims do not suffer lifelong consequences from child sexual abuse, and that many victims are not traumatized, permanently damaged, or wounded for life, we should be happy. But many Americans find this possibility totally unacceptable. Another issue raised by the response to the Rind research triggered a letter to the president of the American Psychological Association from the past and present officers of the Society for the Scientific Study of Sexuality urging him "to staunchly support the right of sexual scientists to engage in free intellectual inquiry—especially in the area of 'controversial' research," such as the sexuality of children and the long-term consequences of child sexual abuse, incest, and adult-child sex.

In the following selections, Schlessinger maintains that the release of the APA study results is harmful because the findings can be interpreted as validating and "normalizing" pedophilia. Sharon Lamb counters that the release of the study results can be viewed in a positive manner. The study can be viewed as evidence to support the idea that not all victims of pedophilia are permanently damaged.

Laura Schlessinger

 **YES**

Evil Among Us

[You may have] heard me on the air lambasting a recent article published in the *Bulletin* of the American Psychological Association, called "A Meta-Analytic Examination of Assumed Properties of Child Sexual Abuse Using College Samples."

In short: The three researchers claim that child sexual abuse does not necessarily cause intense, lasting harm—and go on to suggest that when there is a "willing" sexual encounter between an adult and a child, it be given the "value-neutral" term "adult-child sex"!

I've read and re-read this report until I'm sick to my stomach, and still, putting these words into print leaves me practically speechless—and you know how rare that is.

When I first heard about this, I wanted to disbelieve it. But I've done my research, and I cannot stress strongly enough how deadly serious this is.

This study is the first step on the road toward normalizing pedophilia—just as homosexuality has been mainstreamed, to the point where tolerance is no longer sufficient: We now have to "embrace" it.

I want to recap for you my own journey of discovery in this horrifying story: as I first learned of this study, examined it further, spoke with experts in the field who have excoriated the authors' methodology and their conclusions, and as I received hundreds of outraged, appalled and heartbroken letters from listeners who know all too well the "lasting, pervasive" harm of child sexual abuse—and that it is *never* a "willing," "value-neutral" experience.

The Warning Bell Sounds

It began with a letter.

I was in the middle of my show one day when I received a fax from Don, a father of two, who had just heard Dom Giordano, morning talk show host on my Philadelphia affiliate, WWDB, interview one of the authors of this study. Don wrote:

> "[The author] stated that not all children who engage in sexual contact will-ingly with an adult show any lasting damage. He further stated that to call this sexual contact 'abuse' is a mistake, because it's consensual..." [I believe the researchers had] an agenda that should scare all decent people. The next time some pervert gets caught with a child, I'm sure this is the first study his scum lawyer will drag out to defend his actions."

I immediately thought, "This is a very intelligent letter, but this can't be happening." I didn't believe it. So we started to track it down.

Next we received a fact sheet from NARTH, an organization I respect: the National Association for Research and Therapy of Homosexuality. The name of NARTH's report was: "The Problem of Pedophilia: Adult-Child Sex Is Not Necessarily Abuse, Say Some Psychologists."

The NARTH article pointed out that one of the authors of the *Bulletin* arti-cle had earlier co-authored an article in a special issue of the respected *Journal of Homosexuality* entitled "Male Intergenerational Intimacy." That issue was es-sentially an advertisement for the "benefits" of pedophilia—asserting that the loving pedophile can offer a child "companionship, security and protection" that neither peers nor parents can provide, and that parents should look on the pedophile "as a partner in the boy's upbringing, someone to be welcomed into their home..."!

Here are some excerpts from NARTH's report; I'd like to thank Dr. Joseph Nicolosi, director of NARTH, for giving us permission to quote from it. (I've **boldfaced** some important points.)

> "The American Psychological Association did not denounce the positions advanced within the *Journal of Homosexuality*. In fact, just recently, the APA published a new major study written by one of those same *Journal of Ho-mosexuality* writers. The latest article appears in the APA's own prestigious *Psychological Bulletin*. It provides an overview of all of the research studying the harm resulting from childhood sexual abuse.
>
> **"The authors' conclusion? That childhood sexual abuse is, on the average, only slightly associated with psychological harm, and that the harm may not even be due to the sexual experience, but to the negative family factors in the children's backgrounds. When the sexual contact is not coerced, especially when it is experienced by a boy and enjoyed, it may not be harmful at all....**
>
> **"In fact, the authors of the *Psychological Bulletin* article propose another way of understanding pedophilia: That it may be abuse if the child feels bad about the relationship. They are in effect suggesting a repetition of the steps by which homosexuality was normalized.** In its first step toward removing homosexuality from the Diagnostic Manual, the APA said the condition was normal as long as the person didn't feel bad about it....
>
> "According to the latest diagnostic manual (DSM-IV), a person no longer has a psychological disorder simply because he molests children. To be diagnosed as disordered, he must feel anxious about the molestation,

or be impaired in his work or social relationships. **Thus, the APA has left room for the psychologically 'normal' pedophile."**

Now, I have to reiterate a point here that I've tried to make several times on the air. Psychology has become some kind of holy writ to the general public. It's not. *Psychology is not hard science.* Just because a bunch of psychologists make intellectual-sounding pronouncements about the way things are—it ain't necessarily so!

⋅⟨⊙⟩⋅

So, let me ask a question of the psychologists and psychiatrists of the world: If pedophilia is not a mental disorder, then what is it? Is it normal?

When homosexuality was dropped from the *DSM*, the agenda became, "Homosexuality is normal." If you said anything to the contrary, that meant you were hateful and bigoted. Deviance became redefined as diversity, and tolerance became defined as acceptance, then celebration. It sounds like we're taking the next step with pedophilia.

To return to the NARTH fact sheet:

"If psychology indeed recognizes consensual pedophilia as harmless, then civil law and social norms will be under pressure to follow the lead of so-called social science, as indeed they did in the issue of homosexuality. **When psychiatry declared homosexuality normal, our courts and theologians began to rewrite civil law and moral theology based upon what psychiatry said it had discovered through empirical science."**

Later, Joe Nicolosi sent me a memo that makes some very salient additional points:

1. "The study used a *college-age* sample, which implies that most subjects were likely single. Would the results of this study have been different if they had been conducted with these same subjects ten years later? Would those subjects have been more prone to divorce, alcoholism, and child abuse? Would their spouses agree that they were well-adjusted, sexually and emotionally? We doubt it.

2. "The authors of the study try to make a case for separating 'wrongfulness' (social-moral norms) from 'harmfulness' (psychological damage). We believe that social norms of wrongfulness are not *arbitrary,* but they *evolved* out of the great religious philosophers' time-honored observations of 'harmfulness'—i.e., their finding of psychological damage to the person and society.

3. "The study makes a distinction between *forced* and *consensual* child-adult or adult-teen sex. What minor-age child can make an informed decision to consent to sex?"

The Truth Comes Out

Much as I still didn't want to believe this could be happening, I realized it was time to examine this for myself.

So I got the actual article, published [in July 1998] by the American Psychological Association, in their *Psychological Bulletin*. This is a peer-reviewed publication, which means that some number of clinicians had to read and approve this article for publication. While this may not be a statement of the APA's official position, I hold them accountable for what I have been told by *numerous* professionals is garbage research.

- First of all, let's look at the title of the report: "A Meta-Analytic Examination...": Meta-analysis means you don't do any of your own work; you go into the literature, grab a lot of papers, all done by different people, put them all together, do a lot of math, and publish.
- The researchers chose 59 studies to review. Of these, 38 percent have not been published. They are unpublished master-degree or doctoral dissertations. So 23 of the 59 studies used were not even subject to any kind of peer review—that is, to the technical scrutiny of the psychological community.
- These 59 studies all used self-reporting from college students, who were questioned about the effects of child sexual abuse as they felt them. Think about that term, "self-reporting": That's a brilliant way to do research, right? You have a lot of objectivity there.
- The researchers claim that according to some of these college students' own descriptions, the negative effects of child sexual abuse "were neither pervasive nor typically intense, and that men reacted much less negatively than women." Is this anybody's personal experience? Does this bear any resemblance to anyone you know who was molested as a child?
- According to their findings, two-thirds of sexually abused men and more than one-quarter of sexually abused women "reported neutral or positive reactions." So even in their own study—again keeping in mind the dubious nature of their methods—one-third of the guys and 75 percent of the women were harmed. Aren't statistics a wonderful thing?

⚜

What really frightens me is the idea that this study will now be used to normalize pedophilia—to change the legal system, and further destroy what I feel has been an ongoing plot against the family.

I'm not alone in this view. I had a discussion with Dr. Gerard van den Aardweg of Holland, who has seen firsthand the inroads made in his country by pedophilia activists.

Dr. van den Aardweg has a Ph.D. in psychology, did his dissertation on homosexuality, has been in private practice for many years, and has written several books and articles on homosexuality, pedophilia, neuroses and family issues.

"Their argument is that scores on some tests do not indicate harm—that if harm is not demonstrated by their way of testing, then harm does not exist," Dr. van den Aardweg says.

"**I think these people are so eager to propagate the normality of adult-child sexual contact that they are blind to the obvious alternative: 'If my test did not show harm, maybe my test did not measure harm.'**"

"These tests are sample questionnaires or short interview questions. At best, they can give a very rude indication of subjectively perceived discomfort. But in very many cases they not even do that. Harm is much more than 'I do or do not feel okay,' or 'I didn't like that experience.' Harm after child sexual abuse is often an increased distress with respect to adults; a distorted and unhealthy view of sexuality; a distorted view of their own or the opposite sex. It can be subsequent sexual abnormalities. It can be marriage and other relational problems later in life; problems functioning as a parent; sometimes later promiscuity; and in many cases, inferiority complexes, because children who have been misused often feel worthless.

"**In short, what these psychologists offer us here is an insult to any really credible scientist of true scientific thinking. It is bogus psychology.**"

A Global Crisis

Now here's a further discussion that Dr. van den Aardweg and I had on the telephone:

Dr. van den Aardweg: I think the sexual reform movements of the Western world have as one of their goals to liberate sexuality in all its forms. And so there is a silent—not so silent here in Holland—cooperation of the sexual reform organizations with the cause of the militant pedophiles. Here it is very clear. For example, our Dutch Association for Sexual Reform has special meetings for pedophiles every week in most Dutch cities.

Dr. Laura: This is scary. In this country, such groups gain power and authority by attacking the opposition as phobic, intolerant of diversity, bigoted and mean.

VDA: You will do a wonderful thing if you make people aware of this, and say to them, "Don't let yourself be intimidated. Don't doubt your own common-sense judgment of these things." Because people are overruled and overwhelmed with all kinds of pseudo-science. They think "Who am I? Perhaps I'm wrong, I'm old-fashioned, I'm a victim of my Western culture." But they have to be supported as to their own convictions.

DL: So the point of liberating the sexual mores in general is, ultimately, to have access to kids.

VDA: Yes.

DL: That's what it's for: getting the kids sexually active and then getting sexually active with the kids. So there are a number of ways for people to take our kids. They can recruit them for the Fatherland's master race, they can take them out of villages and force them to become soldiers, or they can support safe-sex education in schools starting in kindergarten, and have them become active and liberated and available and open to new sexual experiences—like sex with an adult.

VDA: Pedophiles have an obsession. It's not a normal kind of sexual drive, it's a pathological obsession. It is the nucleus of their whole life. Like many disturbed people, their attitude is not that "I have to change," but that "the world has to change." And so, they are the ones to crusade to change the world, and really think that they can eventually get normal fathers and mothers to give their children to pedophiles for educational or enlightenment motivations.

Here in Holland, one of the advocates of pedophilia who just died had received royal distinction some years ago for his work to "liberate" homosexuality, as they say. He was in the Dutch senate as a very esteemed and respected senator.

Be aware: The public does not know what is happening. The pedophile network is worldwide.

Outrage and Anguish

You can imagine the firestorm I set off by devoting an entire hour of my radio show to this topic—as well as follow-ups on several subsequent days.

I hadn't even finished speaking when the faxes began pouring in. Listeners were horrified by what they were hearing. . . . The article—and my outspoken opposition to it—received a great deal of media attention. . . .

And, what a surprise, the American Psychological Association was quick to disassociate itself from the article in its own publication, according to a press release they put out:

> "As a publisher of psychological research, APA publishes thousands of research reports every year.
>
> "But, publication of the findings of a research project within an APA journal is in no way an endorsement of a finding by the Association . . .
>
> "Unfortunately, the findings of this meta-analysis . . . are being misreported by some in the media. The actual findings are that for this segment of the population (college students) being the victim of childhood sexual abuse was found to be less damaging to them than generally believed. However, one overall statement of the results was that students who were the victims of child sexual abuse were, on average, slightly less well-adjusted than students who were not victimized as children . . .
>
> "Those who are reporting that the study says that childhood sexual contact with adults is not harmful to children are misreporting the findings."

Perhaps they hadn't read their own publication: The researchers specifically say that "this poorer adjustment *could not be attributed to CSA [child sexual abuse]* [italics mine—DL] because family environment was consistently confounded with CSA...."

Furthermore, the authors clearly state at the end of their report: *"A willing encounter with positive reactions would be labeled simply* adult-child *sex, a value-neutral term.... Moreover, the term* child *should be restricted to nonadolescent children"*—as if a nonadolescent child has the intellectual, psychological or emotional maturity to "willingly" engage in a sexual encounter with an adult!

I'm still flabbergasted by this logic.

NO

Sharon Lamb

Psychology: Some Victims Don't Need Pity

In three weeks, thousands of psychologists will descend on Boston for the American Psychological Association's 107th convention. And it's quite likely that over their clam chowder and steaming lobsters, one hot topic will be a study on child sexual abuse published last year in the APA journal *Psychological Bulletin.*

This is the "meta-analytic" study that looked at 59 earlier reviews of college students who had been sexually abused as children. It found that not all sexually abused children are wounded for life, and not all victims are traumatized.

This is also the study that the House last month voted almost unanimously (13 members abstained) to condemn on the grounds that it supported pedophilia. The APA, after defending the article for several months, eventually caved in and, in a letter from APA President Raymond Fowler to House majority leader Tom DeLay, the organization said it may have erred in publishing the article.

The discussion at the APA's Aug. 20–23 meeting in Boston will be divided, as it often is; experimentalists arguing about the study's methodological accuracy, and clinicians criticizing it for its narrowness of vision and conclusions that go far beyond the findings.

The hottest debate will probably occur in Division 35: Psychology of Women, where feminist psychologists have been defending recovered memories for a decade, and are ready for another fight.

What will be lost in the discussion—and almost certainly won't be covered in the media—is the other feminist point of view which argues that in some ways this study supports women and children who have been abused.

While many—including, unfortunately, The North American Man/Boy Love Association, whose name is self-explanatory—say this study gives a green light to pedophiles, some feminists believe it's great news for victims.

If it is true that many victims do not suffer lifelong consequences from abuse, and that many victims are not traumatized, permanently damaged, or wounded for life, we should be happy. But the culture, and not just feminist psychologists, wants its victims portrayed in a particular way. In a culture supported by a victim-hungry media and made-for-TV movies, we have bought into the idea of a victim as long-suffering and damaged. it is not always accurate, even if it's been carried out in an honest effort to show that abuse of children is wrong.

This may have been a much-needed approach 20 or 30 years ago when it was hard to convince the culture that sexual abuse of children is pretty common. Then, we were battling responses like "She asked for it," or "Mr. Smith is such a decent citizen; he would never do that" or even, "Well, now she's damaged goods." When these attitudes prevailed it was absolutely necessary to point out to the public how innocent children really are, and how devastating sexual abuse can be.

But now, when public awareness of these issues is heightened, a different strategy is needed. We can recognize that abuse comes in all shapes and sizes. One child may have been fondled one time by an uncle in a swimming pool; another may have experienced lifelong incestuous abuse from her father. They are both victims of abuse, but doesn't it make sense to acknowledge that in the first case the child may remember the incident only as something confusing and unpleasant while in the second, the girl may need long-term psychotherapy to deal with the issues of betrayal, exploitation, fear, and sexuality that such abuse often brings?

Children respond in different ways to abuse; they are influenced by their own history, their support systems, and internal resources. For one child who has been fondled by her grandfather several times, the incident may be a defining one in her life, causing her great anguish; for another, who had the family structure and internal wherewithal to tell her mother who then stopped the abuse, she may look back at the experience as unpleasant but not self-defining.

Why can't we let victims "get over it"? We surely don't like to see all the suffering that's trotted out. Most psychologists are decent people who want to help others, and who even take great reductions in their fees to do so; thus this is probably no plot by psychologists to drum up more business by creating patients-for-life.

But psychologists, too, are influenced by cultural expectations, and our culture requires that for a victim to be a "real" victim, she needs to deal with her victimization all her life, and she needs to be devastated.

It is exactly such a presumption—those who have been abused can never be viewed as unharmed or resilient—that is targeted in the study whose authors were Bruce Rind, a professor of psychology at Temple University; Robert Bauserman, an evaluation specialist with Maryland's Department of Health and Mental Hygiene; and Philip Tromovitch, a graduate student at the University of Pennsylvania.

Victims implicitly know what's expected of them. Amanda Konradi, a sociologist at Ohio University, studied rape victims going to trial. She found that they played up their helplessness, their devastation, and their weakness in hopes of influencing the jury's decision. One woman hid the fact that she was an avid backpacker from the lawyers for fear the jury would see her as too self-reliant.

While we need victims to be total victims, the culture also needs its perpetrators to be total monsters. Despite hopeful studies that show that some child molesters can, with therapy, recover, the media consistently put out the view and the public generally believes that the child molester is incurable.

We don't need absolute innocence nor absolute devastation from our victims to make the point that abuse is wrong. Boys and men who are taught respect, and who develop compassion and empathy, have no reason to exploit a child. They would never consider doing something that might be so harmful.

And abuse can be devastating—even if sometimes it is not.

The way to support victims is not to call each and every one a survivor. Some were survivors; others were not. Some experienced horrific abuse akin to torture; others were confused by a mild exploitation. Some are still dealing with the aftereffects; others have moved on.

[The] APA has done a disservice to victims of child sexual abuse in its refusal to support the most important finding of this study. Of course all victims deserve support, therapy, and encouragement when they need it; they also all deserve the right to "get over it" when and if they can.

POSTSCRIPT

Does Recent Pedophilia Research Threaten Accepted Moral Standards?

In 1986, after examining three hundred incest relationships, Warren Farrell, a psychologist teaching at the University of California School of Medicine, concluded that the effects of incest "are perhaps best described as a magnifying glass—magnifying the worst in a poor family environment and the best in a caring and loving family environment." However, in his report titled "The Last Taboo? The Complexities of Incest and Female Sexuality," published in *The Handbook of Sexology, vol. 7* (Elsevier Science, 1991), Farrell noted that "in most family environments it exposes the family fabric to rays of confusion and guilt of such intensity that the magnifying glass burns a hole in all but the strongest."

Whether or not all, most, or only some, children who have been involved in adult-child sexual relationships are emotionally and/or psychologically damaged for life, it is clear that adult-child sexual relationships are regarded as socially unacceptable in American culture. There are currently other societies where noncoercive, consensual sexual relations between adults and minors are quite acceptable. In some countries, including the Vatican State, boys and girls can be given legal consent to sexual relations if they are twelve years old. In the South Pacific, adolescnt Melanesian boys and girls are not allowed to have sex with each other before marriage, but the boys are expected to have sex both with an older male and with a boy of their own age. Their first heterosexual experience comes with marriage. In the Cook Islands, Mangaian boys are expected to have sex with many girls but only after an older woman teaches them about the art of sexual play. However, the values which are acceptable in other cultures are not always acceptable in United States culture.

Obviously, this is a serious issue that raises important questions. Do you believe an adult-child sexual relationships have lifelong damaging effects on the minors involved? Where are the facts, and how should we discover them?

Suggested Readings

J. Duin, "Controversies Cloud APA Convention. Premier Psychological Body's Reports on Child Abuse Still Draw Criticism," *The Washington Times* (August 12, 1999).

G. Goslinga, "Radical Reconsideration of the Concept of Child Sexual Abuse: New Findings by Mauserman, Rind, and Tromovitch," *Koinos* (April 1998).

K. Parker, "Adult-Child Sex Is Abuse, Plain and Clear," *The Orlando Sentinel* (March 28, 1999).

B. Rind and P. Tromovitch, "A Meta-Analytic Review of Findings From National Samples on Psychological Correlates of Child Sexual Abuse," *Journal of Sex Research* (1997).

B. Rind, P. Tromovitch, and R. Bauserman, "A Meta-Analytic Examination of Assumed Properties of Child Sexual Abuse Using College Samples," *Psychological Bulletin* (1998).

ISSUE 11

Should Federal Funding of Stem Cell Research Be Restricted?

YES: George W. Bush, from Remarks by the President on Stem Cell Research (August 9, 2001)

NO: Douglas F. Munch, from "Why Expanded Stem Cell Research and Less Federal Government Interference Are Needed in the U.S.," An Original Essay Written for This Volume (2002)

ISSUE SUMMARY

YES: President George W. Bush explains his decision to permit limited federal funding of embryonic stem cell research for the purpose of seeking treatments for serious diseases.

NO: Douglas F. Munch, a management consultant to the pharmaceutical and biotechnology industries, criticizes President Bush's decision for not fully reflecting the will of the people and for being too restrictive to have any meaningful impact on medical science and the lives of people affected by serious diseases.

For decades Americans have debated the subject of abortion, largely with respect to the question, "When does life begin?" In 2001 this debate took a sharp turn toward arguing the ethics of studying embryonic stem cells for their potential usefulness in treating serious and chronic diseases, like Parkinson's, Alzheimers's, and juvenile diabetes. Embryonic stem cells are derived from human embryos and have the capacity to become any type of human cell. This capacity is a characteristic not shared by fetal tissue or adult stem cells. It is believed that the manipulation and replication of embryonic stem cells can ultimately lead to therapies that could be used to treat diseases that afflict millions.

So, how does this relate to the abortion debate and the question of when life begins? Some opponents of stem cell research believe that a human being is created the moment that sperm and egg meet and cells begin dividing. To these opponents, the scientific use of an embryo's stem cells, which would lead to the embryo's destruction, is no different than killing a human being. Supporters of embryonic stem cell research believe that these embryos, formed a few days after conception and slated for inevitable destruction anyway, are not to be afforded protection at the expense of people with terminal illnesses who could be treated. It is important to note that there are many other subjective opinions about when human life begins, reflecting various individual or religious beliefs.

The surplus of embryos in question is the product of in vitro fertilization, a reproductive process commonly used by infertile couples. In this process, ova (eggs) are fertilized with sperm outside the uterus. The resulting embryo is then implanted inside the uterus. It is a common practice to form several embryos during the in vitro fertilization process, with each serving as "backup" in the event that the preceding implantation fails. Subsequently, most unused embryos are stored indefinitely in a frozen state. Few are intentionally destroyed, and even fewer are donated for medical research.

On August 9, 2001, President George W. Bush informed the nation of his decision to permit limited federal funding of embryonic stem cell research. His decision would permit research on 64 stem cell lines already in existence. Some praised the decision as a fair and reasonable compromise; others feared the limits would prevent any meaningful impact on the lives of millions of people with serious diseases; still others criticized the decision as incongruent with the president's pro-life position. The decision created an atypical rift among "pro-life" individuals and groups. Some, like Pope John Paul II and the National Conference of Catholic Bishops, criticized the decision, while others, like conservative members of Congress (Orrin Hatch, Trent Lott) and the National Right to Life Organization, expressed support for the decision.

A few Hollywood celebrities drew public attention to the subject and lobbied in favor of embryonic stem cell research. Actor Christopher Reeve, also chairman of the Christopher Reeve Paralysis Organization, had previously sued the federal government for withholding federal funds. Following Bush's decision, he expressed concern that "[T]his political compromise may seriously hinder progress toward finding treatments and cures for a wide variety of diseases and disorders that affect 100 million Americans." Actress Mary Tyler Moore, who has battled juvenile diabetes for 30 years, and actor Michael J. Fox, who has Parkinson's disease, were also vocal supporters of federal research funding. Moore voiced her support for the president's decision, while Fox was skeptical about the limitations. Nancy Reagan, whose husband, former President Ronald Reagan is battling Alzheimer's disease, expressed support for stem cell research while staunchly opposing abortion.

In the following selections, Bush explains his decision to authorize limited federal funding of embryonic stem cell research and describes the ethical arguments he considered in making his decision. Douglas F. Munch comments that Bush's decision does not represent the public interest and falls far too short to enable scientists to develop cures for debilitating and terminal diseases.

George W. Bush

 **YES**

Remarks by the President
on Stem Cell Research

THE PRESIDENT: Good evening. I appreciate you giving me a few minutes of your time tonight so I can discuss with you a complex and difficult issue, an issue that is one of the most profound of our time.

The issue of research involving stem cells derived from human embryos is increasingly the subject of a national debate and dinner table discussions. The issue is confronted every day in laboratories as scientists ponder the ethical ramifications of their work. It is agonized over by parents and many couples as they try to have children, or to save children already born.

The issue is debated within the church, with people of different faiths, even many of the same faith coming to different conclusions. Many people are finding that the more they know about stem cell research, the less certain they are about the right ethical and moral conclusions.

My administration must decide whether to allow federal funds, your tax dollars, to be used for scientific research on stem cells derived from human embryos. A large number of these embryos already exist. They are the product of a process called in vitro fertilization, which helps so many couples conceive children. When doctors match sperm and egg to create life outside the womb, they usually produce more embryos than are planted in the mother. Once a couple successfully has children, or if they are unsuccessful, the additional embryos remain frozen in laboratories.

Some will not survive during long storage; others are destroyed. A number have been donated to science and used to create privately funded stem cell lines. And a few have been implanted in an adoptive mother and born, and are today healthy children.

Based on preliminary work that has been privately funded, scientists believe further research using stem cells offers great promise that could help improve the lives of those who suffer from many terrible diseases—from juvenile diabetes to Alzheimer's, from Parkinson's to spinal cord injuries. And while scientists admit they are not yet certain, they believe stem cells derived from embryos have unique potential.

You should also know that stem cells can be derived from sources other than embryos—from adult cells, from umbilical cords that are discarded after

From George W. Bush, Remarks by the President on Stem Cell Research (August 9, 2001).

babies are born, from human placenta. And many scientists feel research on these type of stem cells is also promising. Many patients suffering from a range of diseases are already being helped with treatments developed from adult stem cells.

However, most scientists, at least today, believe that research on embryonic stem cells offer the most promise because these cells have the potential to develop in all of the tissues in the body.

Scientists further believe that rapid progress in this research will come only with federal funds. Federal dollars help attract the best and brightest scientists. They ensure new discoveries are widely shared at the largest number of research facilities and that the research is directed toward the greatest public good.

The United States has a long and proud record of leading the world toward advances in science and medicine that improve human life. And the United States has a long and proud record of upholding the highest standards of ethics as we expand the limits of science and knowledge. Research on embryonic stem cells raises profound ethical questions, because extracting the stem cell destroys the embryo, and thus destroys its potential for life. Like a snowflake, each of these embryos is unique, with the unique genetic potential of an individual human being.

As I thought through this issue, I kept returning to two fundamental questions: First, are these frozen embryos human life, and therefore, something precious to be protected? And second, if they're going to be destroyed anyway, shouldn't they be used for a greater good, for research that has the potential to save and improve other lives?

I've asked those questions and others of scientists, scholars, bioethicists, religious leaders, doctors, researchers, members of Congress, my Cabinet, and my friends. I have read heartfelt letters from many Americans. I have given this issue a great deal of thought, prayer and considerable reflection. And I have found widespread disagreement.

On the first issue, are these embryos human life—well, one researcher told me he believes this five-day-old cluster of cells is not an embryo, not yet an individual, but a pre-embryo. He argued that it has the potential for life, but it is not a life because it cannot develop on its own.

An ethicist dismissed that as a callous attempt at rationalization. Make no mistake, he told me, that cluster of cells is the same way you and I, and all the rest of us, started our lives. One goes with a heavy heart if we use these, he said, because we are dealing with the seeds of the next generation.

And to the other crucial question, if these are going to be destroyed anyway, why not use them for good purpose—I also found different answers. Many argue these embryos are byproducts of a process that helps create life, and we should allow couples to donate them to science so they can be used for good purpose instead of wasting their potential. Others will argue there's no such thing as excess life, and the fact that a living being is going to die does not justify experimenting on it or exploiting it as a natural resource.

At its core, this issue forces us to confront fundamental questions about the beginnings of life and the ends of science. It lies at a difficult moral intersection, juxtaposing the need to protect life in all its phases with the prospect of saving and improving life in all its stages.

As the discoveries of modern science create tremendous hope, they also lay vast ethical mine fields. As the genius of science extends the horizons of what we can do, we increasingly confront complex questions about what we should do. We have arrived at that brave new world that seemed so distant in 1932, when Aldous Huxley wrote about human beings created in test tubes in what he called a "hatchery."

In recent weeks, we learned that scientists have created human embryos in test tubes solely to experiment on them. This is deeply troubling, and a warning sign that should prompt all of us to think through these issues very carefully.

Embryonic stem cell research is at the leading edge of a series of moral hazards. The initial stem cell researcher was at first reluctant to begin his research, fearing it might be used for human cloning. Scientists have already cloned a sheep. Researchers are telling us the next step could be to clone human beings to create individual designer stem cells, essentially to grow another you, to be available in case you need another heart or lung or liver.

I strongly oppose human cloning, as do most Americans. We recoil at the idea of growing human beings for spare body parts, or creating life for our convenience. And while we must devote enormous energy to conquering disease, it is equally important that we pay attention to the moral concerns raised by the new frontier of human embryo stem cell research. Even the most noble ends do not justify any means.

My position on these issues is shaped by deeply held beliefs. I'm a strong supporter of science and technology, and believe they have the potential for incredible good—to improve lives, to save life, to conquer disease. Research offers hope that millions of our loved ones may be cured of a disease and rid of their suffering. I have friends whose children suffer from juvenile diabetes. Nancy Reagan has written me about President Reagan's struggle with Alzheimer's. My own family has confronted the tragedy of childhood leukemia. And, like all Americans, I have great hope for cures.

I also believe human life is a sacred gift from our Creator. I worry about a culture that devalues life, and believe as your President I have an important obligation to foster and encourage respect for life in America and throughout the world. And while we're all hopeful about the potential of this research, no one can be certain that the science will live up to the hope it has generated.

Eight years ago, scientists believed fetal tissue research offered great hope for cures and treatments—yet, the progress to date has not lived up to its initial expectations. Embryonic stem cell research offers both great promise and great peril. So I have decided we must proceed with great care.

As a result of private research, more than 60 genetically diverse stem cell lines already exist. They were created from embryos that have already been destroyed, and they have the ability to regenerate themselves indefinitely, creating ongoing opportunities for research. I have concluded that we should allow federal funds to be used for research on these existing stem cell lines, where the life and death decision has already been made.

Leading scientists tell me research on these 60 lines has great promise that could lead to breakthrough therapies and cures. This allows us to explore the promise and potential of stem cell research without crossing a fundamental moral line, by providing taxpayer funding that would sanction or encourage further destruction of human embryos that have at least the potential for life.

I also believe that great scientific progress can be made through aggressive federal funding of research on umbilical cord placenta, adult and animal stem cells which do not involve the same moral dilemma. This year, your government will spend $250 million on this important research.

I will also name a President's council to monitor stem cell research, to recommend appropriate guidelines and regulations, and to consider all of the medical and ethical ramifications of biomedical innovation. This council will consist of leading scientists, doctors, ethicists, lawyers, theologians and others, and will be chaired by Dr. Leon Kass, a leading biomedical ethicist from the University of Chicago.

This council will keep us apprised of new developments and give our nation a forum to continue to discuss and evaluate these important issues. As we go forward, I hope we will always be guided by both intellect and heart, by both our capabilities and our conscience.

I have made this decision with great care, and I pray it is the right one.

Thank you for listening. Good night, and God bless America.

Douglas F. Munch  **NO**

Why Expanded Stem Cell Research and Less Federal Government Interference Are Needed in the U.S.

On August 9, 2001, President George W. Bush presented his remarks on stem cell research to the American Public. The President cleverly rode the political fence on his decision to allow stem cell research, but only utilizing those 64 stem cell lines already in existence worldwide. Unfortunately, the President's decision does not go far enough in supporting this important research and that in time, perhaps sooner then he expects, the issue will have to be revisited.

The potential of stem cell research will be realized through the invention of new therapies for currently incurable diseases. Diabetes, heart disease, cancer, Alzheimer's disease, Parkinson's disease, multiple sclerosis and ALS [Lou Gehrig's disease] are some of the diseases expected to benefit from the development of knowledge about stem cells. But that is not all. Stem cell research may open the doors to understanding how genes control cell differentiation. It can also give us much improved insight into new drug development and toxicity to human cells as well as organ transplant rejection.

Why is public funding of this research such a contentious decision? The government sits squarely in the middle of the controversy surrounding the subject. On one side is the vast landscape of government funded research, with medical scientists requesting increased access to embryonic stem cells accompanied by substantially increased funding and support from the National Institutes for Health (NIH) and other government sources. On the other side is an equally vast landscape of public opinion that is divided on highly emotional moral and ethical grounds. This question is further complicated by the President's own conservative theological views and his pronounced political support from the conservative Christian right opposing this research. Since public sentiment drives most political positions in our current age of opinion polls, the arbitrator of public money, largely the political party in power, feels obligated to find its own balance between public funding for public good and defining that good. As a result, while the President's remarks cover the waterfront of stem cell research science and ethics, his decision does not go far enough.

As I view this debate, there are very different points of view coming into play across the nation. There is a definite complex of opposing theological perspectives, coupled with medical/scientific, ethical, and economic points of view.

Theological Perspectives

At the core, the theological debate revolves around the issue of when human life begins. Theologians testifying before the National Bioethics Advisory Commission indicated that religious tradition offers no support to the idea that the fertilized egg goes through some earlier human stage before acquiring the moral status of a person. A commonly expressed conservative position states that human life begins at the moment of conception when the sperm and egg cell are united since the fertilized egg has the potential to become a human being. Other positions vary widely. Some hold that human life begins upon implantation of the egg in the uterus. Historical Catholic teaching and a current Jewish position state that human life begins with quickening (when a pregnant woman can feel fetal movements some time in the fourth month of pregnancy).

Few denominations have taken an official position on the appropriateness of stem cell research. Most church leaders of various denominations appear to be undecided about the matter but some are leaning toward supporting the research. In 1997 the United Church of Christ's General Synod approved serious research on "human pre-embryos through the 14th day of fetal development."

The Episcopal, Evangelical Lutheran, and United Methodist churches have declined to take a position on the matter until . . . their national meetings convene. Other religions are similarly noncommittal. As an example, the Unitarian Universalist Association seems to favor the funding of stem cell work within its pro-science and pro-research tradition, but has reportedly not taken an official position. The Church of Jesus Christ of Latter Day Saints (Mormon Church) similarly is noncommittal on the matter stating that it "merits cautious scrutiny." Reformed Jews, Presbyterian Church USA, and the United Church of Christ seem to be generally favoring the research, although their official positions are not developed and there seem to be many nuances to consider.

Judaism discourages interfering with nature's plan for no good reason, but even Conservative Jews may favor stem cell research. Rabbi Elliott Dorff, Vice Chairman of the Conservative Movement's Committee on Law and Standards, indicated that "the research can serve a common good, combating disease."

There is no Islamic official position in the United States, but Moslem teaching holds that life does not begin until the fertilized egg is attached to the uterine wall, a position which would allow research on embryonic stem cells.

The President's personal and political position appears to be largely influenced by his close relationship with the Christian Conservative Right. Strong opposition to stem cell research has been voiced from both the Roman Catholic Church and the Christian Conservative Right. In a recent visit to the Vatican, the Pope told President Bush that "stem cell research devalues and violates human life." However, these views, and the President's decision, may not be reflected by the general public.

Public Opinion

Recent polls indicate that there is wide support among Americans for stem cell research in contrast to the largely undecided official position of religious authorities. As individuals learn more about the promise of this research and the scientific and ethical implications, the polls show that public opinion favors stem cell research. In an NBC news poll on July 12, 2001, fully 70 percent of Roman Catholics support stem cell research versus 69 percent of the overall U.S. population. Among Catholics, only 22 percent oppose the research versus 23 percent of the overall population. In a June 2001 poll in Utah, the overall population was 62 percent in favor of stem cell research and 27 percent against. Of individuals identifying themselves as "very conservative" 47 percent favored the research while only 35 percent opposed.

The point is that there are many independent views about the humanity of a fertilized egg. Human beings are unable to resolve this fundamental issue on any grounds, scientific or theological, leaving the matter to individual conscience. It is therefore not up to the government to impose an ethical or moral standard about this research. That decision should be up to the individual scientist with funding awarded based on merit for creative scientific thinking that enhances human understanding about these cells, their function and usefulness.

The human race has become cocreators of our world with God. Observation of modern man's impact on our society makes this obvious. Scientists have prevented extinction of animal species, produced transgenic animals used for medical research, genetically modified cell lines for the production of medicine, invented and implemented in-vitro fertilization (IVF), prepared gene replacement therapies to treat disease, and introduced new genes into food products to improve yield and reduce susceptibility to disease. Whether one likes it or not, we humans are already using our gift of free will, intelligence and creativity to alter this world and change the natural course of evolution. The die is cast. It will continue to be our responsibility to use our creative powers and scientific knowledge for ethical and moral purpose from which all people benefit. As cocreators, stem cell research will be no different.

Scientific and Medical Grounds

The President's remarks about the scientific and medical benefit are very favorable toward stem cell research. So favorable that it seems his conclusion to limit the stem cell lines to those existing as of August 9, 2001, is inconsistent with his preamble. But, there are also important issues that the President underplayed in his address.

Human stem cell research is a relatively new medical field. It was only in 1981 that British scientists created the first animal stem cell line from mouse embryos. In 1996 Congress banned the use of federal funding for research where human embryos would be destroyed in the process. Hence, private funding from Geron Corporation enabled scientists at the Wisconsin Alumni Research Foundation (WARF) to develop and patent a method to separate stem cells from the blastocyst in 1998. As of August 9, 2001, there were 64 separate lines of human stem cells available worldwide. Sweden has 24 lines, the U.S. has 20, India has 10, Australia has 6, and Israel has 4. Only these lines are eligible for research funded by the federal government. This by itself is potentially problematic.

Among these 64 lines of stem cells that are approved for funding, many are derived from frozen embryos that are known to be much less robust, reportedly having only 1 chance in 100 of developing to the blastocyst stage (a colony of about 200 undifferentiated stem cells). It is still unknown how many of these lines will be satisfactory for research purposes. Research quality stem cells must have normal chromosomes and genes. They must be able to reproduce without limit and they must be capable of differentiation into all other human cells. While scientists anticipate that these cells will reproduce indefinitely, this is an assumption that may not work out in the future. We cannot know how many of these approved cell lines will develop into useful research material or if they will provide adequate quantities of material to meet research standards and demand.

While stem cells may be obtained from adult tissues (i.e. fat, bone marrow, or brain) and other fetal cell lines (umbilical or placenta), these cells may have started down a differentiation pathway and therefore have more limited research potential. Experts recognize that stem cells from the blastocyst stage of the embryo are ideal because they are completely undifferentiated and have the potential to become any of the approximately 260 cell lines in the human body. Today, medical scientists have only limited knowledge about the theoretical and practical issues necessary to derive therapeutic benefit from the science, although the theoretical potential is great. Additionally, today's stem cells are being grown in a mouse cell culture to trick the stem cells to differentiate, which also limits the research and therapeutic potential due to the potential contamination of the human cells. Much work remains to be done and will be done. If not in the U.S., then the work will be engaged by scientists in other countries where fewer barriers are imposed.

Ethical Issues

The President's remarks appropriately address the possibility of misuse of stem cell research potentially leading to the serious abuse of human reproductive cloning which is properly banned in most countries. However, all technologies have potential for misuse by unscrupulous individuals inclined to manipulate the system for their own ill-gotten gain.

The President appropriately states that the U.S. has a "long and proud record of upholding the highest standards of ethics." We have achieved this record through exercise of individual conscience superimposed over a sound foundation of knowledge, ethics, and through peer pressure from other scientists, not through government imposed legislation. There are already safeguards in the research funding system to protect against such activity—specifically, the long established peer review system awards research grants to worthy (and ethical) projects. Investigational review boards (IRB) protect patients against potentially harmful or immoral clinical research. The system works and the government should not meddle with it or use it as an excuse to install barriers or artificially limit funding for this important work.

In-vitro fertilization (IVF) procedures have produced a large number of unused frozen embryos, as the President correctly pointed out in his remarks. Again, his comments do not adequately address the issues. Unused embryos may remain frozen for many years as they are rarely adopted, donated, or destroyed when they are unwanted. We know that extra embryos are a consequence of IVF.

People choosing to avail themselves of this procedure should be required to undertake the moral and ethical responsibility of determining the disposition of their unused cells as part of their overall decision making and medical informed consent process. I believe that this decision should be required at the time people choose IVF to achieve pregnancy. Otherwise, unused embryos are likely to remain frozen as a burden to society. I would suggest that the options include donation of the embryos for stem cell research purposes. This decision is a personal one, and should be driven by individual conscience. After all, when faced with the tragic death of a child, many parents now take comfort in donating some of the child's tissues to help others as transplants. Should not the same opportunity to benefit others be available to IVF "parents"? If morality is the issue, then where is the morality in abandoning human embryos in a frozen and indeterminate state, leaving them as someone else's problem or to deteriorate in the freezer?

Economic Issues

Several economic factors may also be considered. U.S. Government-funded research has been the most important incubator for new ideas in the world. This support has historically been provided without prior assessment of economic potential. Industries have been started as a result and perhaps hundreds of biotech and health care companies owe their existence to government funded research programs. Inadequate support of stem cell research will unwittingly block the creation of entrepreneurial companies focused on the developing new therapies based on knowledge discovered with federal grant support.

U.S. companies, developing state-of-the-art commercial products for health care, make a substantial contribution to our economy and to maintaining our worldwide superiority in medicine and therapeutics. Supporting basic research at the federal level forms the groundwork for establishing important intellectual property positions for American entrepreneurs and corporations. Placing hurdles in the way of U.S. scientists will move discovery to other nations where there are fewer or no impediments to this research. On August 28th, 2001, the *Washington Post* reported an Indian stem cell scientist to say that the Bush policy "creates a windfall for researchers in such countries as

India that do not face such constraints." Another reports that Bush's announcement has opened up a "new pot of gold" for science and business outside the U.S.

By putting political barriers in front of scientists who develop new treatments for disease, we are not only impeding economic and medical progress in the U.S. but also risk losing our leading scientists. Dr. Roger Pedersen, a prominent scientist from the University of California, San Francisco, has announced that he is leaving the U.S. to work in England where research restrictions are not as burdensome. Others will also leave if government restrictions get in the way of science.

Concluding Remarks

Like the President, I have come to express my position on these sensitive matters regarding stem cell research after much thought and personal deliberation. I believe that the views I have presented here support the sanctity of human life. They also allow our American culture to prevail where strong social and ethical values are the underpinnings of the exercise of our gift of free will. Our democratic system enables this to occur. Our federal government should not legislate against its own system by seeking to establish and impose state ethics on our free society.

POSTSCRIPT

Should Federal Funding of Stem Cell Research Be Restricted?

The question of whether or not embryonic stem cell research should be restricted may come down to fundamental beliefs about the origin of human life. Does life begin at the moment of conception, as many "pro-life" individuals contend? If so, what is to be done with excess embryos already created in the in vitro fertilization process but not destined for implantation? "Pro-choice" individuals may have an easier time with this question, as they reject the belief that a fertilized egg is a human being. The opportunity to improve the lives of people with severe illnesses may be seen as no match to the comparative value of a cluster of cells that is not destined for pregnancy.

In his speech, the president raised the issue of human cloning. His statement, "[T]he next step could be to clone human beings to create individual designer stem cells, essentially to grow another you to be available in case you need another heart or lung or liver," requires some clarification. Scientists who have expressed an intention to clone humans are relying on adult stem cells to create a whole cloned human person. Adult cells would be taken from an adult, their DNA injected into a human ovum, and that ovum implanted into a woman's uterus to create a cloned person. Most scientists dismiss this as both unethical and nearly impossible. However, substituting one's DNA for the DNA in embryonic stem cells to create specialized (and perfectly genetically matched cells) is possible.

How do you assess the president's compromise? Did it go far enough or does it fall short of being useful for those afflicted with incurable illnesses? What ethical considerations would guide you in deciding this matter?

Suggested Readings

"Stem Cell Disappointment," *Arizona Daily Star* (August 12, 2001).

"Stem Cells: Not Far Enough," *The Providence Journal* (August 12, 2001).

S. Begley, "Cellular Divide," *Newsweek* (July 9, 2001).

S. Begley, "Did the President Go Far Enough?" *Newsweek* (August 20, 2001).

A. Breznican, "Celebs Supporting Stem Cell Research," *Associated Press* (August 9, 2001).

T. Lindberg, "The Politics of Stem Cell Research: President Bush Got the Headlines He Wanted," *The Washington Times* (August 14, 2001).

The White House, "Fact Sheet: Embryonic Stem Cell Research," available at http://www.whitehouse.gov (August 9, 2001).

K. L. Woodward, "A Question of Life or Death: Untangling the Knottiest of Ethical Dilemmas," *Newsweek* (July 9, 2001).

ISSUE 12

Should States Fund Sexuality Research?

YES: John Bancroft, from "The Medical Community Needs Kinsey's Research Now More Than Ever," *Insight on the News* (March 30, 1998)

NO: Beverly R. Newman, from "Research That Mainstreams Sexual Perversity Does Not Serve the Public Good," *Insight on the News* (March 30, 1998)

ISSUE SUMMARY

YES: John Bancroft, a medical doctor, sexologist, and director of the University of Indiana's Alfred Kinsey Institute for Research in Sex, Gender, and Reproduction, argues that public funding for scientific research on sexuality issues is vital in order to solve some of the major sexual problems that plague the United States.

NO: Beverly R. Newman, a counselor of sexual abuse survivors and a teacher at Ivy Tech College in Indianapolis, Indiana, opposes any public funding of sexuality research by the Kinsey Institute or any other alleged scientific research group because she fears that researchers will follow Alfred Kinsey (1894–1956), whom she calls "a callous, maniacal scientist."

The United States has an unequaled wealth of sexological research. At the end of the nineteenth century, Celia D. Mosher, a physician and college professor, began to survey her women patients, asking them to describe their sexual and reproductive lives. Thanks to Mosher's scientific curiosity, there is a small but intriguing sample of middle-class, married women's sexual histories that allows some tentative comparisons of women's sexuality at the peak of the Victorian Age and today, one hundred years later. In the early part of the twentieth century, gynecologist Robert Latou Dickinson pioneered the scientific study of human sexuality, marital sex, contraception, women's diseases, and sex problems.

In 1938, Alfred Kinsey, a biology professor at the University of Indiana, was determined to interview 100,000 American men and women about their sex lives. By 1959 his team of colleagues were able to interview 18,000 adults, which was the first scientific picture of the sexual lives of American men and women: when they became sexually active, how often they had sex and what kind of sex, homosexuality and bisexuality; premarital, marital, and extramarital sex; and orgasm. Before Kinsey died in 1956, it seemed that opponents of sex research would be successful in discouraging support for his surveys. In the 1960s, William Masters and Virginia Johnson focused public attention on the scientific study of the physiology and psychology of the human sexual response. For 12 years, Masters and Johnson interviewed and observed individuals experiencing orgasm through masturbation and intercourse. Their research revealed the first detailed scientific information about the stages one goes through from sexual desire to arousal, orgasm, and resolution.

Sexological research in the United States today is considered vital to the management of many social and public health problems. Each year, one million teenage girls become pregnant, a rate twice that of Canada, England, and Sweden, and 10 times that of the Netherlands. This disproportion is similar for teenage abortions. The United States spends $25 billion on social, health, and welfare services for families begun by teenagers. One million Americans are HIV positive and almost one-quarter of a million have died of AIDS. Yet only one in ten American children receives sexuality education that includes information about HIV/AIDS transmission and prevention. One in five adolescent girls in grades eight through eleven is subject to sexual harassment, while three-quarters of girls under age fourteen who have had sexual relations have been raped. These and other public health problems are well documented and increasingly understood in the context of poverty, family trauma, ethnic discrimination, lack of educational opportunities, and inadequate health services. However, there is little recognition among the general public and legislators of the need for sexological research to deal effectively with these problems. Congress has several times refused or withdrawn funding for well-designed and important surveys because of pressure from conservative minorities.

In 1995, the Sexuality Research Assessment Project of the Social Science Research Council published a comprehensive sexuality research review entitled *Sexuality Research in the United States: An Assessment of the Social and Behavioral Sciences.* This report identified and described major information gaps that prevent understanding of how sexual behaviors develop in the context of society and culture and how sexual socialization occurs in families, schools, the media, and peer groups. Without that understanding, efforts to effectively address problems and projects in gender, HIV/AIDS, adolescent sexuality, sexual orientation, sexual coercion, and research methodology are crippled.

In the following selections, John Bancroft argues that the lack of federal, private sector, and academic funding for research prevents legislators, educators, and social service and health care professionals from dealing with serious problems in American families and society. Beverly R. Newman opposes any funding for sexuality research that supports the philosophy of Alfred Kinsey and the institute that carries his name. She maintains that all sex research in the United States has been contaminated by Kinsey, whom she says "blithely collected data obtained as results from massive sexual experimentation on babies and children."

John Bancroft  **YES**

The Medical Community Needs Kinsey's Research Now More Than Ever

 T he United States leads the industrialized world in a number of important ways, but they are not all positive. Our country heads the league tables for sex-related problems—teenage pregnancies, sexually transmitted diseases and sexual assaults. We have our fair share of other problems as well, such as child sexual abuse and the common sexual dysfunctions that can undermine the stability of marriage. Yet, we remain ignorant or uncertain about many aspects of these problems. If scientists and policymakers are to tackle them effectively, they must better understand the problems.

Human sexuality is complex; sociocultural and biological determinants must be taken into account. For that reason, we need an ongoing tradition of interdisciplinary scholarship. The Kinsey Institute for Research in Sex, Gender and Reproduction, one of Indiana University's several research institutes, is unique not only in the United States but in the world in its established commitment to such interdisciplinary scholarship.

So why am I asked to defend state funding of the Kinsey Institute? Because there is an ongoing campaign by vocal and well-funded elements to close it down. Their principal target appears to be sex education. They misguidedly believe that by discrediting Alfred Kinsey, who died 42 years ago, they will undermine modern sex education. And what better way to discredit Kinsey than closing down the institute named for him?

In December 1995, the Family Research Council successfully lobbied to introduce a bill into Congress aimed at the institute's federal funding, but that House bill got nowhere. In January 1998, a resolution was passed by the Indiana House of Representatives urging the withdrawal of state funding for the Kinsey Institute; that effort was instigated by Concerned Women for America, or CWA. That measure also died quietly when the Legislature ended its session in February. Both efforts were anchored in a dislike of Kinsey and what he represented— as well as a considerable amount of misinformation.

I recently met with the sponsor of the Indiana resolution, and discovered that his case was based largely on the current campaign of misinformation from CWA. He had read nothing written by Kinsey himself; he knew nothing about the Kinsey Institute's work and mission today and apparently was not interested. He wanted its closure as a symbolic denigration of Kinsey by Indiana University.

The campaign of misinformation is extraordinary, with statement upon statement with no basis in fact. For example: According to some allegations, Kinsey believed that "all sex laws should be eliminated, including laws against rape"; that "there was no moral difference between one sexual outlet and any other"; that the consequences of such beliefs included a 526 percent increase in the number of rapes in the United States; and that Kinsey's "theories" produced a 560 percent increase in crime, a 300 percent increase in out-of-wedlock births, a 200 percent increase in divorce rates and a 200 percent increase in teen suicides. These allegations, and many others like them, are ridiculous.

Sex education today, we are told in this disingenuous campaign, is based on research Kinsey carried out with sexual criminals. Kinsey studied sexual criminals; the Kinsey Institute published a book on "sexual offenders" in 1965 based on this data, which has nothing to do with sex education. Kinsey reported observations of children's sexual responses made by a few of these sexual criminals; the evidence in the much-cited "Table 34" contains information from one such man. The nature of this information, which was made clear in the book, represents a small proportion of the evidence presented about childhood sexuality, a tiny proportion of his two published books, and it has nothing to do with sex education today or in the past. In fact, sex education today is not based on Kinsey's research in any respect. Insofar as sex education relies on research findings, it uses far more recent and relevant research.

Kinsey's research is discredited, we are told by opponents of the institute, because, having interviewed these sexual criminals, he then did not report them to the police.

At the time of Kinsey's research, virtually all forms of sexual activity outside marriage and several forms of sexual activity within marriage (not including raping one's wife) were illegal. He attached great importance to the confidentiality he guaranteed his subjects, and this was crucial to the success of his whole research endeavor.

Kinsey's mission, his detractors claim, was to undermine sexual morality as we know it. In his last book, the volume on the female, he was principally concerned about the lack of sexual understanding between men and women and how this undermined the stability of marriage. Ironically, considering how Kinsey so often has been accused to the contrary, the book underscores that he saw heterosexual marital sex as the norm. True, Kinsey is not beyond criticism. He made mistakes; with the benefit of 50 years of hindsight, one can say that he was naïve in several respects. But he was a pioneer who broke through the social taboos to carry out the first substantial survey of sexual behavior, which remains the largest and richest collection of data on sexual behavior ever collected and is used by researchers today.

What of the institute named for him? The Kinsey Institute fulfills its mission in a number of ways. It has uniquely rich collections of materials relevant to the understanding of human sexuality and how it has changed over time and across cultures. In addition to its extensive library of books and papers, the institute has major collections of photography, art, films and videos as well as archival papers and manuscripts. As we work to preserve these collections and make them more accessible to scholars, so we find a steady increase in demand for access from the academic community.

The institute organizes interdisciplinary meetings, bringing scholars together from around the world and producing publications from these events. The institute has a research program; we are studying the effects of steroidal contraceptives on the sexuality and well-being of women and the impact of such effects on the acceptability and continuation with these methods. This is research that should have been conducted several decades ago. We are exploring with Family Health International how this research methodology can be adapted to address the same questions in other countries in the developing world, tackling an issue of crucial importance to the effectiveness of family-planning programs worldwide. We are investigating the impact of the menstrual cycle on the sexuality of women.

In the area of male sexuality, we have a novel research program studying the neuropsychology of male sexual response. This research not only may prove to be considerably relevant to understanding common problems of male sexual dysfunction but also may shed light on why some men persist in taking sexual risks, an issue crucial to the HIV/AIDS epidemic. We are collaborating with colleagues in the medical school to use brain-imaging techniques to investigate central mechanisms involved in the control of sexual response.

We have been fortunate to have two postdoctoral fellows funded by the Social Science Research Council's, or SSRC's new Sexuality Research Fellowship program. Last year, our SSRC fellow, a historian, used the institute's archives to further her study of the history of transsexualism in the United States between 1930 and 1970. This year and next, we have a fellow studying the relationship between childhood sexual play and adult sexual adjustment by asking young adults to recall their childhood experiences, as well as describing their sexual development during adolescence and since. This data will be compared with data obtained from Kinsey's original survey, permitting the parallel study of two data sets collected 50 years apart. The Kinsey Institute provides specialized clinical services to men and women who have sexual dysfunctions and women with menstrual-cycle-related problems. This form of clinical care, in which both psychological and physical aspects are given equal importance, is threatened by the current health-care system in the United States. Our clinics, and the training of health professionals associated with them, will help to keep these important clinical skills alive and available.

And finally, the institute is attaching increasing importance to its role as an "information service," provided through our World Wide Web site. I would urge anyone who wants to know more about the Kinsey Institute and its current activities to visit us at http://www.indiana.edu/~kinsey/.

We are legally restricted in how we can use many of the materials in our collections, and because of this we restrict access to scholars with bona fide research interests. However, we are progressively "coming out of the closet." For the last three years we have provided courses for the local community through the university's continuing-studies and mini-university programs. Last October, we had our first major public exhibit of items from our art and photography collections. The six-week-long exhibit, "The Art of Desire: Erotic Treasures From the Kinsey Institute," was held in the fine-arts gallery on the Bloomington campus. This effort celebrated the 50th anniversary of the founding of the institute and was a great success. We give tours for an increasing number of visitors to the institute and, following the recent political interest, we have invited state legislators to visit the institute to learn more about our activities. We are proud of the Kinsey Institute, and we believe its role will grow. In fact, the need for interdisciplinary research of this kind is so great today that, rather than closing us down, comparable institutes should be set up on other campuses around the country. Then there will be a reasonable chance that the need for an established tradition of interdisciplinary scholarship in human sexuality will be met.

As for sex education, the Kinsey Institute is not directly involved, but we recognize its importance. It is not a straightforward issue, however. There is need for vigorous debate as well as careful evaluation of the effects of different policies. And, of course, issues of sexual morality will be central to this debate as, I hope, will evidence derived from sound scientific research. But a productive debate only can flourish in a climate of honesty and respect for varying opinions, none of which are in the forecast of the anti-Kinsey movement.

Beverly R. Newman

 NO

Research That Mainstreams Sexual Perversity Does Not Serve the Public Good

Deep in America's heartland is the heart of one of history's biggest cover-ups. Hundreds, perhaps thousands, of sex crimes undoubtedly have been committed in the name of science, and yet a major state university continues to battle for the sake of protecting the name and the reputation of a callous, maniacal scientist who blithely collected data obtained as results from massive sexual experimentation on babies and children. Alfred C. Kinsey is the world's most famous sex researcher, who got unprecedented media attention after the publication of *Sexual Behavior in the Human Male* in 1948 and *Sexual Behavior in the Human Female* in 1953. Less well-known is the fact that he was a classic example of a sexual addict, who induced his own wife to commit adultery on films he made in the attic of their home in Bloomington, Ind.

In recent weeks Bloomington, home to the Kinsey Institute for Research in Sex, Gender and Reproduction, based at Indiana University, has witnessed a raging inferno of citizen anger that is spreading throughout the Hoosier State. While taxpayers foot the bill for the Kinsey Institute through annual appropriations of $750,000, the public is not welcome to use or view the Kinsey Institute, which is cloaked in secrecy. Callers are informed that there are VIP tours set up every so often, but even then a Kinsey representative must accompany the visitors at all times. State Sen. John Waterman made two unannounced visits to the institute last month—one during office hours on a weekday—but was unable even to take the elevator up to the third floor of Morrison Hall, where the institute is housed at public expense. Accompanied by an ex-Indiana University police officer, Waterman was told by the officer that he never had been permitted to have the keys to the third floor of Morrison Hall.

Recently, Waterman and another Indiana legislator, Rep. Woody Burton, led an unprecedented campaign to denounce and defund the institute. On Jan. 21 the Indiana House of Representatives passed Burton's House Concurrent Resolution No. 16, which excoriated the institute's founder and directed that, "No public funds should be used to operate or support institutions that further the claims made by Alfred Kinsey's research."

What are those controversial claims? The most far-reaching is that children naturally are given to initiating sexual acts and that virtually all forms of sexual behavior should be acknowledged as normal and tolerated. Kinsey's verbose prose is hardly quotable but nonetheless radical in its implications. Consider his condescending dismissal of sex between humans and animals: "There is probably no type of human sexual behavior which has been more severely condemned by that segment of the population which happens not to have had such experience, and which accepts the age-old judgment that animal intercourse must evidence a mental abnormality, as well as immorality." Translation: It's all good.

This and other malignant myths manufactured by the Kinsey Institute have metastasized during the last 50 years. Kinsey's books and the publications of the institute have created what I call the "Kinsey dogma," a body of unproven assumptions about sexual behavior which are often not normal, fruitful or truthful. It is built upon vile crimes against captive babies and children in the name of science. Wardell Pomeroy, a devoted fellow researcher of Kinsey, who worked at the Kinsey Institute for 13 years, still is spewing classic Kinsey dogma. According to Pomeroy in his book, *Boys and Sex:* "[F]or boys approaching or entering adolescence (p. 13)... Your sex life, like everybody else's, probably began before you were born (p. 32)... We know now that both male and female babies as young as four to six months have orgasm (p. 33)... Small boys often want to try intercourse with their girl playmates (p. 38)."

This elementary-level sex text then continues to instruct its young audience in homosexual "oral sex," which is portrayed as common oral behavior of young children. This sex text and its companion book, *Girls and Sex,* are found in the children's section of most libraries. The sex text repeatedly instructs girls about the benefits of early intercourse between a boy and a girl as a training ground for marriage. Pomeroy's main message to young girls is that "essentially nothing humans do sexually... can be called abnormal" since humans are mammals, and mammals "engage in practically every kind of sex."

Kinsey's pernicious and fallacious dogma, pervasive in our schools, courts and professions, is poison to children. Children who have been sexualized early in life are often easy to spot. They are the kids who manipulate themselves at school, experience rage and terrifying flashbacks, cannot control their fears and anger, run away from home, drop out of school with early and multiple pregnancies, make repeated suicide attempts throughout their lives and fight lifelong addictions and depression. This is the norm for young survivors, who have been sexualized by acts of incest, child molestation or pornography.

Expert opinion holds that children who are sexually violated, whether through incest, molestation or exposure to pornography, frequently and chronically suffer from post-traumatic stress disorder, dissociation and/or multiple-personality disorder. According to the textbook *Psychology,* by John Santrock, "A summary of the research literature on multiple personality suggests that the most striking feature related to the disorder is an inordinately high rate of sexual or physical abuse during early childhood."

The sex-education programs in U.S. schools are the most catastrophic failure ever witnessed in American education, just in sheer numbers of sexual casualties through unwanted pregnancies, abortions, sexually transmitted diseases and sexual dysfunctions. What else could you expect from a program founded on the works of a man who promoted animal-human sex and, as noted by historian James Jones, Kinsey's biographer, "attempted to put child molesters in a benign light"?

It may be argued—and many psychologists do—that children are not born sexual. When children exhibit sexual or criminal behaviors, these have been learned through harmful acts inflicted upon them or in the presence of children by adults or much-older children. Sexual abuse, for instance, includes pornography or live sex acts displayed in front of children. According to the National Adoption Information Clearinghouse, the classic signs of sexually abused children, which are listed in school manuals and professional training materials throughout the United States, are exactly what Kinsey followers claim to be normal behavior, specifically advanced sexual knowledge and early sexual promiscuity. These are the key indicators of child molestation, not childhood sexuality. Classic Kinsey dogma—that all sex is natural, normal and acceptable—promotes exactly such behaviors by young children.

The Kinsey dogma, which American sex education has been founded upon, is lies built upon crimes. The infamous *Sexual Behavior in the Human Male* acknowledges the cooperation of numerous schools, orphanages and children's homes in which Kinsey or his assistants did "research." Beginning on page 175 of Kinsey's sexual manual are tables of experimental data about babies and children containing such tell-tale phrases as: "Based on actual observation[s]." Table 30 details the sexual responses of hundreds of babies and children, observed but not timed. Table 31 records observations of 317 males from age two months to 15 years old. Table 32 records "observations [of 188 boys] timed with second-hand or stop watch. Ages range from five months of age to adolescence." Table 33 details observed and sometimes timed responses of 182 young males timed by the second. Table 34 includes data from sexual experiments on infants as young as five months old and children, who were sexually tortured for up to 24 hours at a time.

Where did the nine adult males who observed these sexual responses, according to Kinsey, gain access to hundreds of babies and children to time their sexual responses for up to 24 hours at a time?

The enormity and the severity of these sexual crimes against children never have been denounced by the Kinsey Institute despite the data having required the sexual torture of infants and children. The matter that needs to be disclosed is the extent to which Kinsey and his colleagues actually facilitated such research by encouraging it, purchasing the data of sexual predators, training them accurately to time their captive subjects and/or personally conducting the experiments themselves. Somewhere in the history and secrecy of the Kinsey Institute are the answers to these questions.

No matter what good work in which the Kinsey Institute may claim to be engaged in today, its history is based upon criminal acts of the most heinous and vicious kind. Until now, they had not been denounced or even admitted by Indiana officials. Kinsey Institute staff continue to speak of Kinsey as a devoted husband, successful father and a very principled scientist, despite the brutal revelations contained in the recent biography of Kinsey written by Jones, a former member of the science advisory board of the Kinsey Institute. The continuing denial of Kinsey Institute staff in the face of the documented monstrous realities about Kinsey in *Alfred C. Kinsey: A Public/Private Life* speaks volumes about the institute's credibility. According to Jones, "Kinsey was having sex with other men and arranging for his wife, Clara, to be filmed having sex with [Kinsey Institute] staff members," and Kinsey was so sexually addicted that he escalated to performing acts of severe sadomasochism on himself on film. In 1954, says Jones, Kinsey threw a rope over the exposed ceiling pipes of his basement office at Indiana University, tied it to his genitals and jumped off a chair. The fact is, Kinsey delighted in homosexual sadomasochism and simply disregarded sex-crime laws that differed with his own obsessions and addictions to sex.

The citizens of Indiana are beginning to realize that Kinsey should never have been walking the streets freely, let alone administering a major university institution. Kinsey is a prime example of the awful realities of "sexual liberation." Like any sex addict, he could not get enough sex and misused sex. The man perceived to be the founder of sex education in American schools reduced sex to the primitive, mechanical level of plants and animals, and his namesake institute continues to attempt to normalize sexual aberrations in the name of science. The institute boasts of having the nation's best collections on the history of transsexuality and supports fellowships on homosexual parenting. The shameful Kinsey legacy continues to menace the lives of America's children.

POSTSCRIPT

Should States Fund Sexuality Research?

Childhood sexuality appears to be the pivotal issue in the debate over funding for sexuality research. Certainly, of all the areas of human sexual behavior, childhood sexuality remains the prime area that has been largely unexplored by researchers. Childhood is widely seen as a period of asexual innocence. Strong taboos continue concerning childhood eroticism, and childhood sexual expression and learning are still divisive social issues.

John Money, an international gender expert, summed up the question of funding for sexuality research in the United States in his book *The Lovemap Guidebook* (Continuum, 1999). He states that the politics of the forbidden restrict the content of the curriculum in sex education, the procedures for treating sexological maladies, and the scope of what gets approved, funded, and published in sexological research. Restrictions on research apply especially to childhood sexuality. Money believes that it would be the "kiss of death" to submit a grant application for the developmental investigation of childhood sexual rehearsal play or the developmental content of juvenile sexual ideation and imagery.

In trying to ascertain why it is nearly impossible to obtain funding for certain kinds of sexuality research, Patricia Koch and David Weis, coeditors of *Sexuality in America: Understanding Our Sexual Values and Behavior* (Continuum, 1999), believe it might be interesting to determine the extent to which American researchers accept the premise that scientific explorations of sexuality might be harmful to children. For example, the field of child development, a sizable branch of American psychology, has largely ignored the issue of sexuality. An examination of standard developmental texts or reviews of the child development research literature is striking for this omission.

In the selections by Bancroft and Newman, what are the background issues that underlie the surface arguments for and against the funding of sex research? How important do you think this kind of research is? Should it be in America's national priorities?

Suggested Readings

V. L. Bullough, *Science in the Bedroom: A History of Sex Research* (Basic Books, 1994).

P. B. Koch and D. L. Weis, eds., *Sexuality in America: Understanding Our Sexual Values and Behavior* (Continuum, 1999).

W. B. Pomeroy, *Dr. Kinsey and the Institute for Sex Research* (Harper & Row, 1972).

ISSUE 13

Is Cohabitation Before Marriage a Bad Idea?

YES: David Popenoe and Barbara Dafoe Whitehead, from "Should We Live Together? What Young Adults Need to Know About Cohabitation Before Marriage: A Comprehensive Review of Research," A Report of the National Marriage Project (1999)

NO: Dorian Solot and Marshall Miller, from "Ten Problems (Plus One Bonus Problem) With the National Marriage Project's Cohabitation Report," A Revised Report of the Alternatives to Marriage Project (2001)

ISSUE SUMMARY

YES: David Popenoe and Barbara Dafoe Whitehead, directors of the National Marriage Project, http://marriage.rutgers.edu, contend that living together before marriage is not a good way to prepare for marriage or avoid divorce. They maintain that cohabitation weakens the institution of marriage and poses serious risks for women and children.

NO: Dorian Solot and Marshall Miller, founders of the Alternatives to Marriage Project, http://www.unmarried.org, state that while marriage may be a good choice for some people, it should not be pushed as the only acceptable option. They criticize a report by the National Marriage Project for misrepresenting social science research on cohabitation and marriage.

What do Americans think of sexual relationships and living together before marriage? Attitudes have changed dramatically during the past 30 years. In a 1969 Gallup poll of American adults, two-thirds said it was morally wrong for a man and a woman to have sexual relations before marriage. A more recent (2001) poll revealed that only 38 percent of American adults share this opinion today. These two surveys focus on the sexual behavior of young people before marriage. When the question is broadened to examine how today's Americans feel about couples "living together," or cohabiting, 52 percent approve. In practice, more than one-half of Americans live together before marrying.

Many cohabiting couples will live together for a relatively short period of time, with most couples either breaking up or marrying within about one and one-half years, though couples with children are more likely to stay together. In addition, the 2000 U.S. Census indicates that there are almost four million opposite-sex, unmarried households in the United States. (These households include both couples who have been married previously and those who have never been married.) Forty-one percent of these households have at least one child under the age of 18.

Like their married counterparts, infidelity is not seen among the majority of cohabiting couples, though rates are slightly different. According to Robert T. Francoeur's United States chapter of the *International Encyclopedia of Sexuality* (Continuum, 1998), about 94 percent of married persons had sex only with their spouse during the last year, compared with 75 percent of cohabiting persons.

In light of the growing acceptance of cohabitation and concern that marriage is "declining as an institution for childbearing and child rearing," the National Marriage Project was formed at Rutgers University in 1997. The project's mission is to "strengthen the institution of marriage" by providing research and analysis intended to educate the American public and influence public policy. In January 1999 the National Marriage Project released the report from which the following selection has been taken. This report provides commentary and analysis of existing literature on the subject. It warns young people, particularly young women, of the dangers of cohabitation to them and their children.

The Alternatives to Marriage Project was formed in 1998 with a different view of marriage and relationship options. This nonprofit organization provides support and information to people who choose not to marry, are not legally permitted to marry (e.g., gay males and lesbians), and people who elect to live together before marrying. They express their support for marriage as an option but indicate that it is not the *only* option. In responding to the report of the National Marriage Project, the Alternatives to Marriage Project highlights numerous flaws and presumptions that they indicate amount to a misrepresentation of cited research.

In the following selections, David Popenoe and Barbara Dafoe Whitehead present the National Marriage Project's findings and concerns regarding young people who cohabit before marrying. Dorian Solot and Marshall Miller challenge these findings as biased and misleading.

David Popenoe and
Barbara Dafoe Whitehead

 **YES**

Should We Live Together?

Executive Summary

Cohabitation is replacing marriage as the first living together experience for young men and women. When blushing brides walk down the aisle in the 1990s, more than half have already lived together with a boyfriend.

For today's young adults, the first generation to come of age during the divorce revolution, living together seems like a good way to achieve some of the benefits of marriage and avoid the risk of divorce. Couples who live together can share expenses and learn more about each other. They can find out if their partner has what it takes to be married. If things don't work out, breaking up is easy to do. Cohabitating couples do not have to seek legal or religious permission to dissolve their union.

Not surprisingly, young adults favor cohabitation. According to surveys, most young people say it is a good idea to live with a person before marrying.

But a careful review of the available social science evidence suggests that living together is not a good way to prepare for marriage or to avoid divorce. What's more, it shows that the rise in cohabitation is not a positive family trend. cohabitating unions tend to weaken the institution of marriage and pose clear and present dangers for women and children. Specifically, the research indicates that:

- Living together before marriage increases the risk of breaking up after marriage.
- Living together outside of marriage increases the risk of domestic violence for women, and the risk of physical and sexual abuse for children.
- Unmarried couples have lower levels of happiness and well-being than married couples.

Because this generation of young adults is so keenly aware of the fragility of marriage, it is especially important for them to know what contributes to marital success and what may threaten it. Yet many young people do not know the basic facts about cohabitation and its risks. Nor are parents, teachers, clergy and others who instruct the young in matters of sex, love and marriage well acquainted with the social science evidence. Therefore, one purpose of this [selection] is to report on the available research.

At the same time, we recognize the larger social and cultural trends that make cohabiting relationships attractive to many young adults today. Unmarried cohabitation is not likely to go away. Given this reality, the second purpose of this [selection] is to guide thinking on the question: "should we live together?" . . .

Should We Live Together?

What Young Adults Need to Know About Cohabitation Before Marriage: A Comprehensive Review of Recent Research

Living together before marriage is one of America's most significant and unexpected family trends. By simple definition, living together—or unmarried cohabitation—is the status of couples who are sexual partners, not married to each other, and sharing a household. By 1997, the total number of unmarried couples in America topped 4 million, up from less than half a million in 1960. It is estimated that about a quarter of unmarried women between the ages of 25 and 39 are currently living with a partner and about half have lived at some time with an unmarried partner (the data are typically reported for women but not for men). Over half of all first marriages are now preceded by cohabitation, compared to virtually none earlier in the century.

What makes cohabitation so significant is not only its prevalence but also its widespread popular acceptance. In recent representative national surveys nearly 60% of high school seniors indicated that they "agreed" or "mostly agreed" with the statement "it is usually a good idea for a couple to live together before getting married in order to find out whether they really get along." And nearly three quarters of the students, slightly more girls than boys, stated that "a man and a woman who live together without being married" are either "experimenting with a worthwhile alternative lifestyle" or "doing their own thing and not affecting anyone else."

Unlike divorce or unwed childbearing, the trend toward cohabitation has inspired virtually no public comment or criticism. It is hard to believe that across America, only thirty years ago, living together for unmarried, heterosexual couples was against the law. And it was considered immoral—living in sin—or at the very least highly improper. Women who provided sexual and housekeeping services to a man without the benefits of marriage were regarded as fools at best and morally loose at worst. A double standard existed, but cohabitating men were certainly not regarded with approbation.

Today, the old view of cohabitation seems yet another example of the repressive Victorian norms. The new view is that cohabitation represents a more progressive approach to intimate relationships. How much healthier women are to be free of social pressure to marry and stigma when they don't. How much better off people are today to be able to exercise choice in their sexual and domestic arrangements. How much better off marriage can be, and how many divorces can be avoided, when sexual relationships start with a trial period.

Surprisingly, much of the accumulating social science research suggests otherwise. What most cohabiting couples don't know, and what in fact few people know, are the conclusions of many recent studies on unmarried cohabitation and its implications for young people and for society. Living together before marriage may seem like a harmless or even progressive family trend until one takes a careful look at the evidence.

How Living Together Before Marriage May Contribute to Marital Failure

The vast majority of young women today want to marry and have children. And many of these women and most young men see cohabitation as a way to test marital compatibility and improve the chances of long-lasting marriage. Their reasoning is as follows: Given the high levels of divorce, why be in a hurry to marry? Why not test marital compatibility by sharing a bed and a bathroom for a year or even longer? If it doesn't work out, one can simply move out. According to this reasoning, cohabitation weeds out unsuitable partners through a process of natural de-selection. Over time, perhaps after several living-together relationships, a person will eventually find a marriageable mate.

The social science evidence challenges this idea that cohabiting ensures greater marital compatibility and thereby promotes stronger and more enduring marriages. Cohabitation does not reduce the likelihood of eventual divorce; in fact, it may lead to a higher divorce risk. Although the association was stronger a decade or two ago and has diminished in the younger generations, virtually all research on the topic has determined that the chances of divorce ending a marriage preceded by cohabitation are significantly greater than for a marriage not preceded by cohabitation. A 1992 study of 3,300 cases, for example, based on the 1987 National Survey of Families and Households, found that in their marriages prior cohabitors "are estimated to have a hazard of dissolution that is about 46% higher than for noncohabitors." The authors of this study concluded, after reviewing all previous studies, that the enhanced risk of marital disruption following cohabitation "is beginning to take on the status of an empirical generalization."

More in question within the research community is why the striking statistical association between cohabitation and divorce should exist. Perhaps the most obvious explanation is that those people willing to cohabit are more unconventional than others and less committed to the institution of marriage. These are the same people then, who more easily will leave a marriage if it becomes troublesome. By this explanation, cohabitation doesn't cause divorce but is merely associated with it because the same type of people is involved in both phenomena.

There is some empirical support for this position. Yet even when this "selection effect" is carefully controlled statistically a negative effect of cohabitation on later marriage stability still remains. And no positive contribution of cohabitation to marriage has been ever been found.

The reasons for cohabitation's negative effect are not fully understood. One may be that while marriages are held together largely by a strong ethic of commitment, cohabiting relationships by their very nature tend to undercut this ethic. Although cohabiting relationships are like marriages in many ways—shared dwelling, economic union (at least in part), sexual intimacy, often even children—they typically differ in the levels of commitment and autonomy involved. According to recent studies cohabitants tend not to be as committed as married couples in their dedication to the continuation of the relationship and reluctance to terminate it, and they are more oriented toward their own personal autonomy. It is reasonable to speculate, based on these studies, that once this low-commitment, high-autonomy pattern of relating is learned, it becomes hard to unlearn.

The results of several studies suggest that cohabitation may change partners' attitudes toward the institution of marriage, contributing to either making marriage less likely, or if marriage takes place, less successful. A 1997 longitudinal study conducted by demographers at Pennsylvania State University concluded, for example, "cohabitation increased young people's acceptance of divorce, but other independent living experiences did not." And "the more months of exposure to cohabitation that young people experienced, the less enthusiastic they were toward marriage and childbearing."

Particularly problematic is serial cohabitation. One study determined that the effect of cohabitation on later marital instability is found only when one or both partners had previously cohabited with someone other than their spouse. A reason for this could be that the experience of dissolving one cohabiting relationship generates a greater willingness to dissolve later relationships. People's tolerance for unhappiness is diminished, and they will scrap a marriage that might otherwise be salvaged. This may be similar to the attitudinal effects of divorce; going through a divorce makes one more tolerant of divorce.

If the conclusions of these studies hold up under further investigation, they may hold the answer to the question of why premarital cohabitation should effect the stability of a later marriage. The act of cohabitation generates changes in people's attitudes toward marriage that make the stability of marriage less likely. Society wide, therefore, the growth of cohabitation will tend to further weaken marriage as an institution.

An important caveat must be inserted here. There is a growing understanding among researchers that different types and life-patterns of cohabitation must be distinguished clearly from each other. Cohabitation that is an immediate prelude to marriage, or prenuptial cohabitation—both partners plan to marry each other in the near future—is different from cohabitation that is an alternative to marriage. There is some evidence to support the proposition that living together for a short period of time with the person one intends to marry has no adverse effects on the subsequent marriage. Cohabitation in this case appears to be very similar to marriage; it merely takes place during the engagement period. This proposition would appear to be less true, however, when one or both of the partners has had prior experience with cohabitation, or brings children into the relationship.

Cohabitation as an Alternative to Marriage

Most cohabiting relationships are relatively short lived and an estimated 60% end in marriage. Still, a surprising number are essentially alternatives to marriage and that number is increasing. This should be of great national concern, not only for what the growth of cohabitation is doing to the institution of marriage but for what it is doing, or not doing, for the participants involved. In general, cohabiting relationships tend to be less satisfactory than marriage relationships.

Except perhaps for the short term prenuptial type of cohabitation, and probably also for the post-marriage cohabiting relationships of seniors and retired people who typically cohabit rather than marry for economic reasons, cohabitation and marriage relationships are qualitatively different. Cohabiting couples report lower levels of happiness, lower levels of sexual exclusivity and sexual satisfaction, and poorer relationships with their parents. One reason is that, as several sociologists not surprisingly concluded after a careful analysis, in unmarried cohabitation "levels of certainty about the relationship are lower than in marriage."

It is easy to understand, therefore, why cohabiting is inherently much less stable than marriage and why, especially in view of the fact that it is easier to terminate, the break-up rate of cohabitors is far higher than for married partners. Within two years about half of all cohabiting relationships end in either marriage or a parting of the ways, and after five years only about 10% of couples are still cohabiting (data from the late 1980s). In comparison, only about 45% of first marriages today are expected to break up over the course of a lifetime.

Still not widely known by the public at large is the fact that married couples have substantial benefits over the unmarried in terms of labor force productivity, physical and mental health, general happiness, and longevity. There is evidence that these benefits are diluted for couples who are not married but merely cohabiting. Among the probable reasons for the benefits of marriage, as summarized by University of Chicago demographer Linda Waite, are:

1. *The long-term contract implicit in marriage.* This facilitates emotional investment in the relationship, including the close monitoring of each other's behavior. The longer time horizon also makes specialization more likely; working as a couple, individuals can develop those skills in which they excel, leaving others to their partner.
2. *The greater sharing of economic and social resources by married couples.* In addition to economies of scale, this enables couples to act as a small insurance pool against life uncertainties, reducing each person's need to protect themselves from unexpected events.
3. *The better connection of married couples to the larger community.* This includes other individuals and groups (such as in-laws) as well as social institutions such as churches and synagogues. These can be important sources of social and emotional support and material benefits.

In addition to missing out on many of the benefits of marriage, cohabitors may face more serious difficulties. Annual rates of depression among cohabiting couples are more than three times what they are among married couples. And women in cohabiting relationships are more likely than married women to suffer physical and sexual abuse. Some research has shown that aggression is at least twice as common among cohabitors as it is among married partners.

Again, the selection factor is undoubtedly strong in findings such as these. But the most careful statistical probing suggests that selection is not the only factor at work; the intrinsic nature of the cohabiting relationship also plays a role.

Why Cohabitation Is Harmful for Children

Of all the types of cohabitation, that involving children is by far the most problematic. In 1997, 36% of all unmarried-couple households included a child under eighteen, up from only 21% in 1987. For unmarried couples in the 25–34 age group the percentage with children is higher still, approaching half of all such households. By one recent estimate nearly half of all children today will spend some time in a cohabiting family before age 16.

One of the greatest problems for children living with a cohabiting couple is the high rise that the couple will break up. Fully three quarters of children born to cohabiting parents will see their parents split up before they reach age sixteen, whereas only about a third of children born to married parents face a similar fate. One reason is that marriage rates for cohabiting couples have been plummeting. In the last decade, the proportion of cohabiting mothers who go on to eventually marry the child's father declined from 57% to 44%.

Parental break up, as is now widely known, almost always entails a myriad of personal and social difficulties for children, some of which can be long lasting. For the children of a cohabiting couple these may come on top of a plethora of already existing problems. One study found that children currently living with a mother and her unmarried partner had significantly more behavior problems and lower academic performance than children from intact families.

It is important to note that the great majority of children in unmarried-couple households were born not in the present union but in a previous union of one of the adult partners, usually the mother. This means that they are living with an unmarried stepfather or mother's boyfriend, with whom the economic and social relationships are often tenuous. For example, these children have no claim to child support should the couple separate.

Child abuse has become a major national problem and has increased dramatically in recent years, by more than 10% a year according to one estimate. In the opinion of most researchers, this increase is related strongly to changing family forms. Surprisingly, the available American data do not enable us to distinguish the abuse that takes place in married-couple households from that in cohabiting-couple households. We do have abuse-prevalence studies that look at stepparent families (both married and unmarried) and mother's boyfriends (both cohabiting and dating). Both show far higher levels of child abuse than is found in intact families.

One study in Great Britain did look at the relationship between child abuse and the family structure and marital background of parents, and the results are disturbing. It was found that, compared to children living with married biological parents, children living with cohabiting but unmarried biological parents are 20 times more likely to be subject to child abuse, and those living with a mother and a cohabiting boyfriend who is not the father face an increased risk of 33 times. In contrast, the rate of abuse is 14 times higher if the child lives with a biological mother who lives alone. Indeed, the evidence suggests that the most unsafe of all family environments for children is that in which the mother is living with someone other than the child's biological father. This is the environment for the majority of children in cohabiting couple households.

Part of the enormous differences indicated above are probably due to differing income levels of the families involved. But this points up one of the other problems of cohabiting couples—their lower incomes. It is well known that children of single parents face poorly economically when compared to the children of married parents. Not so well known is that cohabiting couples are economically more like single parents than like married couples. While the 1996 poverty rate for children living in married couple households was about 6%, it was 31% for children living in cohabiting households, much closer to the rate of 45% for children living in families headed by single mothers.

One of the most important social science findings of recent years is that marriage is a wealth enhancing institution. According to one study, childrearing cohabiting couples have only about two-thirds of the income of married couples with children, mainly due to the fact that the average income of male cohabiting partners is only about half that of male married partners. The selection effect is surely at work here, with less well-off men and their partners choosing cohabitation over marriage. But it also is the case that men when they marry, especially those who then go on to have children, tend to become more responsible and productive. They earn more than their unmarried counterparts. An additional factor not to be overlooked is the private transfer of wealth among extended family members, which is considerably lower for cohabiting couples than for married couples. It is clear that family members are more willing to transfer wealth to "in-laws" than to mere boyfriends or girlfriends.

Who Cohabits and Why

Why has unmarried cohabitation become such a widespread practice throughout the modern world in such a short period of time? Demographic factors are surely involved. Puberty begins at an earlier age, as does the onset of sexual activity, and marriages take place at older ages mainly because of the longer time period spent getting educated and establishing careers. Thus there is an extended period of sexually active singlehood before first marriage. Also, our material affluence as well as welfare benefits enable many young people to live on their own for an extended time, apart from their parents. During those years of young adulthood nonmarital cohabitation can be a cost-saver, a source of companionship, and an assurance of relatively safe sexual fulfillment. For some, cohabitation is a prelude to marriage, for some, an alternative to it, and for yet others, simply an alternative to living alone.

More broadly, the rise of cohabitation in the advanced nations has been attributed to the sexual revolution, which has virtually revoked the stigma against cohabitation. In the past thirty years, with the advent of effective contraceptive technologies and widespread sexual permissiveness promoted by advertising and the organized entertainment industry, premarital sex has become widely accepted. In large segments of the population cohabitation no longer is associated with sin or social impropriety or pathology, nor are cohabiting couples subject to much, if any, disapproval.

Another important reason for cohabitation's growth is that the institution of marriage has changed dramatically, leading to an erosion of confidence in its stability. From a tradition strongly buttressed by economics, religion, and the law, marriage has become a more personalized relationship, what one wag has referred to as a mere "notarized date." People used to marry not just for love but also for family and economic considerations, and if love died during the course of a marriage, this was not considered sufficient reason to break up an established union. A divorce was legally difficult if not impossible to get, and people who divorced faced enormous social stigma.

In today's marriages love is all, and it is a love tied to self-fulfillment. Divorce is available to everyone, with little stigma attached. If either love or a sense of self-fulfillment disappear, the marriage is considered to be over and divorce is the logical outcome.

Fully aware of this new fragility of marriage, people are taking cautionary actions. The attitude is either try it out first and make sure that it will work, or try to minimize the damage of breakup by settling for a weaker form of union, one that avoids a marriage license and, if need be, an eventual divorce.

The growth of cohabitation is also associated with the rise of feminism. Traditional marriage, both in law and in practice, typically involved male leadership. For some women, cohabitation seemingly avoids the legacy of patriarchy and at the same time provides more personal autonomy and equality in the relationship. Moreover, women's shift into the labor force and their growing economic independence make marriage less necessary and, for some, less desirable.

Underlying all of these trends is the broad cultural shift from a more religious society where marriage was considered the bedrock of civilization and people were imbued with a strong sense of social conformity and tradition, to a more secular society focused on individual autonomy and self-invention. This cultural rejection of traditional institutional and moral authority, evident in all of the advanced, Western societies, often has had "freedom of choice" as its theme and the acceptance of "alternative lifestyles" as its message.

In general, cohabitation is a phenomenon that began among the young in the lower classes and then moved up to the middle classes. Cohabitation in America—especially cohabitation as an alternative to marriage—is more common among Blacks, Puerto Ricans, and disadvantaged white women. One reason for this is that male income and employment are lower among minorities and the lower classes, and male economic status remains an important determinant as to whether or not a man feels ready to marry, and a woman wants to marry him. Cohabitation is also more common among those who are less religious than their peers. Indeed, some evidence suggests that the act of cohabitation actually diminishes religious participation, whereas marriage tends to increase it.

People who cohabit are much more likely to come from broken homes. Among young adults, those who experienced parental divorce, fatherlessness, or high levels of marital discord during childhood are more likely to form cohabiting unions than children who grew up in families with married parents who got along. They are also more likely to enter living-together relationships at younger ages. For young people who have already suffered the losses associated with parental divorce, cohabitation may provide an early escape from family turmoil, although unfortunately it increases the likelihood of new losses and turmoil. For these people, cohabitation often recapitulates the childhood experience of coming together and splitting apart with the additional possibility of more violent conflict. Finally, cohabitation is a much more likely experience for those who themselves have been divorced.

What Are the Main Arguments For and Against Living Together Before Marriage in Modern Societies?

To the degree that there is a scholarly debate about the growth of cohabitation, it is typically polarized into "for" and "against" without much concern for the nuances. On one side is the religiously inspired view that living with someone outside of marriage, indeed all premarital sex, represents an assault on the sanctity of marriage. If you are ready for sex you are ready for marriage, the argument goes, and the two should always go together, following biblical injunction. This side is typically supportive of early marriage as an antidote to sexual promiscuity, and as worthwhile in its own right.

The other side, based in secular thought, holds that we can't realistically expect people to remain sexually abstinent from today's puberty at age eleven or twelve (even earlier for some) to marriage in the late twenties, which is empirically the most desirable age for insuring a lasting union. Therefore, it is better that they cohabit during that time with a few others than be promiscuous with many. This side also finds the idea of a trial marriage quite appealing. Modern societies in any event, the argument goes, have become so highly sexualized and the practice of cohabitation has become so widely accepted that there is no way to stop it.

The anti-cohabitation perspective believes in linking sex to marriage, but fails to answer the question of how to postpone sex until marriage at a time when the age of marriage has risen to an average of almost 26, the highest in this century. Cold showers, anyone? Nor is there evidence to support the idea that marriage at a younger age is a good solution. On the contrary, marrying later in life seems to provide some protection against divorce. Teenage marriages, for example, have a much higher risk of breaking up than do marriages among young adults in their twenties. The reasons are fairly obvious; at older ages people are more emotionally mature and established in their jobs and careers, and usually better able to know what they want in a lifetime mate.

Pro-cohabitation arguments recognize the demographic and social realities but fail to answer another question: if the aim is to have a strong, lifelong marriage, and for most people it still is, can cohabitation be of any help? As we have seen the statistical data are unsupportive on this point. So far, at least, living together before marriage has been remarkably unsuccessful as a generator of happy and long-lasting marriages.

Should Unmarried Cohabitation Be Institutionalized?

If marriage has been moving toward decreased social and legal recognition and control, cohabitation has moved in the opposite direction, steadily gaining social and legal identification as a distinct new institution. Cohabitation was illegal in all states prior to about 1970 and, although the law is seldom enforced, it remains illegal in a number of states. No state has yet established cohabitation as a legal relationship, but most states have now decriminalized "consensual sexual acts" among adults, which include cohabitation.

In lieu of state laws, some marriage-like rights of cohabitors have gradually been established through the courts. The law typically comes into play, for example, when cohabitors who split up have disagreements about the division of property, when one of the partners argues that some kind of oral or implicit marriage-like contract existed, and when the courts accept this position. Whereas property claims by cohabitors traditionally have been denied on the ground that "Parties to an illegal relationship do not have rights based on that relationship," courts have begun to rule more frequently that cohabitors do have certain rights based on such concepts as "equitable principles." The legal changes underway mean that cohabitation is becoming less of a "no-strings attached" phenomenon, one involving some of the benefits of marriage with none of the costly legal procedures and financial consequences of divorce.

In the most famous case, Marvin vs. Marvin, what the news media labeled "palimony" in place of alimony was sought by a woman with whom Hollywood actor Lee Marvin lived for many years. The Supreme Court of California upheld the women's claim of an implied contract. Many states have not accepted key elements of the Marvin decision, and the financial award of palimony was eventually rejected on appeal. Yet the proposition that unmarried couples have the right to form contracts has come to be widely acknowledged.

In an attempt to reduce the uncertainties of the legal system, some cohabitors are now initiating formal "living together contracts." Some of these contracts state clearly, with the intent of avoiding property entanglements should the relationship break down, that the relationship is not a marriage but merely "two free and independent human beings who happen to live together." Others, in contrast, seek to secure the rights of married couples in such matters as inheritance and child custody.

Marriage-like fiscal and legal benefits are also beginning to come to cohabiting couples. In the attempt to provide for gay and lesbian couples, for whom marriage is forbidden, some corporations and municipalities now provide "domestic partnership" benefits ranging from health insurance and pensions to the right to inherit the lease of a rent controlled apartment. In the process, such benefits have commonly been offered to unmarried heterosexual couples as well, one reason being to avoid lawsuits charging "illegal discrimination." Although the legal issues have only begun to be considered, the courts are likely to hold that the withholding of benefits from heterosexual cohabitors when they are offered to same-sex couples is a violation of U.S. laws against sex discrimination.

Religions have also started to reconsider cohabitation. Some religions have developed "commitment ceremonies" as an alternative to marriage ceremonies. So far these are mainly intended for same-sex couples and in some cases the elderly, but it seems only a matter of time before their purview is broadened.

Unlike in the United States, cohabitation has become an accepted new social institution in most northern European countries, and in several Scandinavian nations cohabitors have virtually the same legal rights as married couples. In Sweden and Denmark, for example, the world's cohabitation leaders, cohabitors and married couples have the same rights and obligations in taxation, welfare benefits, inheritance, and child care. Only a few differences remain, such as the right to adopt children, but even that difference may soon disappear. Not incidentally, Sweden also has the lowest marriage rate ever recorded (and one of the highest divorce rates); an estimated 30% of all couples sharing a household in Sweden today are unmarried. For many Swedish and Danish couples cohabiting has become an alternative rather than a prelude to marriage, and almost all marriages in these nations are now preceded by cohabitation.

Is America moving toward the Scandinavian family model? Sweden and Denmark are the world's most secular societies, and some argue that American religiosity will work against increasing levels of cohabitation. Yet few religions prohibit cohabitation or even actively attempt to discourage it, so the religious barrier may be quite weak. Others argue that most Americans draw a sharper distinction than Scandinavians do between cohabitation and marriage, viewing marriage as a higher and more serious form of commitment. But as the practice of cohabitation in America becomes increasingly common, popular distinctions between cohabitation and marriage are fading. In short, the legal, social and religious barriers to cohabitation are weak and likely to get weaker. Unless there is an unexpected turnaround, America and the other Anglo countries, plus the rest of northern Europe, do appear to be headed in the direction of Scandinavia.

The institutionalization of cohabitation in the public and private sectors has potentially serious social consequences that need to be carefully considered. At first glance, in a world where close relationships are in increasingly short supply, why not recognize and support such relationships in whatever form they occur? Surely this is the approach that would seem to blend social justice and compassion with the goal of personal freedom. But is it not in society's greater interest to foster long-term, committed relationships among childrearing couples? In this regard the advantages of marriage are substantial. It is only marriage that has the implicit long-term contract, the greater sharing of economic and social resources, and the better connection to the larger community.

The recognition and support of unmarried cohabitation unfortunately casts marriage as merely one of several alternative lifestyle choices. As the alternatives to it are strengthened, the institution of marriage is bound to weaken. After all, if cohabitors have the same rights and responsibilities as married couples, why bother to marry? Why bother, indeed, if society itself expresses no strong preference one way or the other. It is simpler and less complicated to live together.

The expansion of domestic partner benefits to heterosexual cohabiting couples, then, may be an easy way to avoid legal challenges, but the troubling issue arises: cities and private businesses that extend these benefits are in effect subsidizing the formation of fragile family forms. Even more troublingly, they are subsidizing family forms that pose increased risks of violence to women and children. While the granting of certain marriage-like legal rights to cohabiting couples may be advisable in some circumstances to protect children and other dependents in the event of couple break up, an extensive granting of such rights serves to undercut an essential institution that is already established to regulate family relationships. These issues, at the least, should cause us to proceed toward the further institutionalization of unmarried cohabitation only after very careful deliberation and forethought.

Some Principles to Guide the Practice of Cohabitation Before Marriage

Unmarried cohabitation has become a prominent feature of modern life and is undoubtedly here to stay in some form. The demographic, economic, and cultural forces of modern life would appear to be too strong to permit any society merely to turn back the clock, even if it so desired. Yet by all of the empirical evidence at our disposal, not to mention the wisdom of the ages, the institution of marriage remains a cornerstone of a successful society. And the practice of cohabitation, far from being a friend of marriage, looks more and more like its enemy. As a goal of social change, therefore, perhaps the best that we can hope for is to contain cohabitation in ways that minimize its damage to marriage.

With that goal in mind, are there any principles that we might give to young adults to guide their thinking about living together before marriage? In developing such principles it is important to note that, because men and women differ somewhat in their sexual and mate-selection strategies, cohabitation often has a different meaning for each sex. Women tend to see it as a step toward eventual marriage, while men regard it more as a sexual opportunity without the ties of long-term commitment. A woman's willingness to cohabit runs the risk of sending men precisely the wrong signal. What our grandmothers supposedly knew might well be true: If a woman truly wants a man to marry her, wisdom dictates a measure of playing hard to get.

Pulling together what we know from recent social science research about cohabitation and its effects, here are four principles concerning living together before marriage that seem most likely to promote, or at least not curtail, long-term committed relationships among childrearing couples:

1. **Consider not living together at all before marriage.** Cohabitation appears not to be helpful and may be harmful as a try-out for marriage. There is no evidence that if you decide to cohabit before marriage you will have a stronger marriage than those who don't live together, and some evidence to suggest that if you live together before marriage, you are more likely to break up after marriage. Cohabitation is probably least harmful (though not necessarily helpful) when it is prenuptial —when both partners are definitely planning to marry, have formally announced their engagement and have picked a wedding date.

2. **Do not make a habit of cohabiting.** Be aware of the dangers of multiple living together experiences, both for your own sense of well-being and for your chances of establishing a strong lifelong partnership. Contrary to popular wisdom, you do not learn to have better relationships from multiple failed cohabiting relationships. In fact, multiple cohabiting is a strong predictor of the failure of future relationships.

3. **Limit cohabitation to the shortest possible period of time.** The longer you live together with a partner, the more likely it is that the low-commitment ethic of cohabitation will take hold, the opposite of what is required for a successful marriage.

4. **Do not cohabit if children are involved.** Children need and should have parents who are committed to staying together over the long term. Cohabiting parents break up at a much higher rate then married parents and the effects of breakup can be devastating and often long lasting. Moreover, children living in cohabiting unions are at higher risk of sexual abuse and physical violence, including lethal violence, than are children living with married parents.

Conclusion

Despite its widespread acceptance by the young, the remarkable growth of un-married cohabitation in recent years does not appear to be in children's or the society's best interest. The evidence suggests that is has weakened marriage and the intact, two-parent family and thereby damaged our social well-being, especially that of women and children. We can not go back in history, but it seems time to establish some guidelines for the practice of cohabitation and to seriously question the further institutionalization of this new family form.

In place of institutionalizing cohabitation, in our opinion, we should be trying to revitalize marriage—not along classic male-dominant lines but along modern egalitarian lines. Particularly helpful in this regard would be educating young people about marriage from the early school years onward, getting them to make the wisest choices in their lifetime mates, and stressing the importance of long-term commitment to marriages. Such an educational venture could build on the fact that a huge majority of our nation's young people still express the strong desire to be in a long-term monogamous marriage.

These ideas are offered to the American public and especially to society's leaders in the spirit of generating a discussion. Our conclusions are tentative, and certainly not the last word on the subject. There is an obvious need for more research on cohabitation, and the findings of new research, of course, could alter our thinking. What is most important now, in our view, is a national debate on a topic that heretofore has been overlooked. Indeed, few issues seem more critical for the future of marriage and for generations to come.

 **NO**

Ten Problems (Plus One Bonus Problem) With the National Marriage Project's Cohabitation Report

What's Wrong With the Work of the National Marriage Project?

Based on Rutgers University, the National Marriage Project was founded in 1997 and has taken a leading role in attracting attention for its marriage-only agenda. Though the Project describes itself as a "nonpartisan, nonsectarian, and interdisciplinary initiative," its reports misrepresent social science research in a politicized attempt to argue that marriage is the only acceptable way to form a relationship or a family.

The National Marriage Project regularly releases reports to promote its political agenda. Below, we consider one recent report, "Should We Live Together? What Young Adults Need to Know About Cohabitation Before Marriage." Released in February 1999, the report's authors described it as "a comprehensive review of recent research," but our analysis reveals it to be seriously flawed. The ten problems we point out below are only the tip of an iceberg of reasons why the report cannot be considered fair or accurate.

Although we strongly critique this report, the Alternatives to Marriage Project[1] is neither anti-marriage nor pro-cohabitation. We count both married people and cohabitors among our organization's supporters, along with people who live alone or in a variety of other household and family structures. We recognize that different types of relationships work best for different people, and that this can change over the course of a lifetime. Marriage is a good choice for many people. Most people under age 40 cohabit at some point in their lives, as well. Diverse relationships and families need social and legal recognition and fair treatment regardless of whether they are married, living together before marriage (as most marrying couples do today), cannot marry (such as gay, lesbian, bisexual, and transgender people in same-sex relationships), or decide, for whatever reason, that marriage is not for them.

Unmarried people may experience pressure to marry from their family, friends, and communities, and they may face discrimination on the basis of their marital status. This pressure and discrimination can be fueled by reports like "Should We Live Together?" that push marriage as the only acceptable option.

The Problems

1. The cohabitation report says: "Living together before marriage increases the risk of breaking up after marriage."

Yet the research the report cites on this isn't nearly as straightforward as its authors represent it to be. For instance, one study they cite found that the only situation in which cohabitation is associated with a higher divorce rate is among "serial cohabitors"—people who have cohabited with more than one partner. That's a small portion of all cohabitors. The study actually concluded that for first-time cohabitors who then marry their partners, there's no increased risk of divorce.

Also, the National Marriage Project misrepresents the research by saying that cohabitation *increases* the risk of divorce, implying a casual relationship. Some research has found a correlation between the two, but correlation (the fact that two things happen at the same time) is not the same as causation (one thing causing the other). There can be other factors that explain the difference in divorce rates, as seen in several of the studies the National Marriage Project cites. As people who do not live together before marriage become a smaller and smaller minority, they begin to show some distinct characteristics. On average they are more religious and have more "traditional" views about marriage and family. They tend to be more strongly opposed to divorce and less likely to see divorce as an option for ending a bad marriage. It's no surprise when, as a result of these attitudes, they have a lower divorce rate.

People who cohabit and those who don't are two very different groups of people—an apples and oranges comparison. As University of California sociologist Judith Seltzer wrote recently in the *Journal of Marriage and the Family,* "Claims that individuals who cohabit before marriage hurt their chances of a good marriage pay too little attention to this evidence."

2. The cohabitation report says: "Cohabiting unions tend to weaken the institution of marriage."

Concern about a weakened institution of marriage is only a problem when you've started with the pre-conceived "truth" that marriage must be "revitalized"—one of the National Marriage Project's stated key missions. If your first goal is to help people have happy, healthy families and relationships, and you're open to learning about how that can best happen, promoting marriage may be much less important.

In fact, one of the studies the National Marriage Project cites seems to disagree with them. It says, "Because marriage has declined more than cohabitation has increased, there is little reason to think that the rise in cohabitation has caused the decline in marriage. What is much more likely is that the same set of factors are responsible for both the rise in cohabitation and the fall in marriage." Setting up cohabitation and marriage as battling opponents is akin to arguing that making ice cream available will decrease people's interest in eating pie. In fact, most people today both cohabit and marry, just as pie consumption seems to be doing fine with ice cream right on top.

    3. The cohabitation report says: "Cohabitants tend not to be as committed as married couples in their dedication to the continuation of the relationship."

As you can imagine, commitment is difficult to assess using a survey. Those studies that have tried to compare commitment between cohabiting and married couples have found only small differences between the two groups. The first one the National Marriage Project cites found that on a 20 point "commitment" scale where a lower score supposedly indicated more commitment, married women who had never cohabited with their husbands rated themselves at 13.1, while cohabiting women rated themselves 11.4, a difference of 1.7 points. For men, the difference was even smaller. It may be true that cohabitors were less committed on average, but does a difference so negligible mean anything in the real world?

Of course some cohabitors are not committed to each other, just as we've all known married couples who were not very committed to their marriage and soon got divorced. Other cohabitors' level of commitment easily matches the most loving, stable married couples—some have plans to marry and just haven't done so yet, while others stay together for decades without getting married. Cohabitors make up a varied group: the demographic category includes couples who own a home and have lived together for 30 years, as well as couples who just moved in together last week when one of them couldn't afford to pay rent, and those who are trying out living together to see if they want to get married. Because of the enormous variation within the group, it's meaningless to come up with an objective average level of commitment among cohabitors. Understanding commitment requires an understanding of an individual's relationship, not just one's marital status.

    4. The cohabitation report says: "Cohabiting couples report . . . lower levels of happiness [than married people]."

According to the 1987 National Survey of Families and Households, 83% of cohabitors say they are 5s, 6s, or 7s (out of a happiness scale of 1 to 7)—heavily on the happy end. Only 7% put themselves on the "unhappy" side of the scale (1s, 2s, or 3s). Pro-marriage-only groups like to talk about how much happier married people are, implying that cohabitors are unhappy. In reality, the difference between the two is quite minimal, with both groups saying they are quite happy.

There are lots of reasons why some married people could be happier, on average, than some unmarried people. One is the societal support and benefits married people receive. Another is the fact that on average, married people are a wealthier, more privileged group than unmarried people, and that the unmarried group average includes a variety of "disadvantaged" people (people with poor social skills or poor personal hygiene, alcohol or drug additions, etc.) who might affect the group's average. Finally, averages don't tell us anything about individual lives. On average pet owners may be happier than non-pet owners, but does that mean that those with severe allergies would be happier if they got a pet! Even if it is true that many married people are happier than many unmarried ones, it does not follow that getting married will make any individual happier.

5. The cohabitation report says: "Married couples are better connected than cohabitors to the larger community. This includes other individuals and groups (such as in-laws)."

This theory was disproved by a study cited later in the National Marriage Project's report. The researcher, who set out to examine whether cohabitors are "socially isolated," found that cohabiting couples are actually *more* likely to be tied to informal networks of family and friends than married couples.

6. The cohabitation report says: "Some research has shown that aggression is at least twice as common among cohabitors as it is among married partners."

They've misrepresented this research. The study the National Marriage Project cites here, by Jan Stets, actually found that the probable explanation for the difference in aggression can be found in demographics: "cohabitors . . . are more likely to be youthful and black; . . . and they tend to possess certain psychological and behavior problems, including depression and alcohol problems." Although the National Marriage Project would like the reader to believe that the aggression is because they're not married, it's more likely because of other factors, which are all linked more with poverty than with marital status. Again, correlation is not the same as causation.

In addition, the difference may be explained by another piece of simple common sense: cohabitors with aggressive partners may have made the wise decision not to get married. Rather than marriage making relationships peaceful, it's entirely logical that people in more peaceful relationships are the ones who choose to marry.

7. The cohabitation report says: "The great majority of children in unmarried-couple households were born not in the present union but in a previous union of one of the adult partners, usually the mother. This means that [the children] are living with an unmarried stepfather or mother's boyfriend. . . . These children have no claim to child support should the couple separate."

This implies that children born to unmarried parents have no claim to child support. But children have the right to child support from their parents whether the parents are married or unmarried at the time of the child's birth. The number of previously married deadbeat dads shows that marriage is not a very strong guarantee of paternal support during the marriage or after it ends. While financial responsibility for children, and whether married or cohabiting stepparents should share this responsibility, are important issues, the allegation that cohabitors' children have no claim to child support is baseless.

> *8. The cohabitation report says: "By all of the empirical evidence at our disposal, not to mention the wisdom of the ages, the institution of marriage remains a cornerstone of a successful society."*

This sweeping generalization begs to be disproved—and the report itself provides several counterexamples. Just a few pages earlier, the report calls Sweden and Denmark "the worlds' cohabitation leaders" (in these countries, about half of babies are born to unmarried parents, compared with one-third of babies in the U.S.). This seems to be the perfect contradiction to the report's own claim that nations need marriage to succeed: these high-cohabitation countries exceed the United States and other more "married" countries on many scales of well-being. For example, in Sweden 3.7% of children live in poverty and in Denmark 4.6%, compared with 18.5% in the United States. This is not to say that cohabitation is the answer, but to point out how high levels of cohabitation and lower levels of marriage do not equal automatic doom for a society or its children.

In fact, many people may be surprised to learn that the marriage rate in the United States is 65% higher than the marriage rate in the European Union (and 110% higher than Sweden's). Anthropologist Leanna Wolfe discusses other successful societies where marriage is less than a "cornerstone" in her book *Women Who May Never Marry.*

> *9. The cohabitation report says: "Children living in cohabiting unions are at higher risk of sexual abuse and physical violence, including lethal violence, than are children living with married parents."*

The National Marriage Project cites two studies to support its claim that the children of cohabitors are more likely to be abused. As sociologist Wendy Manning, a leading expert on children in cohabiting families, points out, one of these is based on interviews with seven cohabiting mothers in one Iowa county and another sample from Iowa that does not distinguish between live-in and non-live-in boyfriends. The other is based on 32 children in cohabiting families in Great Britain between 1982 and 1988. The samples from both studies are far too small and geographically narrow to be assumed representative of millions of children living with cohabiting parents in the United States. As Manning writes, "These results should be interpreted with extreme caution and other researchers should not base their understanding of cohabitation on these results."

> *10. In this supposedly "comprehensive review of recent research," the National Marriage Project overlooked many studies that weaken its hypothesis.*

For instance, one study threw out the traditional marital status categories and instead divided people into 4 categories: married, living with a partner, having a partner you don't live with, and people without partners. It found that people living with a partner had the highest levels of emotional support (higher than married couples) and the same low distress levels as married couples.

In addition, the report's claims that married people enjoy better physical and mental health are undercut by multiple studies finding that it is living with a partner in a positive, mutually supportive relationship—not necessarily being married to that partner—that correlates with healthier outcomes. Happy cohabitors seem to be just as healthy as happy married couples.

Plus one bonus: The cohabitation report says: "If a woman truly wants a man to marry her, wisdom dictates a measure of playing hard to get."

It's revealing that the National Marriage Project promotes dishonest game playing as a route to marriage.

Note

1. To learn more about the Alternatives to Marriage Project, see www.unmarried. org.

POSTSCRIPT

Is Cohabitation Before Marriage a Bad Idea?

There is a common misperception that premarital sex is a cultural phenomenon that was introduced to American society during the sexual revolution of the 1960s and 1970s. Sexologist Robert T. Francoeur dispels this myth by commenting on the prevalence of premarital sex dating back to colonial American times. As an example, Francoeur describes the courtship ritual of "bundling," which helped frontier farmers know that a bride-to-be was fertile and could produce children to work the farm. A courting couple was permitted to sleep together, fully dressed, in a small bed in the corner of a small, often single-room log cabin or sod house. A bundling board between the couple or a bundling bag for the woman was not an insurmountable obstacle to sexual intercourse. When the prospective bride became pregnant, the marriage was announced. This is but one example of historically positive and functional attitudes toward premarital sexual intercourse in the United States.

Other countries have experienced growing trends in relationship patterns that contrast with the United States' rise in cohabitation. In Sweden and other Scandinavian countries, for example, a concept called "LAT" (living alone together) has become increasingly popular. Adult couples who "live alone together" maintain a committed interpersonal relationship but also maintain separate households. In Italy, mammoni (literally, "mama's boys") are adult men who continue to live at home with their parents. While calling a man a "mama's boy" may be an insult in American culture, it is not so in Italy, where more and more men are avoiding marriage into their later adult years, regardless of whether or not they are involved in a committed relationship. Not surprisingly, this growing trend has resulted in a drastic lowering of the Italian birth rate.

In the United States, why would a couple want to choose cohabitation before marriage, or as a relationship option instead of marriage? The following reasons have been identified:

- Some couples are not legally allowed to marry because they are members of the same sex, and some heterosexual couples avoid marriage in objection to an institution that is not legally available to all.
- Some couples believe that one's intimate relationship does not require the endorsement of government or religion.
- Some people are troubled by the divorce rate, or have experienced a divorce themselves, and wish to avoid the risk (or stigma) of divorce.
- Some people believe that a relationship does not need to be a lifelong commitment.

- Some people are not sure if their current partner is the one they would select for a lifetime commitment. They might try cohabitation as a precursor to marriage.
- Some people feel their relationship is working fine without marriage.
- Some people might lose financial benefits if they decide to marry (such as from the pension of a prior spouse).
- Some people are uncomfortable with marriage's historical view toward women as property.

Some opponents of cohabitation before marriage are concerned primarily about the sexual aspect of these relationships; namely, they believe that sexual intercourse before marriage is impermissible. However, sexual and marital trends indicate that most young people begin having intercourse in their mid-to-late teens, about *eight years before they marry.* Is it better for young people to begin having sex later, or consider marrying earlier? Are the main issues the timing of sex and the marital decision, or the health and happiness of the couple?

Suggested Readings

R. T. Francoeur, "Challenging Common Religious/Social Myths of Sex, Marriage, and Family," unpublished manuscript submitted to the *Journal of Sex Education and Therapy* (July 24, 2001).

T. Ihara, R. Warner, and F. Hertz, *Living Together: A Legal Guide for Unmarried Couples* (Nolo Press, 2001).

L. M. Latham, "Southern Governors Declare War on Divorce," http://www.salon.com (January 24, 2000).

K. S. Peterson, "Changing the Shape of the American Family," *USA Today* (April 18, 2000).

K. S. Peterson, "Wedded to Relationship but Not to Marriage," *USA Today* (April 18, 2000).

R. Schoen, "The Ties That Bind: Perspectives on Marriage and Cohabitation," *Journal of Marriage and Family* (August 1, 2001).

P. J. Smock, "Cohabitation in the United States: An Appraisal of Research, Themes, Findings, and Implications," *Annual Review of Sociology* (2000).

ISSUE 14

Is the Model of Normal and Vandalized Gendermaps/Lovemaps Biased?

YES: Pat Califia, from *Sex Changes: The Politics of Transgenderism* (Cleis Press, 1997)

NO: John Money, from "An Interview With John Money," *Omni* (April 1996)

ISSUE SUMMARY

YES: Pat Califia, a feminist and self-described sex radical, argues that John Money's concept of lovemaps reflects a high-handed, moralistic division of the world into "normal" and "abnormal" sexuality. She maintains that many "differently pleasured" persons, including homosexuals, are at risk because of the moralistic distinctions implicit in Money's model of lovemaps.

NO: John Money, an expert on gender development, contends that every society has taboos and establishes its own sexual ethic. Money suggests that Califia's idea of a sexual democracy where people can love whomever they please, in whatever fashion they please, is unachievable because of those taboos.

The cover story of the March/April 1993 issue of *The Sciences* was "The Five Sexes: Why Male and Female Are Not Enough." The author of the article, medical biologist Anne Fausto-Sterling, argued that "biologically speaking, there are many gradations running from female to male; along that spectrum lie at least five sexes—perhaps even more." Along with males and females, Fausto-Sterling counted the 4 percent of babies who are born hermaphrodites (herms), female pseudo-hermaphrodites (ferms), or male pseudo-hermaphrodites (merms).

If a person's gender identity is relevant to the question "How many sexes are there?" then we can add to Fausto-Sterling's list of sexes people who describe themselves as transgendered—transvestites (or cross-dressers) and transsexuals, or people whose psyche (gender identity) conflicts with their sexual bodies. If one's "gender orientation" is part of one's "sex," then we may need to consider people who are sexually attracted to people of their own sex or gender, those who fall in love with people of the opposite sex, people who are sexually attracted to both sexes, and asexual people, who have no interest in sexual intimacy at all. And then we have to figure out where people who enjoy fetishes and unconventional sexual outlets fit into our schema.

"How many sexes are there?" is not a simple question, because it cannot have a simple answer. It is now known that a person's sexual nature is not a simple given, male or female, set at conception, birth, or any other point in time. Most experts believe that a person's sex is the result of both nature (genes, hormones, and anatomy) and nurture (learning) interacting from conception to death.

Few scientists have contributed more to the understanding of human sexual development than John Money. For over 50 years Money has studied "nature's experiments," the not-so-rare children with anomalies of sex organs and hormone systems. Money views the complex path that people follow as they develop their gender identity, gender role, and gender orientation as a "gendermap." Part of this gendermap is a "lovemap."

As described in the introduction to the *Omni* interview with Money that is reprinted in the second selection of this issue, the concept of a lovemap represents the personal template, or imprint, of all the neural pathways that develop in the brain. Its development is influenced by hormones, genes, and learning. Its contours affect whom we are sexually attracted to, whom we fall in love with, and what kind of sex we like, including when, how often, and under what circumstances. In adulthood individuals seek to match their lovemaps with someone else's to form pair-bonding relationships.

The main contours of the lovemap are etched during childhood sex-rehearsal play. When the lovemap is allowed to grow naturally, the child at puberty matures into a healthy lover. When the child is subjected to traumatic experiences, his or her lovemap may be vandalized or distorted. Thwarted childhood sex play can vandalize a lovemap. Adult functioning of the sex organs in lovemaking will be impaired. There may be no sex at all. Or the lovemap owner may defy defacement by using the sex organs with compulsive frequency. A third solution is paraphilia where the lovemap is redesigned with detours that include new elements or relocations of old ones. In paraphilia, both love and lust are compromised. The genitals will work but only in the presence of some special substitute imagery, object, or ritual. This is because in the lovemap of a paraphiliac, where love and lust cannot be reconciled, the solution is to find a way to reconcile them temporarily. The means can be as benign as a shoe fetish, as complex as cross-dressing, or as deadly as asphyxophilia (purposely cutting off one's air supply to increase the pleasure of masturbating).

This brings us to the issue raised by Pat Califia, who argues in the following selection that Money's concept of lovemaps discriminates against people whose lovemap does not fit the conventional expectations of society. Califia suggests that terms like *vandalized, abnormal, deviant,* and *distorted* are cultural constructs that unnecessarily stigmatize some individuals. Money counters that every society has its taboos, so these terms are unavoidable, even though we must constantly reevaluate and challenge them in the light of new knowledge.

Pat Califia

 **YES**

Sex Changes: The Politics
of Transgenderism

[John] Money (with his collaborators) is the author of hundreds of scientific papers and more than two dozen books in the field of sexology and psychoendocrinology. He is an enormously influential intellectual and researcher who clearly sees himself as a humanitarian who advocates better treatment for those he views as being less sexually fortunate than normal people. But he does not seem to understand how precarious the scientific basis is for his high-handed division of the world into "normal sexuality" and "paraphilias." Money is essentially a moralist masquerading as a scientist, and he gets away with it because of his medical credentials and his prolific output of technical-sounding publications about sexuality. In fact, it is the sort of attitudes toward sex, gender, and pleasure that he promotes which are the underpinnings of such things as sodomy laws and psychiatric incarceration of "differently-pleasured" people.

Nowhere is this moralism made more clear than in Money and Margaret Lamacz's 1989 *Vandalized Lovemaps: Paraphilic Outcome of Seven Cases in Pediatric Sexology....* Money and Lamacz advocate intervention in the lives of sexually different children without conclusive proof that such interventions have any impact on adult sexual orientation, gender identity, or pleasure-seeking behavior. In fact, the dedication of this book is to "Those whose lovemaps will be paraphilia-free in the twenty-first century if this book promotes the founding of pediatric sexology clinics and research centers, worldwide, as we hope." The prospect makes me shudder.

Money says:

> The lovemap is the personal imprint or template of whatever turns a person on. The beginning topography of the lovemap evolves in the womb, where the developing brain is open to the influence of the sex hormones. Spontaneous erections begin in the womb. And throughout childhood erotic play for most youngsters seldom voluntarily stops. The main contours of the lovemap are etched during this childhood sex-rehearsal play; when the lovemap is allowed to grow naturally, the child at puberty matures into a healthy lover. In adulthood an individual seeks to match lovemaps with someone else in a pair-bonding relationship.

This explanation of the genesis of the lovemap has as much to do with objective reality as the fad that swept the country a few years ago for female ejaculation, which supposedly took place because of the G-spot, a mythical organ that no anatomist could even find in the female body. All Money is really doing is recycling a bunch of very questionable assumptions about the genesis of pleasure-seeking behavior in adults. He moves readily from the "circulating fetal hormones" explanation of the structure of the lovemap to a "traumatic childhood event" explanation, without managing to document that either one is true. This is his "theory" about the etiology of sadomasochism: "The classic example is the kid who gets a hard-on while in a state of abject terror because he's been called down to the principal's office for punishment.... Suddenly you've got the connection between an erection, sexual feeling, and getting beaten up. So you've got a sadomasochist in the making."

Money, of course, is not troubled by the fact that there are plenty of sadomasochists who had little or no childhood experience with corporal punishment. Nor does it occur to him to ask why the kid who is about to be punished has a hard-on in the first place. Perhaps a predisposition to enjoy exposure, verbal rebukes, and a blow upon the buttocks existed before this make-belief teenager was chastised—or perhaps the potential to respond with arousal to this set of circumstances exists in all of us. The right question to ask may not be, "Why do some people grow up to be perverts?" but "Why doesn't everybody grow up with more sexual diversity and the ability to enjoy polymorphous pleasure?"

Though sexually conservative, Money does not consciously refer to the Bible or English common law to justify his fairly traditional views about what constitutes appropriate sexual conduct. Instead, he makes reference to the secular religion of the West, romantic love. It is the inability to enjoy romantic fulfillment that makes Money's paraphile a sad figure. The paraphiliac, according to Money, has accomplished a triumph in spite of the tragedy of having her or (more often) his lovemap defaced. The paraphiliac rescues lust from total wreckage and obliteration and constructs a new map that gives the erotic side of relationships a new chance. But there is a terrible price to be paid. In Money's world view, paraphiliacs cannot have both love and lust; they sacrifice committed, intimate, romantic partnerships in order to have their strange pleasures.

Having known many people Money would call "paraphiliacs" who do indeed enjoy romance and committed relationships, this generalization seems dubious to me. But Money has a double-bind to cover any exceptions to his rule. He simply pathologizes any relationships that sexually-different people might construct. In an interview, he typified such relationships as "spooky" and added, "I have never really gotten to the bottom of this strange collusional business between a paraphile and the partner. Do they smell each other out at the time of courtship? Does one grow into the paraphilia of the other —or a bit of both? Well, I have to call it a spooky collusional relationship. They know what they're doing. They're not ignorant, but both are powerless to not do it."

As powerless, perhaps, as two heterosexual vanilla people who are deeply in love? When he enters the shadow side of human sexuality, Money leaves Occam's Razor at home.

In case being threatened with the loss of love doesn't convince us that the intense pleasures of the paraphilias are to be shunned, he makes ominous references to epilepsy among paraphiliacs and warns us that it is "terribly dangerous" to have "people who've got too much power" (i.e., politicians) with hidden paraphilias. In an interview, he equated the use of atomic weapons with fetishism and masochism. This, and his attempt to make paraphiliac sex sound radically different from vanilla heterosexual lovemaking, fall rather flat. He says there "must be neurochemical changes" when paraphiliacs "go into a trance-like state and carry out their rituals. . . . They have no self-governance over their behavior"—as if neurochemical changes do not take place during all sexual activity! Money has absolutely no evidence that a fetishist, sadomasochist, or transsexual is in any more of a "trance," engaging in a "ritual," or lacking self-control than a teenage boy who's getting some at a drive-in movie or a couple of newlyweds during their first night in the honeymoon hotel.

By the way, according to the 1996 edition of *Who's Who*, Money never married and has no children. It seems that what's sauce for the goose is not sauce for the sexologist. I guess it would verge on ad hominem to speculate about what might have happened to *his* lovemap.

Money has gotten big street cred in academia for boldly and calmly confronting dreadful things. He says he made a decision to allow the first sex-change surgery in the United States to take place in February of 1965 at Johns Hopkins because he was interested in the welfare of transsexuals and wanted to change the medical profession's attitude toward people with sexual problems. This kind of talk has made some people see Money as an advocate for positive social change. But the fact is, he wants to get rid of all the weird, scary people who made him so esteemed and famous. When asked by an interviewer if transsexuals would still seek sex reassignment in a "sexual democracy," Money replied, "I have a very strong suspicion that if we had a genuine sexual democracy, we would not create all of these problems in our children." Conformity, not increased tolerance, is Money's recipe for the Sexually Great Society.

Money believes that societies such as an aboriginal community in north central Australia have no "paraphilias or even bisexual or homosexual stuff either. They had no sexual taboo; the kids were allowed to play sex-rehearsal games without being punished." He continues:

> We need a better ethnographic survey of peoples who don't have sexual taboos to find out to what extent we're actually creating these paraphilias by so zealously trying to beat out sex from the development of young children. Perfectly reasonable, nice mothers and fathers go berserk when they encounter the first appearance of normal sexual rehearsal play in their children. If we were truly committed to having our children grow up to be plain, ordinary heterosexuals, we'd treat them exactly as if we wanted them to be athletes—get them practicing and reward them every time we saw them doing it.

It never seems to have occurred to him that small, isolated groups of people are able to do a much better job of controlling and repressing unacceptable sexual conduct than a handful of vice cops and fundamentalist preachers in a big, modern city. Nor has he considered the possibility that the respondents may have lied to whoever was studying them, or not understood the sexual categories used by Westerners. While I can certainly support Money's goal to get parents to stop punishing their children for age-appropriate sex play, it seems intellectually dishonest for him to simply overlook the large amount of such childish "sexual rehearsal" that is unconventional, to say the least. Piaget may not have noticed that, but Freud certainly did. I can't say I relish the prospect of "normal" sexplay being imposed on homosexual or transsexual children as a form of behavioral therapy. Money doesn't prescribe this specifically, but it seems consistent with his philosophy.

. . . The overwhelming sense that I get from this examination of the history of transsexuality and sex reassignment is that "help" from doctors is truly a double-edged sword for sexual minorities.

Transsexuals became the abused darlings of sexologists and medical doctors because they could be "cured" by using hormones and surgery. Those who see themselves as gender scientists are invested in trying to discover a physiological explanation for human sexual variation. Instead of simply accepting this variation as a normal part of the spectrum of human experience, and seeing its intrinsic worth, these people inappropriately apply a medical model of health versus disease to gender identity and pleasure-seeking behavior.

Once sex hormones were discovered, doctors tried to use them to treat every sex disorder from impotence to homosexuality; in no case were they successful enough to set up a treatment industry. Transsexuality is an exception. By creating a "treatment" process that is intended to churn out feminine heterosexual women and masculine heterosexual men, the gender scientists have turned their backs on the most liberating and revolutionary implications of what they call "gender dysphoria"—the possibility that the categories of "male" and "female" are unrealistic and smothering us all.

It doesn't matter whether sex deviation is caused by social learning or biology; or at least it doesn't matter to the "deviate." If it weren't for loneliness, discrimination, and stigma, most sexual-minority members would never consider giving up or altering their fantasies and pleasures. But it does matter to the doctors and scientists and researchers because these issues give them government grants, publishing contracts, and tenure at universities. We need to question the so-called experts who are too quick to pathologize behavior or self-concepts that are not inherently self-destructive and that don't necessarily interfere with people's ability to love or pleasure one another. We can only do that if we jettison our own guilt and apply the same intellectual standards to sex research that we would apply to a piece of research in the field of astronomy or physics.

Queer activists who believe it would be politically advantageous for us to be able to prove that homosexuality has a genetic basis should consider transsexuals' experience with the father figures of gender science. Doctors have believed that transsexuality is a medical problem with a biological cause for nearly two decades, and the position of transgendered people in society has barely advanced a notch or two. Transsexuals are still perceived as the tragic victims of a delusion that may or may not have a chromosomal or hormonal origin. Not a single recognized authority on this issue has said that transgendered people have intrinsic value and worth, or something important to contribute to the rest of us and our understanding of what it means to be human. Money [and his colleagues] would have absolutely no ethical problem with genetically engineering transsexuals out of existence. It would be interesting to see what their recommendations might be if amniocentesis could detect the potential for transgenderism in a fetus.

Gay men, lesbians, and bisexuals would be foolish and deluded if we imagined the gender scientists have a more positive picture of us than they do of transsexuals. To them, we are all manifestations of the same disease, gender identity disorder. As long as we are operating in a social context where sexual or gender difference is seen as a bad thing, the medical model will further stigmatize homosexuals as sick or developmentally flawed people in need of a cure—not equal civil rights. It is very possible that homosexuality does have a biological basis. But the belief that our difference springs from our genes, hormones, or brain chemistry is no guarantee that social policy toward us will be liberalized.

Finally, how very sad it is that even the people who viewed themselves as transsexuals' allies and advocates at the same time saw them as sick, delusional, and inferior people.... And how frustrating it is that... lengthy technical texts were constructed to explain gender dysphoria and justify sex reassignment, when the thing that really needs to be explained is our insistence on gender dimorphism, despite all the hard medical evidence that this is not uniformly natural to our species. It is our fear and hatred of people who are differently-gendered that need to be cured, not their synthesis of the qualities we think of as maleness and femaleness, masculinity and femininity.

An Interview With John Money

Omni: Why have the sexual passions so long been considered anarchistic, dangerous, something to suppress?

Money: At the recent Seventh World Congress of Sexology, in India, quite a clear contrast emerged for me between the sexual philosophy of the Kama Sutra and that of Ayurvedic medicine. This traditional Indian herbal medicine, totally in contrast with the celebration of joy and sex in the Kama Sutra, espouses the conservation of "vital fluids," that is, semen. This is a teaching of extreme antiquity and is widespread in Asia and Africa, probably antedating the discovery of writing. While we'll never know when taboos originated, I associate their invention with this concept of seminal retention. In my imagination I place taboo as a means of controlling human behavior in the hands of some priestly rulers in the Magdalenian Age, when the drawings were done in the caves of Lascaux and Altamira.

It's a pretty simple piece of psychology that if you terrorize small children, making them afraid of doing something the human organism normally does in healthy development, then you've put in place a lever of guilt and shame. All you need to do after that is pull the lever and they jump to attention and do whatever you tell them. So taboos are extremely widespread, the most common by far being the taboo against sex. While some tribes in New Guinea, Melanesia, or Amazonia still may exist without a taboo, the Polynesians, covering a large part of the earth's surface, are the prime example of a people who've managed not to have a sexual taboo. They raise teenagers with a totally different morality for sex. But they have a fearful taboo about the desecration of the bodies, spirits, and burial places of the dead.

Omni: Is there evidence that taboos enable societies to function in orderly ways?

Money: It would be challenging to find out, with comparative ethnographic studies, why humans invented the concept of taboo, used it to raise their children, and adhered to it so wonderfully all these millennia. Still, we can say that every society establishes a sexual ethic, regardless of the conditions and constraints. This century reevaluated the sexual ethic in the presence of contraception. The contraception revolution that got going around 1870 simply *dictated* this change to us. It's not the whimsy of a bunch of pointy-eared Easterners, as some Bible Belt people would have it. The so-called sexual revolution was necessitated by the universalization of birth control, which culminated in the discovery of the pill. Although the diaphragm had been in existence for ages, the pill's incredible value was that you put it in your mouth, not your vagina. So it wasn't sex. It was so completely de-eroticized, it was acceptable.

Omni: Do you think there's a struggle going on now over sexual morality?

Money: The rules of social behavior tend to be self-perpetuating except when something new—a cultural artifact either invented or borrowed—comes in to upset the balance. The American automobile changed the landscape, really everything. And there's almost a complete chronological overlap with the invention of the automobile and of birth control. The pivotal factor of the universalization of birth control was the vending machine. It was very important that young people could drive up to a gas station, slip in a quarter, and get a condom; and avoid a red-faced confrontation at a counter, especially with a female clerk. Even today some people will risk pregnancy rather than the humiliation of asking for birth control in public.

Omni: Are there new strategies for love as a result of this historical imperative?

Money: Historically, there are different traditions of pair-bonding in establishing marriages, breeding relationships. The familiar European one, endorsed by the Church, came through Imperial Rome, by way of the Middle East. This system of the arranged marriage, the virgin bride, and the double standard was also adapted by the Moslems. In contrast was the pre-Roman, pre-Christian European one that I call the betrothal system. It's still intact in Iceland and parts of the Arctic north in Scandinavia. In the betrothal system lasting relationships were based on a ritualistic sequence of the love affair, falling in love.

The breeding customs of any society are almost in the Marxist sense intimately related to the method of production and distribution of wealth. The betrothal system was a natural for a society of small farmers, fishermen, and woodspeople, where the family was the production unit. In the Middle East the system evolved with the growth of cities. Very rich and powerful people would commandeer the girls for their harems, leaving the public harem—the whorehouse—to take care of all the unattached men.

Today's college students, without necessarily any blueprint for it, have resumed the pattern of the betrothal by living together before getting married. Birth control, of course, has made the system viable again. You don't live together to try for a pregnancy but to see how well you make it as a sexual couple in advance of the contractual obligations of marriage. Many young people are vaguely aware that they grew up in erotically rather joyless families, and they are searching for a better way. Many people, being so obsessed with sex and conformity to the old mores, forget that people fall in love, and the romantic affair is as important a part of the equation as the sex-organ relationship. Young people are very much involved in romantic love attraction to one another.

Omni: Can a sexual democracy—where people can love whomever they please, in whatever fashion they please—exist?

Money: Yes, but it would cause a kaleidoscopic reshuffling, because everything within a society is integrated with everything else. All the institutions have their feelers out interdigitating with one another. Some of the Moral Majority expect young people to have no sex, not even to masturbate, until they're old enough to marry at twenty-eight. But a true sexual democracy doesn't dictate to children. With adequate economic support, there's a perfectly good argument for young parenthood.

Omni: Will AIDS have an effect on this historical progression?

Money: Yes, AIDS has already made a big, big change in sexual-life patterns. But not big enough to stop the spread of AIDS; it never will. Nothing ever stopped people from spreading syphilis and gonorrhea. In the eighteenth century [Swiss physician Simon André] Tissot was obsessed with the terrifying effects of the social vice. Syphilis and gonorrhea were considered one disease. His book on the terrible dangers of onanism said it's not only losing your vital seminal fluids (women were problematic vis-à-vis vital fluids), but it's also yielding to your concupiscent thoughts and letting your passions go wild that gets you out on the streets with the whores and catching the disease. Tissot was really tangling with issues of sexual behavior and morality as related to disease. The great appeal of his teaching, summed up as degeneracy theory, was that it gave doctors an explanation for disease. You degenerated yourself, and then you were vulnerable to everything. After the previous theory—the demon possession theory, which faded when the Inquisition burned itself out—the medical profession had no theory of health or disease until Tissot formulated this wonderful degeneracy theory.

His book was profoundly influential, in America particularly through Sylvester Graham, who had many followers in the 1830's. By 1870 Kellogg made his mark with degeneracy theory. Kellogg is important historically because he sat on the fence between degeneracy theory and germ theory. He couldn't make change and absorb germ theory, so he became a sort of mastodon of medical theory embalmed in ice. Yet his antisexual teachings are still explicitly used by the Seventh Day Adventists and Jehovah's Witnesses in their books on sex education. Neither differ much from the Mormons.

Omni: In a sexual democracy, will transsexuals and others with complex gender identity/roles still try to make sex changes?

Money: At the New Delhi Congress, Margaret Lamacz and I ran a symposium on gender transposition. Gender transposition means that as compared with the standard stereotypes, which may or may not be biologically, historically, or culturally based, some people are transposed away from what you'd expect if you looked only at their sex organs. Instead of being male, they're committed to a whole lot that's female, and vice versa. Since there was a terminological problem, I suggested we use the concept of miming, so you get men who are gynemimetic, impersonating women; and women who are andromimetic, impersonating men.

In India you find the hijra, whose history is lost in the mists of time, but essentially these people replenish their ranks with teenagers who run away from home because they are disgracing their families by being too effeminate. They like to have sex with men and want to be women—they're obsessed with it, the same as our patients here are. The ultimate stage of the hijra is to get up the courage to go through with amputation of penis and testicles. They had no anesthetic. No hormone treatment. So in their ancient ways, they looked like men impersonating women. Now some of them are beginning to take hormones.

I have a large group of gynemimetic patients—so does anybody who deals with gender problems—who do *not* want their penises removed, do *not* want a vagina constructed, and the corresponding is true for the women-to-men. They simply want to take hormones and live their lives as members of the opposite sex. Now if we had a sexual democracy, we'd have a place for both kinds of people. A book called *The Transsexual Empire* argues that it's only these cruel, vicious, and heartless members of the medical profession who are forcing these poor darlings to go and get themselves cut up and mutilated, whereas we should leave them alone. Well, I have news for whoever wrote that book: You'd have lots of patients willing to get a gun and blow off their own genitals if you don't do it. I've had several who got knives and cut themselves trying to get rid of their sex organs. That's their obsession!

Then there are the transvestophiles, who dress up occasionally, often doing incredibly good impressions of the other sex. It's almost always men who cross-dress, and it gives them a real thrill, but that's not why they do it. The major reason is that it's the only way they can get an erection and reach orgasm. Ideally, one finds a partner who's as turned on by your dressing up as you are. It's incredibly hard to find. I've never met a woman partner who was really turned on by having her man with his legs and body shaved, wearing perfumes and ladies' clothing. It just makes her go sexually, erotically dead. Numb. I've met those who go along with it, but basically it's a nasty taste in their mouths. That's transvestophilia.

Now with a partial degree of transposition you have people whom you'd never recognize as being gender transposed. Everything, except their choice of sex partner, conforms to the stereotypes of masculinity or femininity. Many a person is surprised to discover the boyfriend, husband, brother, or guy at work is gay. They don't look or act gay in social situations. The only way you know they are—like the big football player who comes out and announces himself on TV—is that he's said he likes to have a boyfriend he sucks penis with. In terms of total life pattern, that is a minor degree of transposition because it only applies to the sexual activity and not to the other trimmings and trappings of acting masculine or not. Then you have bisexual people.... Now all I've dealt with is gender transposition, and I haven't even gone through the whole list of them. So in a sexual democracy, you'd find a place for all of those people. But I have a very strong suspicion that if we had a genuine sexual democracy, we would not create all of these problems in our children.

Omni: Your critics note that you talk about these people as if their behavior is natural, and yet you say they've got problems. Do they have problems?

Money: Why don't you just define problem! Whose criterion? Many people with varying degrees of gender transportation do experience it in some contexts of their lives as a problem. I've seen many a youngish person in a panic about whether he or she's gay. For some, the biggest help is for someone to tell them, yes, you can find a niche for yourself in life as a gay person. Others will blow up, practically pull a gun if you tell them it's okay to be gay. Because their attitude is: Nobody's going to tell me that, damn it; you've got to change me! A big part of this business is whether people define themselves as having a problem or not.

Omni: Why the variety of lovemaps, gender identifications, and paraphilias?

Money: I've never found an explanation for why the human race has so many languages. When the brain became a language brain, it obviously needed to develop an intense degree of plasticity. Such plasticity allows languages to be logical, coherent systems and yet be extremely variable. The same brain that thinks in words and symbols is also a brain that has to be freed up with regard to sexual turn-on and partnering. God knows why sex attitudes have been subject to the corresponding degrees of modification and variety as language. I suspect there's a close parallel between the two.

The brain doesn't seem incredibly efficient with regard to sex. I can't find a rational or sensible explanation for why a man needs his partner to dress him in diapers, feed him a baby bottle, let him pee in his diapers, smack his bottom, and tell him what a naughty boy he is—so that then and only then he can get a hard-on and come. I have patients like that, and I can go through my list of forty-odd paraphilias and say, Okay, why should I inveigh against people who have to wear diapers to copulate, or any of the others? But I really can't recommend that person to a partner because I haven't yet met any woman who really gets turned on by diapering her husband.

It's all right if you've a perfect match. And those who do sometimes match are the paraphiliacs of amputation, who get turned on by the stumps. That is, if they don't feel too guilty once they actually admit their paraphilia to an amputee! Perhaps all they can do is establish a friendship; many can't allow it to become erotic, but a few make it wonderfully by marrying an amputee.

Omni: Would there be any paraphilias in a sexual democracy?

Money: I made a study of an aboriginal community way up in north central Australia. I could not find any paraphilias or even bisexual or homosexual stuff either. They had no sexual taboo; the kids were allowed to play sexual-rehearsal games without being punished. My big surprise was that this play was inconspicuous, socially unobtrusive. Their taboo was about with whom you were allowed to use your vocal chords, not your sex organs. And if you weren't allowed to talk to them, you weren't allowed to have sex with them. In some relationships, usually an uncle/nephew relationship, the child could talk to him only if he used a joking relationship, and all the jokes were sexual.

We need a better ethnographic survey of peoples who don't have sexual taboos to find out to what extent we're actually creating these paraphilias by so zealously trying to beat out sex from the development of young children. Perfectly reasonable, nice mothers and fathers go berserk when they encounter the first appearance of normal sexual rehearsal play in their children. If we were truly committed to having our children grow up to be plain, ordinary heterosexuals, we'd treat them exactly as if we wanted them to be athletes—get them practicing and reward them every time we saw them doing it.

But you can't say things like that in this society without convincing people you're an idiot! Yet there's not a single university hospital in the Western world with a department of adult or pediatric sexual health. Children in trouble with their healthy sexual development have no experts and no clinic to go to. Piaget never dealt with sexual, erotic, or genital concepts. He never wrote about boys and girls, really. And he certainly never got down between their legs and looked at their concepts of themselves that way. It's quite an accomplishment, to live to Piaget's age and wear horse blinders about sexual concepts in the development of childhood.

Omni: The fertilized egg is basically hermaphroditic, undifferentiated, but by the eighth week, depending on chromosomal sex, one set of sexual apparatus grows and the other atrophies. Why does nature have a dual pattern like that?

Money: I don't know, but I use that question as a challenge to think about which pattern is used in the development of the sexual part of the brain. The best evidence now says that within the brain, the biochemical—mainly hormonal—process of differentiation occurs so that both masculinizing and feminizing are able to take place together. It has now been established that masculinizing and feminizing and demasculinizing and defeminizing are four processes. The fool who jumps in where angels fear to tread would say that the opposite of masculine is feminine, but it's not; it's demasculine. And that's probably crucial for understanding bisexual feelings and dispositions in love affairs—that people can have either or both. I don't think we can escape the evidence that there's a sexual disposition shaped by hormones influencing the brain.

Omni: What do you think of East German endocrinologist Gunter Dörner's attempt to prove that homosexuality is caused by hormonal differences? In 1980 he tried to show that gay males have a bigger response to estrogen injections than do straight males.

Money: Dörner reported that the effect of estrogen shots on LH [luteinizing hormones, a pituitary regulator that triggers the gonads to secrete sex steroids] in homosexuals resembled that of heterosexual women and differed from that of heterosexual and bisexual men. In 1984 Brian Gladue of Stony Brook obtained similar findings. But this year L. Gooren in Amsterdam not only failed to replicate these findings but showed that the difference in receptivity was due to a previously neglected variable. He showed that abnormal response to the estrogen might result from poor functioning of the hormone-producing cells in the testicles [Leydig cells]. This phenomenon appeared in both hetero- and homosexual men.

Gooren went one step further. He had an additional test group: male-to-female transsexual applicants who were not yet on hormonal therapy. They did not show the higher sensitivity to the estrogen injections, nor the weak Leydig cell function. Since then, he told me, he's been able to repeat this same test on transsexuals before they had their testicles removed and after. When they had their testicles, they didn't show the higher sensitivity. And after, when, of course, they'd lost their Leydig cells along with their testicles, their response was up to females' levels. So Gooren has gone further and pinned it down to the Leydig cells instead of something in the brain. He found it didn't make any difference if they were gay or straight.

It's hard to know if, in your group of homosexuals, you're going to pick up some who may have damaged Leydig cells. Dörner wasn't too fussy about reviewing his patients for unexpected contamination from, for instance, regular drug use. The question is: Is there a greater proportion of gays to straights with Leydig cell impairment? And how will you test for it?

Omni: Isn't science a bit deterministic in insisting on a purely physiological cause?

Money: Yes, and I don't know why. But I get attacked from both sides of the fence. Some homosexuals want to make it all a matter of moral choice, and I tell them they're crazy. They couldn't fall in love with a woman if they got a million dollars. They might be able to fuck her, but falling in love is *the* key. You can't force yourself if you don't have your heart and soul in it.

The problem reduces itself to a simple scientific issue: How do you get your gender status, a lovemap that makes you fall in love with your own sex? When, and through what channel, does it get into the body? Through your genes, your prenatal hormones, the kind of food your mother ate when she was pregnant, the food you ate in your first years, pollutants in the air? Or does it get in through your eyes, ears, and skin senses? And it doesn't really matter, does it? What matters is that science has been totally defeated in being able to change straight people into gays, and vice versa.

Omni: Could we create new human genders from the procreation of groups with the same sexual anomalies?

Money: Such as girls with precocious onsets of puberty? Would we create a class of three-year-old whores? Why not capitalize on what could be a new development in the human species and put all the early-developing children together to breed so that you have a new subspecies? Why not make it into a total irony by having a kennel-club show every year and see who gets the prize in each category of human subspecies? It's provocative to suggest that instead of viewing these conditions as pathological diseases to be attacked, you could twist it around and say maybe this is a new design in nature that we should help her with, exploit. And then, it's fascinating to pursue all the implications of abolishing childhood.

Omni: Do paraphiles have more intense erotic or love experiences?

Money: Something I find scientifically provoking beyond my capability to deal with since I haven't big money for PET [positron emission tomography] scanning and such, is what happens to so many of these paraphiles when they go into a trancelike state and carry out their rituals. There must be neurochemical changes. But it's not terribly different from how far out we go when we're in a hopeless love affair. And we can get pretty carried away with a really good sexual experience. So paraphiles probably are not terribly different from ordinary people. They have no self-governance over their behavior once it takes over because it's the only intensity they know.

Omni: Why do suppressed paraphilias sometimes explode during a midlife crisis?

Money: Usually they haven't been suppressed in mental imagery, fantasy, or erotic dreams. Most paraphilias appear to be developmentally induced, except where tumors screw up the sexual pathways in the brain. Paraphilias are induced mostly by biochemical malfunctions, not by three-dimensional lesions in the brain. The paraphilia is somehow a response to stress at a critical period of childhood when sexual-rehearsal play was handicapped, or even induced prematurely under wrong conditions. Years later, when there's gigantic stress in a person's life, this accommodation to the earlier stress reaffirms itself as an answer to the present stress.

Many years ago, I saw a sixty-something-year-old transsexual-candidate applicant. He had spent years of his adult life married to a woman physician, and they had raised two children to college age. He had invested very successfully on the stock market, so he could stay at home on a small farm that he ran, as well as invest. He established that life because he dressed as a lady every day, just about.

In his early sixties he developed abdominal cancer, had surgery, and was apparently okay for several years—no recurrence or metastases. But his response to the life-threatening tragedy of cancer was a complete blowup of his cross-dressing into an obsession with becoming a transsexual. Always able to keep that at bay by dressing up as a lady, he now had to go all the way to surgery. The first clinic turned him down, saying it was merely a depressive reaction to his close brush with death. And like all good transsexuals, he got his dander up and told them he was going to teach them a lesson or two.

He finally got through the barricades down here. I told him, "If you think this is going to be the salvation of your life, then you've got to get your affairs in order for a major change. You can't go into this lightly; you've got to pass the two-year real-life test [the act of living and passing in the role of the opposite sex]. You've got to get your wife in here to talk to me."

Omni: Was she against it?

Money: Not exactly. Not for it, either. It was spooky. I have never really gotten to the bottom of this strange collusional business between a paraphile and the partner. Do they smell each other out at the time of courtship? Does one grow into the paraphilia of the other—or a bit of both? Well, I have to call it a spooky collusional relationship. They know what they're doing. They're not ignorant, but both are powerless to not do it.

Anyway, considering the pragmatics of marriage, it worked out marvelously for this physician to have someone doing the housekeeping, bookwork, and accounting. And I admire him for the deftness of his shenanigans: He finally got the evaluations he needed and managed to get the surgery done on Canadian national insurance. That's just one of many stories illustrating the point that he would've spent his whole life as just a cross-dresser, except for the stress of cancer that precipitated the complete transsexualism. I could see it as plain as day: He wasn't changing into a sixty-five-year-old lady; he changed to be a little girl. Talk about Alice in Wonderland or Scarlett O'Hara! This was the formula for rescue....

Omni: Maybe future societies will allow love and lovesickness as an excuse for missing an exam or not coming to work for a week.

Money: It's an important speculation because the amount of time spent at work is obviously going to be diminished as everything becomes microchips. What else is there left in life, really, when you get down to absolute fundamentals, except food, shelter, clothing, and love and lust?

POSTSCRIPT

Is the Model of Normal and Vandalized Gendermaps/Lovemaps Biased?

What criteria should psychologists and society use in deciding how to treat people we choose to describe as having "transposed" or "cross-coded" gender identities (transsexuals) or cross-coded gender roles (transvestites). How should people who engage in sadomasochistic sexual behavior or some other paraphilic behavior that injures no one and the partners enjoy be treated? Money describes these people as having a "vandalized lovemap."

Money and most other gender specialists talk about some people having a gendermap or lovemap with a gender identity, gender role, or gender orientation that somewhere in the developmental process became "cross-coded" or "transposed" from the male path to the female path (or vice versa), or from a heterosexual to a homosexual or bisexual orientation, or from "normophilic" to "paraphilic."

Califia objects to Money's terminology as judgmental, discriminatory, biased, unjustified, and moralistic. She asks us to consider "the possibility that the categories of 'male' and 'female' are unrealistic and smothering us all." She argues that "differently pleasured" people are just as normal and functional as "conventionally pleasured" people.

In a similar vein, members of the Intersex Society of North America recently began describing themselves as "gender fluid." In their newsletter *Hermaphrodites With Attitude,* they argue that infants born with ambiguous genitals or an intersex condition should not be forced by doctors or their parents into undergoing sex-change surgery or other forms of treatment. Instead, society should accept their conditions and allow them to make their own decisions about possible treatment when they are adults.

Suggested Readings

P. Califia, *Sex Changes: The Politics of Transgenderism* (Cleis Press, 1997).

A. Fausto-Sterling, "The Five Sexes: Why Male and Female Are Not Enough," *The Sciences* (March/April 1993).

A. Fausto-Sterling, "How Many Sexes Are There?" *The New York Times* (March 12, 1993).

J. Money, *Gendermaps: Social Constructionism, Feminism, and Sexosophical History* (Continuum Publishing, 1995).

J. Money, *The Lovemap Guidebook* (Continuum Publishing, 1999).

On the Internet ...

Marriage Equality

This Marriage Equality Web site is dedicated to securing the right of same-sex couples to enter into legally recognized civil marriage.

http://www.marriageequality.com

Bay Area Sex Worker Advocacy Network (BAYSWAN)

The Bay Area Sex Worker Advocacy Network (BAYSWAN) provides information for sex workers and information about sex industries on its Web site. On this site is a Prostitute's Education Network that includes links to other Web sites concerning sex workers' rights.

http://www.bayswan.org

Promise

The Promise Web site offers services and support to women who have chosen to get out of prostitution.

http://www.sirius.com/~promise

Sex Criminals

The Sex Criminals Web site includes information on sex crimes and links to state registries of sex offenders.

http://www.sexcriminals.com

PART 3

Legal Issues

*T*he democratic ideal holds that government should make only those laws that are absolutely necessary to preserve the common good. Unless government can demonstrate a "compelling need," it should not infringe on the privacy and personal rights of individual citizens. This principle raises some perplexing questions when applied to the rights of individuals to engage in sexually intimate relationships. This section examines three such questions involving interpersonal relationships and also examines legal questions related to the punishment of sex offenders and the liability of schools in cases of sexual harassment.

- Should Same-Sex Marriage Be Legal?

- Is "Covenant Marriage" a Good Idea?

- Should Prostitution Be Legal?

- Is Chemical Castration an Acceptable Punishment for Sex Offenders?

- Should Schools Pay Damages for Student-on-Student Sexual Harassment?

ISSUE 15

Should Same-Sex Marriage Be Legal?

YES: Jonathan Rauch, from "Leave Gay Marriage to the States," *The Wall Street Journal* (July 27, 2001)

NO: Robert H. Bork, from "Stop Courts From Imposing Gay Marriage," *OpinionJournal*, http://www.opinionjournal.com/editorial/feature.html?id=95000931 (August 7, 2001)

ISSUE SUMMARY

YES: Jonathan Rauch, senior writer for the *National Journal,* argues that the proposed constitutional amendment to define marriage sidesteps the democratic process and violates conservatives' own principles regarding states' rights. Rauch maintains that the legalization of same-sex marriage would benefit all of society.

NO: Robert H. Bork, former federal appeals court judge, contends that the proposed constitutional amendment to define marriage is necessary to stop gay activists from redefining marriage. Bork asserts that gay activists have misused liberal lower courts to gradually redefine the traditional, heterosexual institution of marriage.

In December 1999 the state supreme court of Vermont ruled in favor of several gay couples who sued for the right to marry in the state. The court ruled that the state must provide an institution that gives same-sex couples the same benefits and protections as married heterosexual couples. The court left it up to the state to decide if this institution were to be marriage or some other formal, state-recognized partnership.

In April 2000 Vermont's "civil unions" bill was signed into law by Governor Howard Dean. The new law permitted gay males and lesbians to enter into "civil unions," which were legally equivalent to heterosexual marriage. When the law took effect July 1, 2000, dozens of gay and lesbian Vermont citizens applied for a civil union license. Citizens from other states traveled to Vermont to obtain civil union licenses. Although these unions are recognized in Vermont, they are not necessarily recognized in the applicants' home state. The Defense of Marriage Act, signed into law by President Bill Clinton in 1996, holds that states do not have to recognize same-sex marriages that are performed in another state. In addition, 35 states have adopted laws that would define marriage as the "union of a man and a woman," thereby prohibiting same-sex marriage. However, the prohibitions of these states remain subject to challenge by same-sex couples that file suit with state courts for the right to marry. To stem off any possibility of same-sex marriage being recognized by individual state courts (or, ultimately, by the U.S. Supreme Court), opponents of same-sex marriage proposed a constitutional amendment to define marriage as heterosexual only. An advocacy group known as the Alliance for Marriage proposed the Federal Marriage Amendment, which states:

> "Marriage in the United States shall consist only of the union of a man and a woman. Neither this constitution or the constitution of any state, nor state or federal law, shall be construed to require that marital status or the legal incidents thereof be conferred upon unmarried couples or groups."

The significance of amending the U.S. Constitution is that it would effectively remove the courts as recourse for same-sex couples who wish to marry. Further, state and federal legislators would be prohibited from establishing laws permitting same-sex marriage, since such laws would now be considered "unconstitutional."

In the following selections, Jonathan Rauch asserts that the proposed constitutional amendment to define marriage is a violation of states' rights. Robert H. Bork maintains that the amendment is necessary to stop misuse of lower courts by gay activists who do not represent the views of the majority.

Jonathan Rauch  **YES**

Leave Gay Marriage to the States

The other day I attended what seemed an unusually disingenuous press conference, even by Washington's standards. The event was the unveiling, by a coalition of church and community groups called the Alliance for Marriage, of a proposed 28th Amendment to the Constitution. The "Federal Marriage Amendment" was soon to be introduced in Congress, the Alliance announced. National Review, a conservative bellwether, had already endorsed it.

What, exactly, would the amendment do? Speaker after speaker affirmed that its only effect would be to stop unelected judges from ramming homosexual marriage down the throats of an unwilling public. The intent was merely to require proponents of homosexual marriage to "go through the democratic process" rather than the courts. This seemed odd, because in full view, on an easel next to the podium, was displayed the text of the amendment, whose operative sentence read: "Marriage in the United States shall consist only of the union of a man and a woman."

Strips Power

You didn't have to be James Madison to see that the proposed amendment strips power not from judges but from states. For centuries, since colonial times, family law, including the power to set the terms and conditions of marriage, has been reserved to the states, presumably because this most domestic and intimate sphere is best overseen by institutions that are close to home. The marriage amendment would withdraw from states the power to permit same-sex marriage even if 100% of the voters and legislators of some state wanted to allow it.

One reason to revoke such a core state power might be to prevent a single state from effectively adopting same-sex marriage for the whole country. In 1996, however, Congress and President Clinton foreclosed that possibility by enacting the Defense of Marriage Act, which holds that no state need recognize a same-sex marriage performed or sanctioned in any other state. Meanwhile, three dozen states have legislatively passed pre-emptive bans on same-sex marriage. The country is thus almost 75% of the way to a national ban.

Under those circumstances, there can be only one reason for a constitutional amendment putting gay marriage out of the reach of not just state judges but of states. The sponsors must be worried that eventually some state's legislators or voters, acting in the old-fashioned democratic way, will decide that same-sex marriage suits their state's temperament or helps solve their state's problems.

That conservatives would contemplate so striking a repudiation of federalism is a sign of the panic that same-sex marriage inspires on the right. As people usually do when they act in a panic, conservatives are making a mistake. Even if you don't believe, as I do, that same-sex marriage is good because it is just and humane, the attempt to pre-empt federalism is bad policy from a conservative point of view.

For there is a compelling and deeply conservative case for thinking that homosexual marriage, far from being the end of civilization as we know it, would be a win-win-win proposition: good for homosexuals, good for heterosexuals, and good for marriage itself. The reason is one that conservatives have long understood: Love and marriage go together. Marriage transmutes love into commitment. Love is often fleeting and crazy-making. Marriage is lasting and stabilizing. For all the troubles that divorce, fatherlessness and illegitimacy have brought, marriage remains far and away the most durable bond that two caring people can forge.

Though some homosexuals have children, even childless homosexuals—in fact, especially childless homosexuals—need and benefit from the care of, and promise to care for, another, till death do you part. Society stands to benefit when all people, including gay people, have this care and make this commitment.

Before rushing to ban same-sex marriage, conservatives ought to remember that the real-world alternative is not the status quo or the status quo minus 30 years. Same-sex unions, however viewed by law, are real and increasingly honored by the growing number of Americans who have gay friends and family members. I take my partner, Michael, to the company Christmas party every year, and my colleagues treat him as my spouse. Because governments, businesses, religions and ordinary people are increasingly supportive of these unions, the likely result of a national ban on same-sex marriage would be the profusion of partnership programs and other versions of "marriage lite"—many of which, majoritarian politics being what it is, will inevitably be opened to heterosexual as well as homosexuals.

Some left-wing gay activists favor the establishment of diverse alternatives to marriage as a way to weaken the real thing, which they regard as rigid and oppressive. It is odd for conservatives to try to help them. Marriage, like voting and property ownership and other encompassing civic institutions, is strongest when it is universal and unique, without carve-outs or special cases. It works best when society and law send a clear message that marriage is for everyone—gay and straight alike—and that the only way to secure the benefits and recognition of marriage is to get married.

The retort, of course, is that unyoking marriage from its traditional male-female definition will destroy or severely weaken it. But this is an empirical proposition, and there is reason to doubt it. Opponents of same-sex marriage have done a poor job of explaining why the health of heterosexual marriage depends on the exclusion of a small number of homosexuals. Moreover, predictions that homosexual integration would wreck civic communities and public institutions have a perfect record: They are always wrong. When same-sex couples started holding hands on the street and buying houses in the suburbs, neighborhoods did not turn into Sodoms and otherwise solid families did not collapse. The British military, after protesting for years that morale would be ruined by open homosexuals, has instead found their admission to be a nonevent. Integration of open homosexuals into workplaces has not replaced pinstripe suits with stud collars or ruined the collegial spirit in offices across the country.

Like it or not, homosexuality exists and is not going away. The question is how to ensure that it is pro-social rather than antisocial. I believe that marriage, the greatest civilizing institution ever devised, is the answer. I could be wrong; but the broader point, in any case, is that same-sex marriage bears potential benefits as well as risks. The way to find out is to try, which is what federalism is for.

Separate Ways

Thanks to America's federalist structure and the existence of the Defense of Marriage Act, the United States is uniquely positioned among all the world's countries to get same-sex marriage right, by neither banning it preemptively nor imposing it nationally. Instead, same-sex marriage could be tried in a few places where people feel comfortable with it and believe it would work. Letting states go their separate ways, moreover, is the way to avert culture wars, as the misguided nationalization of abortion law so unpleasantly and frequently reminds us.

Same-sex marriage should not be a federal issue. Conservatives, of all people, should not be attempting to make it one. They have been trumpeting the virtues of federalism for years. Here is a particularly compelling opportunity to heed their own wisdom.

NO

Robert H. Bork

Stop Courts From Imposing Gay Marriage

Of all the contested terrain in the culture war, the subject of homosexual rights is the most awkward to discuss. Almost all of us know homosexuals who are decent, intelligent and compassionate people, and we have no inclination to wound them.

Yet "gay rights" have come to the fore and we must have a discussion, free of ad hominem accusations, about whether homosexual acts and relationships are to be regarded as on a par with the marital relationships of a man and a woman. The immediate problem is the homosexual activists' drive for same-sex marriage.

❦

The activists want it as an expression of moral approbation of homosexual conduct. Many Americans have no desire to impose criminal sanctions on homosexual sodomy. Nevertheless, it is clear that most Americans do not want to create special rights for homosexuals or to consider their behavior morally neutral.

For that reason, the activists have concentrated their efforts on courts, knowing that judges have pushed, and continue to push, the culture to the left. One of the last obstacles to the complete normalization of homosexuality in our society is the understanding that marriage is the union of a man and a woman.

The activists breached that line when the supreme courts of Hawaii and Vermont, purporting to interpret their state constitutions, held that those states must recognize same-sex marriage. The Hawaiian electorate quickly amended their constitution to override that decision. The Vermont Constitution was extremely difficult to amend, and so the Legislature capitulated and enacted a civil-unions law, marriage in all but name, as the less repugnant of the alternatives the court allowed. More state courts are sure to follow.

Many court watchers believe that within five to 10 years the U.S. Supreme Court will hold that there is a constitutional right to homosexual marriage, just as that court invented a right to abortion. The chosen instrument will be the Equal Protection Clause of the 14th Amendment. After all, if state law forbids Fred to marry Henry, aren't they denied equal protection when the law permits

Tom and Jane to marry? The argument is simplistic, but then the argument for the result in *Roe v. Wade* was nonexistent.

To head off the seemingly inexorable march of the courts toward the radical redefinition of marriage, the Alliance for Marriage has put forward the proposed Federal Marriage Amendment: "Marriage in the United States shall consist only of the union of a man and a woman. Neither this Constitution or the constitution of any state, nor state or federal law, shall be construed to require that marital status or the legal incidents thereof be conferred upon unmarried couples or groups."

The first sentence means that no legislature may confer the name of marriage on same-sex unions and no court may recognize a same-sex marriage contracted in another country. We would hope that if people understand the principle behind the amendment, they would not try to contrive counterfeit forms of marriage. We would oppose such attempts, but are prepared to debate the matter in the political forum. So far as legislatures are concerned, the primary thrust of the sentence's prohibition is symbolic, reserving the name of marriage to its traditional meaning. But symbolism is crucial in cultural struggles.

The second sentence expresses the main thrust of the amendment. It recognizes that liberal activist courts are the real problem. If courts are prevented from ordering same-sex marriage or its equivalent, the question of arrangements less than marriage is left where it should be, to the determination of the people through the democratic process.

To try to prevent legislatures from enacting permission for civil unions by constitutional amendment would be to reach too far. It would give opponents the opening to say we do not trust the people when, in fact, we are trying to prevent courts from thwarting the will of the people. The history of the effort to obtain a constitutional amendment relating to abortion is instructive. There was a chance to get an amendment overturning *Roe v. Wade* and returning the issue to the state legislatures. Purists opposed to abortion would not settle for that. They demanded an amendment prohibiting abortion altogether. The result was that they got nothing. An amendment against judicial validation of same-sex marriages would similarly be doomed by pressing for too much.

﹡◐﹡

Some proponents of gay marriage, such as Jonathan Rauch, have tried to split cultural conservatives by invoking federalism. Family law, he argues, has always been governed [by] the states. Though that is not entirely true, it is entirely irrelevant. A constitutional ruling by the Supreme Court in favor of same-sex marriage would itself override federalism.

Activists are already trying to nationalize same-sex unions: Same-sex couples will travel to any state that allows them to marry or have civil unions, relying on the constitutional requirement that states give full faith and credit to the judgments of other states to validate their status in their home states. They will attack the constitutionality of the federal Defense of Marriage Act, which seeks to block this. One way or another, federalism is going to be over-ridden. The only question is whether the general rule will permit or prohibit the marriage of same-sex couples.

Traditional marriage and family have been the foundations of every healthy society known in recorded history. Only in the past few decades of superficial liberal rationalism has marriage come under severe attack. The drive for same-sex marriage ordered by courts is the last stage of the assault. The Federal Marriage Amendment is an attempt, and perhaps the only hope, to preserve marriage as an institution of incalculable value.

POSTSCRIPT

Should Same-Sex Marriage Be Legal?

While the United States considers a constitutional amendment that would prohibit same-sex marriage, several European countries have given legal status to same-sex couples, including Denmark, France, Germany, the Netherlands, Sweden, Iceland, and Norway. At press time, Belgium and Finland are considering same-sex marriage laws.

In the United States, attitudes remain divided. According to a Gallup poll conducted in 2000, 62 percent of Americans believed that same-sex marriages should not be recognized. A 2001 Gallup poll revealed, however, that only 52 percent of Americans opposed civil union laws, with 44 percent supportive and 4 percent expressing no opinion. The percentage of Americans who are supportive of civil union laws is noteworthy, since the vast majority of Americans are heterosexual.

Bork contends that heterosexual marriage and family has been the foundation of every healthy society throughout recorded history. If more lesbian and gay couples raise children (bringing children into their family through adoption or fertility methods), would they contribute more to the health of society?

Rauch focuses on the legal rather than the ethical arguments for same-sex marriage. Should there be other considerations for or against same-sex marriage? How do you view the argument to amend the U.S. Constitution? What potential benefits or difficulties do you foresee resulting from this action? Finally, what do you believe is the *purpose* of marriage? Is marriage primarily about love? rights? children and family? monogamy? other characteristics? Do you regard it as primarily a religious institution or a legal institution? Is there any *single, predominant* purpose of marriage, or are there many purposes worthy of consideration?

Suggested Readings

K. A. Appiah, "The Marrying Kind," *The New York Review* (June 20, 1996).

R. M. Baird and S. E. Rosenbaum, eds., *Same-Sex Marriage: The Moral and Legal Debate* (Prometheus Books, 1997).

E. J. Graff, *What Is Marriage For?* (Beacon, 2000).

S. N. Kurtz, "What Is Wrong With Gay Marriage?" *Commentary* (September 5, 2001).

G. Rotello, "To Have and to Hold: The Case for Gay Marriage," *The Nation* (June 24, 1996).

M. Strasser, *Legally Wed: Same-Sex Marriage and the Constitution* (Cornell University Press, 1997).

A. Sullivan, ed., *Same-Sex Marriage, Pro and Con: A Reader* (Random House, 1997).

A. Sullivan, "Unveiled: The Case Against Same-Sex Marriage Crumbles," http://www.andrewsullivan.com.

J. Q. Wilson, "Against Homosexual Marriage," *Commentary* (March 1996).

ISSUE 16

Is "Covenant Marriage" a Good Idea?

YES: Katherine Shaw Spaht, from "Stop Sacrificing America's Children on the Cold Altar of Convenience for Divorcing Spouses," *Insight on the News* (October 6–13, 1997)

NO: Ashton Applewhite, from "It Won't Lower the Divorce Rate and Will Raise the Human and Economic Cost of Divorce," *Insight on the News* (October 6–13, 1997)

ISSUE SUMMARY

YES: Professor of law Katherine Shaw Spaht states that the main benefit of allowing couples to commit to stricter covenant marriages will be to reduce the devastating, long-term damage that divorce inflicts on America's children. She maintains that there are other "compelling values" that counterbalance "the siren song of self-improvement."

NO: Author Ashton Applewhite counters that repealing or rewriting U.S. no-fault divorce laws and championing a stricter covenant marriage will not reduce the divorce rate because divorce is the "result of sweeping social changes that cannot be wished away with a piece of sanctimonious and punitive legislation." She concludes that covenant marriages are sexist, will hurt children, and will raise the economic and emotional cost of divorce.

Between 1970 and 1990 the divorce rate jumped by 34 percent in the United States. Twenty million Americans, close to one in ten, are divorced. Practically every state has adopted a no-fault divorce policy. With half of all marriages now ending in divorce, compared with about one-third in 1970, about 1.2 million American couples get divorced each year. Despite the popular inclination to blame no-fault divorce laws for this increase, experts are not sure how much of this is due to the ease with which divorces can be obtained. Other factors may have an equal or greater impact on the divorce rate.

In past centuries, a couple's personal expectations of married bliss were much more limited than they are for Americans today. In earlier times a woman could expect to spend most of her adult life rearing children and providing domestic support for her husband, who worked from sunup to sundown six or seven days a week. It was not until 1945 that 50 percent of the American workforce began to enjoy a 40-hour, 5-day workweek. Also, with an average life expectancy somewhere between 35 and 47 years and with one in five mothers dying in childbirth, death often brought a marriage to an early end. With an average life expectancy now pushing age 80; couples having only one, two, or no children, and aging baby-boomers establishing the "graying of America"; divorce ends marriage more often than death does.

The current issue focuses on a law enacted by the state of Louisiana in the summer of 1997. Following several failed attempts to revoke no-fault divorce legislation in several states, including Michigan and Iowa, Louisiana lawmakers adopted a new tactic in an attempt "to slow down the hemorrhaging of the American family through the no-fault divorce system." The new law recognizes two kinds of marriage and requires a couple to choose between a traditional marriage, which can be dissolved by a no-fault divorce, and a new kind of marriage, called a "covenant marriage," with stricter limits on both separations and divorce.

Before entering a covenant marriage, a couple must participate in a pre-marital counseling program and discuss the requirements of a covenant marriage with a clergy person or other counselor. If a covenant marriage goes sour, the couple can be granted a separation only if there is proof that one spouse has committed adultery, has abandoned the matrimonial home for at least a year, has been sentenced to prison or death for a felony, or has physically or sexually abused the spouse or a child. A separation can also be granted if there is proof of "cruel treatment" or "habitual intemperance" by one spouse. A divorce can only be granted if the couple has been legally separated for at least one year to eighteen months if the couple have a minor child—or if they have lived apart for two years. The grounds for a divorce in a covenant marriage are limited to proven adultery, imprisonment, abandonment for a year, or physical/sexual abuse.

A Louisiana couple who choose a traditional marriage can be granted a no-fault divorce after they have lived apart for 6 months or immediately if one spouse is guilty of adultery or has been sentenced to prison or death for a felony.

In the following selection, Katherine Shaw Spaht defends covenant marriages as a major step in reducing too-easy divorces. Ashton Applewhite counters that covenant marriages ignore the complexities of modern society and that they are just "the first step in a nationwide movement led by conservative Christians and 'pro-family' activists to rewrite or repeal no-fault divorce laws."

Katherine Shaw Spaht

 **YES**

Stop Sacrificing America's Children on the Cold Altar of Convenience for Divorcing Spouses

On June 6 [1997] I listened to Judith Wallerstein, a prominent psychologist from California, relate the results of her most recent interviews with children of divorce. Wallerstein has followed 130 children since the divorces of their parents in 1971. Twenty-five years later these children, who were between the ages of 2 and 6 at the time of the divorce, expressed to her in their own words their sentiments about the divorce in the following terms: "The day of the divorce my childhood ended."

They confided that at the time of the divorce they were terrified of being left by both parents. Their closest relatives could not be trusted and, as a consequence, life was dangerous. One child stated, "I would go days at a time without speaking one word." All of the children suffered from a lack of nurturing, and each has lost the ability to be dependent. All of the children would have been shocked to learn that any person considered "their best interests."

The entry of these children into adulthood was shaped by the divorces of their parents. At 18 most stopped receiving child support; they were expected to support themselves. One-third of the children ended their careers with graduation from high school. Only six received full support from their parents or stepparents; the other children who pursued more education worked their way through school and, as a consequence, could not pursue demanding careers. All of these children wound up in occupations below those of their parents.

These children of divorce expressed the view that the law was unjust; if their parents had not divorced, all of them would have received full support. They felt that they were bearing the brunt of their parents' divorces. Child-father relationships were far less stable than in an intact family. Most of the fathers remarried, and their second wives resented the children of the first marriage. Many of the fathers sent their stepchildren through college, but not their own children from the previous marriage. In cases of court-ordered and unmodified child-custody arrangements, not a single child had a good relationship with the non-custodial parent. Wallerstein stated her conclusion in the following terms:

Adults get over the divorce, but their children's suffering doesn't reach a peak at divorce. The impact of the divorce increases over time—throughout the first three decades of life and in all developmental stages.

Wallerstein's results and her conclusion defy the conventional understanding of the 1960s and 1970s, particularly among members of the therapeutic profession, that children would benefit from divorce because they suffered greater harm living in a household where the parents no longer loved each other. The focus should be on the happiness of the spouses; after all, children are remarkably resilient. Peter Kramer, a clinical professor of psychiatry at Brown University, summarizes this view in the Aug. 29 [1997] issue of the *New York Times*: "For most of the past 50 years, enhanced autonomy has been a goal of psychotherapy." The self-help movement, he concludes, resulted in the view that "[o]nce both partners are allowed to be autonomous, the continuation of marriage becomes more truly voluntary. In this sense, an increase in divorce signals social progress. So it seems to me the question is whether any other compelling value counterbalances the siren song of self-improvement."

Therapeutic professions have been disastrously wrong about divorce, and they continue to be wrong. Not only have we failed the children by concentrating on the happiness of the two adults—or, in many cases, of only one—but we also have failed the larger community. Unlike Kramer, I believe there are other "compelling values" that counterbalance "the siren song of self-improvement," which is a perfect choice of words to describe the worship of self. The larger community is paying the price for the phenomenon of "broken homes" because the therapeutic community has discounted the compelling value of such neglected virtues as self-sacrifice, altruism, keeping one's promises, bearing responsibility and performing one's duty.

Unlike Kramer, we in Louisiana believe that the two-parent home in which husband and wife are committed to each other is the ideal institution for rearing children. We therefore have considered how we can encourage that commitment, which often runs counter to an individual's selfish impulses.

Louisiana has launched a noble experiment to help determine the answer to both questions. The subjects of the experiment are fully informed volunteers who choose to contract into a "covenant marriage." Covenant marriage is more difficult to enter into than a standard marriage and it involves more-onerous obligations once it has been celebrated—hence the name covenant marriage. The choice provokes a conversation between bride and groom about each one's expectations of marriage.

If the expectations of bride and groom are reflected in their choosing to contract into a covenant marriage, then they undergo premarital counseling by a trained clergyman or secular marriage counselor of their choice. For couples receiving premarital counseling in the form contemplated by the covenant-marriage law the opportunity exists for a deeper discussion of the truly serious nature of marriage, the inevitable difficulties that will arise during the marriage, the need to resolve them amicably if at all possible and the community's expectations for the couple's union.

The opportunity for seriously examining the meaning of marriage will help to prevent hasty and ill-advised marriages and it will impress upon couples that do marry the gravity of the marriage contract. It will provide them with a firmer foundation upon which to build a lifelong relationship and stable family.

Equally as important as premarital counseling, the couple bound by a covenant marriage commit to marital counseling and other "reasonable steps" to preserve their union "if difficulties arise during the marriage." Difficulties are inevitable, but by agreeing in advance to seek steps to preserve the marriage the couple commit to the virtuous task of preserving their union if at all possible. The bride and groom who contract into a covenant marriage are sacrificing selfish interests in advance for a higher purpose, a purpose which society should encourage—sacrifice for those whom you love. Such self-sacrifice is imperative in the necessarily unselfish task of rearing children. The commitment to take "reasonable steps" to preserve the marriage, including marital counseling, can only help strengthen marriages.

If the efforts at preserving the union in a covenant marriage are unsuccessful, terminating the marriage by no-fault divorce requires a significantly longer waiting period of two years, rather than the current 180 days required for a "standard" marriage. Within that two-year period, moreover, the covenanting spouse who has kept his or her marriage promises may seek a legal separation or a divorce against the spouse who has not kept the promises. Conduct considered a breach of promise in a covenant marriage consists of adultery, being convicted of a felony, abandoning the other spouse for one year and physical or sexual abuse of a spouse or child. Such conduct constitutes such a serious breach of the promises undertaken in the marriage covenant that the offended spouse is permitted to seek an end to the marriage. Interestingly, domestic violence now is a ground for divorce for the first time under Louisiana law and then only in a covenant marriage, which is a strong statement about the community's collective view about such behavior.

By permitting only the offended spouse who kept the marriage promises to seek an immediate end to a covenant marriage, the community makes a powerful statement through law about the conduct of the breaching spouse. It is similar to an ordinary business contract, where the law permits only the party who kept the contract's promises to sue the other party for breach of contract. In the context of an ordinary contract the court assesses blame by identifying the party that breached the contract and either orders the breaching party to perform or awards the injured party damages. By granting an exclusive right to initiate divorce to the innocent spouse in a covenant marriage, the offended spouse enjoys some power to determine when the marriage ends and, potentially, the terms of the divorce—a power that often is described as "bargaining in the shadow of the law."

Restoration of power to the innocent spouse provides important protection for women and their children, particularly where the wife has chosen to forego or to interrupt her career for the purpose of bearing and rearing children. A woman undoubtedly risks more by assuming that her marriage is a lifelong relationship. If we accept that she should have a choice either to pursue a career or to sacrifice it for the good of the family, then a covenant marriage provides a wife a mechanism for gaining greater security than provided by a standard marriage. In some cases it will permit a woman the choice of rearing her own children, a choice that the community should foster.

In the final analysis, Louisiana's covenant marriage experiment is about nourishing our children by strengthening marriage as an institution.

If, as Professor Kramer wrote in the *New York Times*, "an increase in divorce signals social progress," how do we explain to the children of divorce that "social progress" is defined without considering their welfare? Are we willing to look each one of those children in the eye and respond to them as Kramer would that their parents' willingness to stay together would have been " ... out of touch with [Americans'] traditional values: self-expression, self-fulfillment, self-reliance"? Should we shrug our shoulders and say, as he suggests, "that the divorce rate reflects our national values with great exactness, and that conventional modern marriage—an eternal commitment with loopholes galore—expresses precisely the degree of loss of autonomy that we are able to tolerate" regardless of its effect on children?

In at least one state, Americans are insisting that there indeed are "compelling values" that counterbalance "the siren song of self-improvement"—that there indeed are shared "national values," which strengthen rather than destroy our families. My hunch is that many more states will follow Louisiana's lead in pursuing innovative solutions to a very real problem.

Ashton Applewhite

NO

It Won't Lower the Divorce Rate and Will Raise the Human and Economic Cost of Divorce

Covenant marriage," now legally available in Louisiana and pending before numerous other state Legislatures, is the first step in a nationwide movement led by conservative Christians and "pro-family" activists to rewrite or repeal no-fault divorce laws. Under covenant marriage, divorce would be permitted only on narrow grounds such as adultery, abuse, abandonment, felony imprisonment or a mutually agreed-upon two-year separation. It seeks to "fortify" marriage by making divorce harder and thus less common. It won't work.

The prevalence of divorce in America is a result of sweeping social changes that cannot be wished away with a piece of sanctimonious and punitive legislation. Anticipating litigation, the covenant-marriage contract is really a postnuptial agreement, guaranteeing that those who make mistakes will suffer exceedingly in their undoing, hardly a Christian attitude. If anything, it should be harder to get married, not to end a union gone wrong.

There lies the sole benefit of this legislation: By forcing engaged couples to think a little harder about what they're getting into, covenant marriage should prevent a number of disastrous unions from occurring in the first place. Many more couples, however, pressured into feeling that "marriage lite" is a cop-out, will ignore their misgivings and live to regret it.

Covenant marriage won't affect the divorce rate. Covenant marriage will not succeed in its primary objective because there never has been any correlation between the incidence of divorce and the laws on the books. The surge of divorces in the 1960s well preceded no-fault legislation, for example, and the American divorce rate has in fact declined slightly in recent years. As sociologist Andrew Cherlin of Johns Hopkins University in Baltimore, a noted scholar in the field, puts it, "The great misconception is that divorce laws change people's behavior. People's behavior changes divorce laws." That's why there is no indication that public attitudes support the current backlash.

Many conservatives maintain that if just one spouse can file for divorce, or if the legal hurdles are low, more couples will separate. It's a logical argument, but not an accurate one, because restrictive laws simply are not an effective deterrent. Just as capital punishment does not lower the crime rate and restricting access to abortion only results in more back-alley operations, people who want out of their marriages will find a way—legally if they have the resources, illegally if not. The incidence of desertion and fraud, which *does* correlate with stricter divorce laws, would increase, as would marital homicides.

Covenant marriage will raise the human and economic cost of divorce. Because responsibility no longer had to be assigned, no-fault divorce eliminated the need for one spouse to sue the other. This made the whole process more humane, simpler and much less expensive—and is precisely what covenant marriage legislation would undo. Assets would be spent on lawyers instead of building new lives or providing for children, a real irony given the pro-fault movement's "pro-family" stance. Energy would go into excruciating struggles about offspring and property, instead of into figuring out how to maintain decent relations with the person around whom life once centered, and to moving on.

Described in a *New York Times* article, aptly subtitled "Blame is Back," as "an emerging campaign to restore notions of guilt to divorce law," the repeal of no-fault would result in a tragic increase in the kind of hostilities that can turn divorce proceedings into scorched-earth campaigns. As anyone who has been through a "fault" divorce knows, coming up with grounds is the most demoralizing and wounding part of the process. Ruling out mediation or civil compromise, this bitter exercise mires the couple in accusations and repudiations, making it all the harder to heal and move forward. Blame only damages, but the notion of retribution has endless appeal for the self-righteous. Perhaps the blame lobby would find no-fault divorce more palatable if it were renamed "bi-fault."

Covenant marriage will hurt children. Both sides in this debate can cite countless expert opinions as to the effect of divorce on children, whether devastating or benign. Clearly, divorce does not guarantee maladjustment any more than growing up in an intact home guarantees mental health. The real issue is how children of divorce who live in one, or two, calm and happy homes fare compared to those who grow up in intact homes filled with turmoil or icy silence.

One thing all the experts agree on, though, is that witnessing or being party to parental conflict is what harms children. By making their parents' divorce more difficult and more hostile, covenant marriage ensures the prolonged exposure of children to the most damaging possible circumstances: parents who fight. Too often their deliverance is left in the hands of strangers and overburdened courts. Fractured into warring camps, families often never fully recover. Significantly, even psychologist Judith Wallerstein, author of one of the most-cited studies about the negative effects of divorce on children, opposes legal efforts to make divorce harder.

Covenant marriage raises hurdles that already are high enough. The current outcry that divorce has gotten "too easy" is a periodic complaint, recalling Horace

Greeley's displeasure in the late 19th century that too many people were getting "unmarried at pleasure." This charge is cheap to make but impossible to substantiate. Everyone believes divorce is a bad thing, yet everyone knows individuals who divorced for good reasons. By the same token, many think divorce is "too easy," but would be hard put to name a single person for whom the process was anything but painful and arduous—as it should be. Fault or no-fault, divorce is not lightly undertaken.

Neither is matrimony, the Donald Trumps of the world notwithstanding. To act as though the Louisiana Legislature had just invented a way to make marriage binding and meaningful demeans the vows which have joined men and women for millennia.

Covenant marriage is sexist. One of the principal rationales behind covenant marriage is that it will provide wives with legal recourse against errant husbands the way the old laws did. They linked property to "fault," forcing the divorcing wage-earner to continue to support his family and giving "innocent" wives considerable leverage in negotiating settlements. The loss of this bargaining power concerns women's-rights advocates as well, joining them in an unlikely alliance with "pro-family" forces.

But the automatic assumption that wives are victims does women no favors and is unfair to the many "innocent" husbands whose wives leave them. The underlying notion of innocence vs. guilt should be jettisoned. It reinforces the age-old link between goodness (innocence) and passivity, a big step backward for authentic women's rights. It also completely disregards the fact that divorce is twice as likely to be initiated by the wife as the husband, and that advancements in women's social and political status correlate with access to affordable divorce. Divorce indeed would become less accessible to women under covenant marriage because it would cost so much more.

Covenant marriage ignores social reality. Profoundly reactionary, the covenant-marriage movement invokes a return to a way of life that was rooted in postwar prosperity, only available to a privileged minority and never all that golden. Of course it would be wonderful if everyone lived happily ever after and all children were raised by loving parents who made it home by 3 o'clock. But, like it or not, most parents must work outside the home. Like it or not, the American family is changing shape: 60 percent of families are headed by a single parent, more than half of whom have never been married. Like it or not, marriage is becoming less relevant: about 3.5 million unmarried opposite-sex couples now share living quarters, up from 2 million a decade ago; men and women now marry later, separate from one another more frequently and, once separated, are less likely to remarry.

Because of these and other wide-ranging cultural forces, divorce is here to stay. As sociologist Arlie Hochschild puts it, "Women have gone into the labor force, but... we have not rewired the notion of manhood so that it makes sense to participate at home. Marriage then becomes the shock absorber of those strains." To cope, husbands and wives need help figuring out fairer ways to distribute responsibility and authority. Meanwhile, the question is not whether these changes are good or bad, but how Americans can adapt wisely and compassionately to a domestic landscape in profound transition.

Idealizing the traditional nuclear family excludes not just the divorced, but also widows and widowers, adopted and foster children and all those who love and are loved outside of a legal contract. It sanctions job discrimination against working parents who need all the help they can get. It ignores the fact that divorce often brings terrible problems to light (problems that continue to seethe privately and damagingly in many intact families) and that divorce very often is the right decision for both the adults and the children involved. It denies the reality that many divorced parents continue to cooperate successfully in raising healthy children. And it perpetuates the myth that divorced people do not honor or value marriage. It is time for our religious and political leaders to stop looking back at outmoded models and reach ahead to innovative solutions.

Covenant marriage is morally problematic. Who really believes that physical abuse or abandonment must take place to render a marriage intolerable? Certainly no victim of mental cruelty, verbal abuse, confinement, financial or sexual withholding, threats against children or dozens of other reprehensible behaviors against which covenant marriage will offer no recourse.

Even more troubling is the quality of married life implicitly sanctioned by this legislation. The threat of an ugly, protracted legal battle indeed will immobilize a number of deeply unhappy spouses. But the thought that someone would want to stay married against his or her partner's desires runs contrary to any humane notion of how people who once cared deeply about each other—and may still—should treat each other. What kind of marriage can it be when one spouse is present against his or her will? What kind of life can be lived in rooms full of rage and despair? Wedlock indeed, but no place for children, nor for responsible adults.

POSTSCRIPT

Is "Covenant Marriage" a Good Idea?

Originally the church and the state became involved in regulating marriage out of self-interest in providing security for the children on whom the future stability of society would depend and also to clarify inheritance. Nowadays the interests of the child in the permanence of marriage seem to have taken second place to the self-expression, self-fulfillment, and self-reliance of the divorcing parents. In recent decades the divorce rate for couples with children has gone up much faster than the divorce rate for childless couples. Today most divorces involve children, and every year more than one million youngsters are involved in a divorce situation.

Debates rage about the short- and long-term effects of parental divorce on children. Most studies focus on the negative impact of divorce in many areas of children's lives as they struggle to cope. Other studies have found that some children who have to deal with parental divorce have shown enhanced maturity, self-esteem, empathy, and less rigid gender roles.

Similar debates rage over the alleged disadvantages experienced by children in single-parent families. Psychologist June Stephenson, for instance, has reported on her research showing that the case for two-parent families being "the best" is grossly overstated. Her studies show that a variety of family forms, including single-parent families, can produce children who are as well adjusted as or better adjusted than those reared in two-parent families.

Martha Kegel, staff attorney with the Louisiana chapter of the American Civil Liberties Union, raised another consideration you may want to consider as you weigh the argument of Spaht, supporting the option of a traditional or covenant marriage, and Applewhite's argument that covenant marriage will not work because American culture does not support the expectations and behavioral values needed to sustain life-long marriages. Kegel has called the covenant marriage bill a "Trojan horse," which would in some cases harm children by holding them hostage to bad marriages. "It has the laudable goal of keeping families together, but it makes divorce difficult or even impossible in many unfortunate situations where divorce would be in the best interests of the children." Kegel also criticized the bill "as an attempt to use the government to enforce one religious doctrine regarding divorce."

One of the more interesting and pragmatic aspects of this debate is raised by columnist James Carville when he mused about what would have happened if, after stalling for a year before asking Mary Matalin to be his wife, he had suggested going with Marriage Option B—the quickie kind. "Or worse yet: What if I asked Mary to be my wife and she only wanted Option B? Will this new law result in legions of young Louisiana lovers avoiding the so-called choice altogether by hopping in the Chevy and heading for Las Vegas?"

Suggested Readings

M. F. Brinig, "Economics, Law, and Covenant," *Gender Issues* (January 1, 1998).

J. Carville, "It'll Make You Think Twice," http://www.salon.com (June 1997).

R. T. Francoeur, "Covenants, Intimacy, and Marital Diversity," *Humanistic Judaism* (Winter 1994).

D. Gately and A. I. Schwebel, "Favorable Outcomes in Children After Parental Divorce," *Journal of Divorce and Remarriage* (vol. 18, no. 3, 1992).

D. Radosh, "Covenant Marriage: Tightening the Ties That Bind," *Playboy* (December 1997).

J. Stephenson, *The Two-Parent Family Is Not the Best* (Diemer, Smith Publishing, 1991).

B. D. Whitehead, "Dan Quayle Was Right," *Atlantic Monthly* (April 1993).

K. Zinsmeister, "Divorce's Toll on Children," *The American Enterprise* (May/June 1996).

ISSUE 17

Should Prostitution Be Legal?

YES: James Bovard, from "Safeguard Public Health: Legalize Contractual Sex," *Insight on the News* (February 27, 1995)

NO: Anastasia Volkonsky, from "Legalizing the 'Profession' Would Sanction the Abuse," *Insight on the News* (February 27, 1995)

ISSUE SUMMARY

YES: Author James Bovard asserts that legalizing sex work would help stem the spread of AIDS and free up the police to focus on controlling violent crime.

NO: Anastasia Volkonsky, founding director of PROMISE, an organization dedicated to combating sexual exploitation, maintains that decriminalizing prostitution would only cause more social harm, particularly to women.

$\mathbf{P}$rior to the Civil War, prostitution was tolerated in the United States to a limited extent, even though it was socially frowned upon. Few states had specific laws making prostitution a crime. After the Civil War, however, some states passed laws to segregate and license prostitutes operating in "red light districts." In 1910 Congress tried to eliminate the importation of young women from Asia and South America for purposes of prostitution by passing the Mann Act, which prohibited any male from accompanying a female across a state border for the purpose of prostitution, debauchery, or any other immoral purpose. During World War I concern for the morals and health of U.S. soldiers led the U.S. Surgeon General to close down all houses of prostitution near military training camps, especially the famous whorehouses of the French Quarter and Storyville, New Orleans. By 1925 every state had enacted an antiprostitution law.

The effectiveness and the social and economic costs of criminalizing prostitution have been continually questioned. The sexual revolution and the women's movement have added new controversies to the debate. Some advocates of women's rights and equality condemn prostitution as male exploitation of women and their bodies. Others champion the rights of women to control their own bodies, including the right to exchange sexual favors for money. This new attitude is reflected in the term *sex worker*, which has recently begun to replace *prostitute*. New social problems confuse the issue further: the growing concern over drug abuse, the risk of human immunodeficiency virus (HIV) infection among street prostitutes, and the exploitation of teenage girls and boys.

European countries have taken different approaches to prostitution. In Germany, where prostitution is legal and regulated, there are efficient and convenient drive-in motels—often owned and run by women—where customers can arrange a pleasant, safe encounter with a sex worker. Italy and France, longtime bastions of regulated prostitution, have abandoned this approach because of organized efforts of women to abolish it and evidence that other approaches to prostitution could reduce the spread of venereal disease more effectively than legalization and regulation. Since 1959 solicitation on the streets of Great Britain has been a crime, but prostitution per se is no longer against the law. The British authorities have concluded that prostitution cannot be controlled simply by making it a crime. However, they do have laws prohibiting sex workers from advertising their services by posting their business cards in public phone booths. In the Soviet Union in the 1920s, the government provided job training, employment, housing, and health care for former prostitutes. In the 1930s the government's attitude changed to intolerance when it became apparent that working women were turning to prostitution as a way of achieving a higher standard of living than they would otherwise be able to maintain. After the collapse of the Soviet Union, sex work in Russia and abroad became an acceptable career choice for many young women.

In the following selections, James Bovard advocates legalizing sex work to help stem the spread of AIDS and to allow police to focus their time and energy on violent crimes. Anastasia Volkonsky argues that decriminalizing sex work would hurt society in general and allow males to continue exploiting women, particularly those who are poor and vulnerable.

James Bovard

 **YES**

Safeguard Public Health: Legalize Contractual Sex

The call to legalize prostitution once again is becoming a hot issue. Columnists have been complaining about the conviction of Heidi Fleiss, the "Hollywood madam," saying it is unfair that the law punishes her but not her clients. San Francisco has appointed a task force to analyze the issue of legalizing prostitution. (A similar task force in Atlanta recommended legalization in 1986, but the city has not changed its policies.)

As more people fear the spread of AIDS, the legalization of prostitution offers one of the easiest means of limiting the spread of the disease and of improving the quality of law enforcement in this country.

Prostitution long has been illegal in all but one state. Unfortunately, laws against it often bring out the worst among the nation's law-enforcement agencies. Since neither prostitutes nor their customers routinely run to the police to complain about the other's conduct, police rely on trickery and deceit to arrest people.

In 1983, for example, police in Albuquerque, N.M., placed a classified advertisement in a local paper for men to work as paid escorts—and then arrested 50 men who responded for violating laws against prostitution. In 1985, Honolulu police paid private citizens to pick up prostitutes in their cars, have sex with them and then drive them to nearby police cars for arrest. (One convicted prostitute's lawyer complained: "You can now serve your community by fornicating. Once the word gets out there will be no shortage of volunteers.") In San Francisco, the police have wired rooms in the city's leading hotels to make videotapes of prostitutes servicing their customers. But given the minimal control over the videotaping operation, there was little to stop local police from watching and videotaping other hotel guests in bed.

Many prostitution-related entrapment operations make doubtful contributions to preserving public safety. In 1985, eight Fairfax County, Va., police officers rented two $88-a-night Holiday Inn rooms, purchased an ample supply of liquor and then phoned across the Potomac River to Washington to hire a professional stripper for a bachelor party. The stripper came, stripped and was busted for indecent exposure. She faced fines of up to $1,000 and 12 months in jail. Fairfax County police justified the sting operation by claiming it was necessary to fight prostitution. But the department had made only 11 arrests on prostitution charges in the previous year—all with similar sting operations.

In 1992, police in Des Moines, Wash., hired a convicted rapist to have sex with masseuses. The local police explained that they hired the felon after plainclothes police officers could not persuade women at the local Body Care Center to have intercourse. Martin Pratt, police chief in the Seattle suburb, claimed that the ex-rapist was uniquely qualified for the job and, when asked why the police instructed the felon to consummate the acts with the alleged prostitutes, Pratt explained that stopping short "wouldn't have been appropriate."

A New York sting operation [in 1994] indirectly could have helped out the New York Mets: Two San Diego Padres baseball players were arrested after speaking to a female undercover officer. A Seattle journalist who also was busted described the police procedure to *Newsday:* "He said that he was stuck in traffic when he discovered that a miniskirted woman in a low-cut blouse was causing the jam, approaching the cars that were stopped. 'She came up to the windows, kind of swaggering,' he said. He said that she offered him sex, he made a suggestive reply, and the next thing he knew he was surrounded by police officers who dragged him out of his car and arrested him."

Many police appear to prefer chasing naked women than pursuing dangerous felons. As Lt. Bill Young of the Las Vegas Metro Police told Canada's *Vancouver Sun,* "You get up in a penthouse at Caesar's Palace with six naked women frolicking in the room and then say: 'Hey, baby, you're busted!' That's fun." (Las Vegas arrests between 300 to 400 prostitutes a month.) In August 1993, Charles County, Md., police were embarrassed by reports that an undercover officer visiting a strip joint had had intercourse while receiving a "personal lap dance."

In some cities, laws against prostitution are transforming local police officers into de facto car thieves. Female officers masquerade as prostitutes; when a customer stops to negotiate, other police rush out and confiscate the person's car under local asset-forfeiture laws. Such programs are operating in Detroit, Washington, New York and Portland, Ore. The female officers who masquerade as prostitutes are, in some ways, worse than the prostitutes—since, at least, the hookers will exchange services for payment, while the police simply intend to shake down would-be customers.

Shortly after the Washington police began their car-grabbing program in 1992, one driver sped off after a plainclothes officer tried to force his way into the car after the driver spoke to an undercover female officer. One officer's foot was slightly injured, and police fired six shots into the rear of the car. The police volley could have killed two or three people—but apparently the Washington police consider the possibility of killing citizens a small price to pay for slightly and temporarily decreasing the rate of prostitution in one selected neighborhood.

The same tired, failed antiprostitution tactics tend to be repeated ad nauseam around the country. Aurora, Colo., recently announced plans to buy newspaper ads showing pictures of accused johns. The plan hit a rough spot when the *Denver Post* refused to publish the ads, choosing not to be an arm of the criminal-justice system. One Aurora councilman told local radio host Mike Rosen that the city wanted to publish the pictures of the accused (and not wait until after convictions) because some of them might be found not guilty "because of some legal technicality."

In recent years, the Washington police force has tried one trick after another to suppress prostitution—including passing out tens of thousands of tickets to drivers for making right turns onto selected streets known to be venues of solicitation. (Didn't they see the tiny print on the street sign saying that right turns are illegal between 5 p.m. and 2 a.m.?) Yet, at the same time, the murder rate in Washington has skyrocketed and the city's arrest and conviction rates for murders have fallen by more than 50 percent.

The futile fight against prostitution is a major drain on local law-enforcement resources. A study published in the *Hastings Law Journal* in 1987 is perhaps the most reliable estimate of the cost to major cities. Author Julie Pearl observed: "This study focuses on sixteen of the nation's largest cities, in which only 28 percent of reported violent crimes result in arrest. On average, police in these cities made as many arrests for prostitution as for all violent offenses.

Last year, police in Boston, Cleveland, and Houston arrested twice as many people for prostitution as they did for all homicides, rapes, robberies, and assaults combined, while perpetrators evaded arrest for 90 percent of these violent crimes. Cleveland officers spent eighteen hours—the equivalent of two workdays—on prostitution duty for every violent offense failing to yield an arrest." The average cost per bust was almost $2,000 and "the average big-city police department spent 213 man-hours a day enforcing prostitution laws." Pearl estimated that 16 large American cities spent more than $120 million to suppress prostitution in 1985. In 1993, one Los Angeles official estimated that prostitution enforcement was costing the city more than $100 million a year.

Locking up prostitutes and their customers is especially irrational at a time when more than 35 states are under court orders to reduce prison overcrowding. Gerald Arenberg, executive director of the National Association of the Chiefs of Police, has come out in favor of legalizing prostitution. Dennis Martin, president of the same association, declared that prostitution law enforcement is "much too time-consuming, and police forces are short-staffed." Maryland Judge Darryl Russell observed: "We have to explore other alternatives to solving this problem because this eats up a lot of manpower of the police. We're just putting out brush fires while the forest is blazing." National surveys have shown that 94 percent of citizens believe that police do not respond quickly enough to calls for help, and the endless pursuit of prostitution is one factor that slows down many police departments from responding to other crimes.

Another good reason for reforming prostitution laws is to safeguard public health: Regulated prostitutes tend to be cleaner prostitutes. HIV-infection rates tend to be stratospheric among the nation's streetwalkers. In Newark, 57 percent of prostitutes were found to be HIV positive, according to a *Congressional Quarterly* report. In New York City, 35 percent of prostitutes were HIV-positive; in Washington, almost half.

In contrast, brothels, which are legal in 12 rural Nevada counties, tend to be comparative paragons of public safety. The University of California at Berkeley School of Public Health studied the health of legal Nevada brothel workers compared with that of jailed Nevada streetwalkers. None of the brothel workers had AIDS, while 6 percent of the unregulated streetwalkers did. Brothel owners had a strong incentive to police the health of their employees, since they could face liability if an infection were passed to a customer.

Prostitution is legal in several countries in Western Europe. In Hamburg, Germany, which some believe has a model program of legalized prostitution, streetwalkers are sanctioned in certain well-defined areas and prostitutes must undergo frequent health checks. Women with contagious diseases are strictly prohibited from plying their trade. (While some consider Amsterdam a model for legalization, the system there actually has serious problems. A spokesman for the association of Dutch brothels recently told the Associated Press: "The prostitutes these days are not so professional any more. In the past, prostitutes had more skills and they offered better services. Most of them now work only one or two evenings per week, and that's not enough time for them to become good.")

Bans on prostitution actually generate public disorder—streetwalkers, police chases, pervasive disrespect for the law and condoms littering lawns. As long as people have both money and sexual frustration, some will continue paying others to gratify their desires. The issue is not whether prostitution is immoral, but whether police suppression of prostitution will make society a safer place. The ultimate question to ask about a crackdown on prostitution is: How many murders are occurring while police are chasing after people who only want to spend a few bucks for pleasure?

In 1858, San Francisco Police Chief Martin Burke complained: "It is impossible to suppress prostitution altogether, yet it can, and ought to be regulated so as to limit the injury done to society, as much as possible." Vices are not crimes. Despite centuries of attempts to suppress prostitution, the profession continues to flourish. Simply because prostitution may be immoral is no reason for police to waste their time in a futile effort to suppress the oldest profession.

Anastasia Volkonsky

 **NO**

Legalizing the "Profession" Would Sanction the Abuse

Prostitution commonly is referred to as "the world's oldest profession." It's an emblematic statement about the status of women, for whom being sexually available and submissive to men is the oldest form of survival.

As the "world's oldest," prostitution is presented as an accepted fact of history, something that will always be with us that we cannot eradicate. As a "profession," selling access to one's body is being promoted as a viable choice for women. In an era in which the human-rights movement is taking on some of history's most deeply rooted oppressions and an era in which women have made unprecedented strides in politics and the professions, this soft-selling of prostitution is especially intolerable.

Calls for legalization and decriminalization of prostitution put forth by civil libertarians are not forward-thinking reforms. They represent acceptance and normalization of the traffic in human beings. Moreover, the civil-libertarian portrayal of the prostitute as a sexually free, consenting adult hides the vast network of traffickers, organized-crime syndicates, pimps, procurers and brothel keepers, as well as the customer demand that ultimately controls the trade.

In studies replicated in major cities throughout the United States, the conditions of this "profession" are revealed to be extreme sexual, physical and psychological abuse. Approximately 70 percent of prostitutes are raped repeatedly by their customers—an average of 31 times per year, according to a study in a 1993 issue of the *Cardozo Women's Law Journal*. In addition, 65 percent are physically assaulted repeatedly by customers and more by pimps. A majority (65 percent and higher) are drug addicts. Increasingly, prostituted women are HIV positive. Survivors testify to severe violence, torture and attempted murders. The mortality rate for prostitutes, according to Justice Department statistics from 1982, is 40 times the national average.

What can be said of a "profession" with such a job description? How can it be said that women freely choose sexual assault, harassment, abuse and the risk of death as a profession? Such a term might be appealing for women who are trapped in the life, as a last-ditch effort to regain some self-respect and identify with the promises of excitement and glamor that may have lured them into prostitution in the first place. A substantial portion of street-walkers are homeless or living below the poverty line. Even most women who work in outcall or escort services have no control over their income because they are at the mercy of a pimp or pusher. Most will leave prostitution without savings.

Prostitution is not a profession selected from among other options by today's career women. It comes as no surprise that the ranks of prostitutes both in the United States and globally are filled with society's most vulnerable members, those least able to resist recruitment. They are those most displaced and disadvantaged in the job market: women, especially the poor; the working class; racial and ethnic minorities; mothers with young children to support; battered women fleeing abuse; refugees; and illegal immigrants. Women are brought to the United States from Asia and Eastern Europe for prostitution. In a foreign country, with no contacts or language skills and fearing arrest or deportation, they are at the mercy of pimps and crime syndicates.

Most tellingly, the largest group of recruits to prostitution are children. The average age of entry into prostitution in the United States is approximately 14, sociologists Mimi Silbert and Ayala Pines found in a study performed for the Delancey Foundation in San Francisco. More than 65 percent of these child prostitutes are runaways. Most have experienced a major trauma: incest, domestic violence, rape or parental abandonment. At an age widely considered too young to handle activities such as voting, drinking alcohol, driving or holding down a job, these children survive by selling their bodies to strangers. These formative years will leave them with deep scars—should they survive to adulthood.

⋘◉⋙

Sensing this contradiction between the reality of prostitution and the rhetoric of sexual freedom and consensual crime, some proposals to decriminalize prostitution attempt to draw a distinction between "forced" prostitution and "free" prostitution. A June 1993 *Time* article about the international sex industry notes that "faced with the difficulty of sorting out which women are prostitutes by choice and which are coerced, many officials shrug off the problem," implying that when one enters prostitution, it is a free choice. The distinction between force and freedom ends in assigning blame to an already victimized woman for "choosing" to accept prostitution in her circumstances.

"People take acceptance of the money as her consent to be violated," says Susan Hunter, executive director of the Council for Prostitution Alternatives, a Portland, Ore.-based social-service agency that has helped hundreds of women from around the country recover from the effects of prostitution. She likens prostituted women to battered women. When battered women live with their batterer or repeatedly go back to the batterer, we do not take this as a legal consent to battering. A woman's acceptance of money in prostitution should not be taken as her agreement to prostitution. She may take the money because she must survive, because it is the only recompense she will get for the harm that has been done to her and because she has been socialized to believe that this is her role in life. Just as battered women's actions now are understood in light of the effects of trauma and battered woman syndrome, prostituted women suffer psychologically in the aftermath of repeated physical and sexual assaults.

To make an informed choice about prostitution, says Hunter, women need to recover their safety, sobriety and self-esteem and learn about their options. The women in her program leave prostitution, she asserts, "not because we offer them high salaries, but because we offer them hope.... Women are not voluntarily returning to prostitution."

Proponents of a "consensual crime" approach hold that the dangers associated with prostitution are a result of its illegality. Legal prostitution will be safe, clean and professional, they argue; the related crimes will disappear.

Yet wherever there is regulated prostitution, it is matched by a flourishing black market. Despite the fact that prostitution is legal in 12 Nevada counties, prostitutes continue to work illegally in casinos to avoid the isolation and control of the legal brothels. Even the legal brothels maintain a business link with the illegal pimping circuit by paying a finder's fee to pimps for bringing in new women.

Ironically, legalization, which frequently is touted as an alternative to spending money on police vice squads, creates its own set of regulations to be monitored. To get prostitutes and pimps to comply with licensing rules, the penalties must be heightened and policing increased—adding to law-enforcement costs.

Behind the facade of a regulated industry, brothel prostitutes in Nevada are captive in conditions analogous to slavery. Women often are procured for the brothels from other areas by pimps who dump them at the house in order to collect the referral fee. Women report working in shifts commonly as long as 12 hours, even when ill, menstruating or pregnant, with no right to refuse a customer who has requested them or to refuse the sexual act for which he has paid. The dozen or so prostitutes I interviewed said they are expected to pay the brothel room and board and a percentage of their earnings—sometimes up to 50 percent. They also must pay for mandatory extras such as medical exams, assigned clothing and fines incurred for breaking house rules. And, contrary to the common claim that the brothel will protect women from the dangerous, crazy clients on the streets, rapes and assaults by customers are covered up by the management.

Local ordinances of questionable constitutionality restrict the women's activities even outside the brothel. They may be confined to certain sections of town and permitted out only on certain days, according to Barbara Hobson, author of *Uneasy Virtue*. Ordinances require that brothels must be located in uninhabited areas at least five miles from any city, town, mobile-home park or residential area. Physically isolated in remote areas, their behavior monitored by brothel managers, without ties to the community and with little money or resources of their own, the Nevada prostitutes often are virtual prisoners. Local legal codes describe the women as "inmates."

Merely decriminalizing prostitution would not remove its stigma and liberate women in the trade. Rather, the fiction that prostitution is freely chosen would become encoded into the law's approach to prostitution. Decriminalization would render prostitution an invisible crime without a name. "The exchange of money [in prostitution] somehow makes the crime of rape invisible" to society, says Hunter.

Amy Fries, director of the National Organization For Women's International Women's Rights Task Force, speaks from experience in studying and combating the sex trade both internationally and in the Washington area. Decriminalization, she says, does not address the market forces at work in prostitution: "[Prostitution] is based on supply and demand. As the demand goes way up, [the pimps] have to meet it with a supply by bringing in more girls."

Ultimately, changing the laws will benefit the customer, not the prostitute. Legalization advocates identify the arrest as the most obvious example of the abuse of prostitutes. But, surprisingly, former prostitutes and prostitutes' advocates say the threat of jail is not a top concern. Considering the absence of any other refuge or shelter, jail provides a temporary safe haven, at the very least providing a bunk, a square meal and a brief respite from johns, pimps and drugs. This is not to make light of abuses of state and police power or the seriousness of jail—the fact that for many women jail is an improvement speaks volumes about their lives on the streets.

It is the customers who have the most to lose from arrest, who fear jail, the stigma of the arrest record and the loss of their anonymity. The argument that prostitution laws invade the privacy of consenting adults is geared toward protecting customers. Prostitutes, working on the streets or in brothels controlled by pimps, have little to no privacy. Furthermore, decriminalization of prostitution is a gateway to decriminalizing pandering, pimping and patronizing—together, decriminalizing many forms of sexual and economic exploitation of women. A 1986 proposal advocated by the New York Bar Association included repeal of such associated laws and the lowering of the age of consent for "voluntary" prostitution. Despite the assertion that prostitutes actively support decriminalization, many women who have escaped prostitution testify that their pimps coerced them into signing such petitions.

Of the many interests contributing to the power of the sex industry—the pimps, the panderers and the patrons—the acts of individual prostitutes are the least influential. Yet, unfortunately, there are incentives for law enforcement to target prostitutes for arrest, rather than aggressively enforcing laws against pimps, johns and traffickers. It is quicker and less costly to round up the women than to pursue pimps and traffickers in elaborate sting operations. The prostitutes are relatively powerless to fight arrest; it is the pimps and johns who can afford private attorneys. And, sadly, it is easier to get a public outcry and convictions against prostitutes, who are marginalized women, than against the wealthier males who are the majority of pimps and johns.

Prostitution is big business. Right now, economics provide an incentive for procuring and pimping women. In all the debates about prostitution, the factor most ignored is the demand. But it is the customers—who have jobs, money, status in the community, clean arrest records and anonymity—who have the most to lose. New legal reforms are beginning to recognize that. An increasing number of communities across the country, from Portland to Baltimore, are adopting car-seizure laws, which allow police to impound the automobiles of those who drive around soliciting prostitutes. This approach recognizes that johns degrade not only women who are prostitutes, but also others by assuming that any females in a given area are for sale. Other towns have instituted, legally or as community efforts, measures designed to publicize and shame would-be johns by publishing their names or pictures and stepping up arrests.

Globally, a pending U.N. Convention Against All Forms of Sexual Exploitation would address the modern forms of prostitution with mechanisms that target pimps and johns and that hold governments accountable for their policies.

Hunter supports the use of civil as well as criminal sanctions against johns, modeled after sexual harassment lawsuits. "People will change their behavior because of economics," she points out, using recent changes in governmental and corporate policy toward sexual harassment as an example of how the fear of lawsuits and financial loss can create social change.

At the heart of the matter, prostitution is buying the right to use a woman's body. The "profession" of prostitution means bearing the infliction of repeated, unwanted sexual acts in order to keep one's "job." It is forced sex as a condition of employment, the very definition of rape and sexual harassment. Cecilie Hoigard and Liv Finstad, who authored the 1992 book *Backstreets,* chronicling 15 years of research on prostitution survivors, stress that it is not any individual act, but the buildup of sexual and emotional violation as a daily occurrence, that determines the trauma of prostitution.

Cleaning up the surrounding conditions won't mask the ugliness of a trade in human beings.

POSTSCRIPT

Should Prostitution Be Legal?

There are a number of ways in which lawmakers could deal with the "world's oldest profession":

- Outlaw prostitution entirely. Enforcing such a law would run the risk of draining a community's resources.
- Outlaw some behavior associated with prostitution, such as street solicitation or loitering, but this can raise difficult distinctions. When, for instance, does casual flirtation and overt come-ons to a stranger become illegal solicitation?
- Legalize sex work and control it by licensing "body work therapists," requiring regular medical checkups, and setting aside specific areas where sex workers can ply their trade.
- Decriminalize all sexual activities between consenting adults, whether or not money changes hands. Advertising and solicitation could be limited by social propriety, and minors could be protected against recruitment and exploitation by the laws regulating child abuse and age of consent. (Note that age of consent laws vary greatly state to state, from 14 in Hawaii to 18 in several states, with additional restrictions that depend on the age differences between partners.)

What is your opinion on this issue now that you have thought about the reasons proposed by Bovard and Volkonsky? What alternative solutions not mentioned here would you propose?

Suggested Readings

N. J. Almodovar, "Prostitution and the Criminal Justice System," *The Truth Seeker* (Summer 1990).

S. Bell, *Reading, Writing, and Rewriting the Prostitute Body* (Indiana University Press, 1994).

V. Bullough and B. Bullough, *Women and Prostitution: A Social History* (Prometheus Press, 1987).

H. Moody and A. Carmen, *Working Women: The Subterranean World of Street Prostitution* (Little, Brown, 1995).

L. Primoratz, "What's Wrong With Prostitution?" *Philosophy* (1993).

L. Shrage, "Prostitution and the Case for Decriminalization," *Dissent* (Spring 1996).

ISSUE 18

Is Chemical Castration an Acceptable Punishment for Sex Offenders?

YES: Douglas J. Besharov, from "Sex Offenders: Yes: Consider Chemical Treatment," *ABA Journal* (July 1992)

NO: Andrew Vachhs, from "Sex Offenders: No: Pragmatically Impotent," *ABA Journal* (July 1992)

ISSUE SUMMARY

YES: Douglas J. Besharov, a resident scholar at the American Enterprise Institute in Washington, D.C., argues that carefully conducted research in Europe and the United States shows that chemical castration is effective, more humane, and much less expensive than imprisonment for some convicted compulsive sex offenders.

NO: Andrew Vachhs, a juvenile justice advocate and novelist, asserts that chemical and surgical castration both fail to address aggression as an underlying motive for repeat sex offenders.

Rapists and child molesters in California can choose between chemical castration and indefinite incarceration. Whether we live in California or another state, we and the politicians we elect to make our laws will have to learn what the facts are about this very controversial and emotional issue.

Until 1996, this issue surfaced occasionally, but it never quite received serious public attention. That situation is changing, as research continues with Depo-Provera, a synthetic form of the hormone progesterone that suppresses the male hormone testosterone and thus eliminates sex drive. As news of this research spreads, convicted sex offenders are starting to ask the courts to allow them to choose between being sent to prison or being sentenced to counseling and ongoing treatment with Depo-Provera.

It is important to note that the procedure in question here is *chemical* castration, not permanent *surgical* castration. In Texas, for instance, Steven Allen Butler, who had raped a 13-year-old girl, asked for surgical castration and 10 years of probation as his punishment instead of imprisonment. The district court initially agreed to his request but later withdrew its approval after protests by civil liberties groups and the refusal of physicians to perform the procedure. Butler himself had second thoughts about the operation. While some view surgical castration as "a return to the Dark Ages," chemical castration with antiandrogenic hormones has been an accepted treatment for many sex offenders.

A case study reported by John Money, founder and director of the Psychohormonal Research Unit at the Johns Hopkins Medical Institutions, illustrates the ambivalence raised by this issue: A young man came to the Hopkins clinic seeking help with a compulsive behavior he did not understand. At intervals he would find himself driving around searching for a church. He then went into an trance state where he could not recall what he did between finding the church and some time later. For 18 months, with counseling and a weekly shot of Depo-Provera, his compulsive behavior was eliminated. Then, while on his way to an appointment at the clinic, he felt a need to follow a school bus that had triggered his compulsion as it passed a church.

The patient's premonition had been only partly fulfilled on this particular occasion for, on the far side of the church, there was only a little boy playing. "I didn't stop," the patient said. "I went on past, but I had to come back again. And after I came back the third time, I just, I just like, uh, relaxed; and I was able to pull myself together, and come on into the city. I don't know what happened. There was a change. Just all of a sudden I quit driving around."

The patient's agitation over this relapse to his compulsive driving around in search of a church allowed Money to uncover what had been happening during his trance states. Before being treated with Depo-Provera, when the patient found a church he would look around to "find a youth at the age of puberty with whom he would strike up a friendly conversation, and then, utterly without warning, punch and kick him, and drive away." For 18 months, Depo-Provera freed him of his compulsive search and the trance-state and subsequent assault that followed his finding a church. Money was then able to uncover the childhood history behind the compulsive assault behavior and treat it. However, as successful as the Depo-Provera was for 18 months, there was still the chance of a mild or even dangerous relapse.

This risk of relapse is a major factor in the following debate between Douglas J. Besharov and Andrew Vachhs. Watch for other points of disagreement and concern as you read their brief statements. Think about what additional information you would like to have on this issue.

Douglas J. Besharov  **YES**

Sex Offenders: Consider Chemical Treatment

Surgical castration has never been very popular in this country, although it has been used sporadically in a number of states for more than 100 years, and was a common remedy in Germany and Denmark as late as the 1960s.

Although many castrated men may be capable of intercourse, the limited research that exists suggests that the repeat-offense rate is low. On humanitarian and civil liberties grounds, however, most experts now oppose the procedure and it is unlikely that many courts will turn to it as an alternative to incarceration—especially since there is a better option.

First tried more than 25 years ago, the use of hormone suppressors—also known as "chemical castration"—has proven highly effective for certain sex offenders. The most common drug used is medroxyprogesterone acetate, a synthetic progesterone originally developed as a contraceptive marketed as Depo-Provera.

According to a 1990 article in the *American Journal of Criminal Law*, this treatment, when given to men, "reduces the production and effects of testosterone, thus diminishing the compulsive sexual fantasy. Formerly insistent and commanding urges can be voluntarily controlled." It creates what another writer called "erotic apathy." Fifty sex offender clinics in this country now use chemical therapy, and it is even more widely used in Europe.

Low Recidivism

Carefully conducted research indicates that hormone therapy works—when coupled with appropriate counseling—for most paraphiliacs (sex offenders driven by overwhelming sexual fantasies). Recidivism rates are under 5 percent.

Just as in surgical castration, the subject can still have erections, and many successfully impregnate their wives. For this reason, hormone treatment does not work for antisocial personalities or for those whose sex offenses are motivated by feelings of anger, violence or power. The treatment does not reach the causes of their harmful behavior. Thus, proper diagnosis is essential.

Some may argue that hormone treatment as an alternative to incarceration is too lenient for serious sex crimes. First, it is possible to combine treatment with incarceration. But more importantly, we should remember how frequently serious offenders serve very short sentences. Nationally, convicted rapists serve less than 6 years in jail, and that does not include all those who plead guilty to a lesser offense. For too many offenders, the sexual abuse and violence in prisons merely heightens their propensity to commit further crime.

Recognizing the sexual side of some rapes in no way seeks to blame the victim, or denies the violent, hateful aspect of rape. Promoting an apparently effective therapy does not condone the behavior, but it does protect future victims.

Others will oppose using these drugs because, even though they work, they are an invasion of bodily integrity and reproductive freedom. (Side effects include weight gain, hot flashes and hypertension.) But it is more accurate to see them as equivalent to the psychotropic drugs, which include antidepressants, antipsychotics and tranquilizers, now routinely used to treat many mental disorders.

Some would even deny defendants the right to accept the treatment in lieu of imprisonment—because the choice is inherently coercive. Perhaps it is. But the question is this: When faced with the certainty of incarceration, wouldn't we all want to be able to make such a choice? To ask the question is to answer it.

After all the sensationalism, the use of hormone-suppressing drugs, in certain cases, holds great promise for reducing the level of sexual violence against women and children. As a voluntary alternative, it is in both the defendant's and society's interest.

Andrew Vachhs

 **NO**

Sex Offenders: Pragmatically Impotent

As a criminal justice response to the chronic, dangerous sexual psychopath, castration of any kind is morally pernicious and pragmatically impotent. Even if we could ignore the implications of mutilation-as-compensation for criminal offenses, castration must be rejected on the most essential of grounds: The "cure" will exacerbate the "disease."

Proponents of castration tell us: 1) It will heal the offender (and thus protect society), and 2) it would be the offender's own choice.

Violent sex offenders are not victims of their heightened sex drives. Rapists may be "expressing their rage." Predatory pedophiles may be "replaying their old scripts." But any sexual sadist, properly interviewed, will tell you the truth: They do what they do because they want to do it. Their behavior is not the product of sickness—it is volitional.

Castration will not remove the source of a violent sex offender's rage—only one single instrument of its expression. Rapes have been committed with broomsticks, coke bottles—any blunt object. Indeed, most criminal statutes now incorporate just such a possibility.

And imagine a violent rapist whose hatred of women occupies most of his waking thoughts. Imagine him agreeing to castration to avoid a lengthy prison sentence. Imagine his rage festering geometrically as he stews in the bile of what "they" have done to him. Does anyone actually believe such a creature has been rendered harmless?

An escalating pattern is characteristic of many predatory sex offenders—castration is likely to produce an internal demand for even higher levels of stimulation.

The castration remedy implies some biomedical cause for sexual offenses. Once fixed, the offender ceases to be a danger. This is nonsense—the motivation for sexual assault will not disappear with the severed genitalia or altered hormones.

In Germany, Klaus Grabowski avoided a life sentence by agreeing to castration. Released, he began covert hormone injections. In 1980, he strangled a 7-year-old girl and buried her body. At trial, his defense was that the castration had removed any sexual feelings, that he had lured the child to his apartment because he loved children and killed her in response to blackmail threats.

High Predatory Drive

Even the most liberal of Americans have become suspicious of a medical model to explain sex offenders. Such offenders may plot and plan, scheme and stalk for months, utilize the most elaborate devices to avoid detection, even network with others and commercially profit from their foul acts.

But some psycho-apologist can always be found to claim the poor soul was deep in the grip of irresistible impulse when he was compelled to attack. Imagine the field day the expert-witness fraternity will have explaining how the castrated child molester who later killed his new victims was rendered insane as a result of the castration itself.

Sex offender treatment is the growth industry of the 1990s. Chemical castration already looms as a Get-Out-of-Jail-Free Card.

Castration validates the sex offender's self-portrait: He is the victim; he can't help himself. It panders to our ugliest instincts, not the least of which is cowardice—the refusal to call evil by its name.

Nor can castration be defended because the perpetrator chooses it. Leaving aside the obvious issue of coercion, under what theory does a convicted criminal get to select his own (non-incarcerative) sentence?

America loves simple solutions to complex problems, especially solutions with political utility, like boot camp for youthful offenders. The last thing our cities need is muggers in better physical shape.

When it comes to our own self-interest (and self-defense), the greatest sickness is stupidity. Castration qualifies . . . on all counts.

POSTSCRIPT

Is Chemical Castration an Acceptable Punishment for Sex Offenders?

The history of castration as a penalty for sexual assaults in America can be traced back to colonial times, when laws and courts sought to protect American society from "unnatural and inordinate copulations" between black men and white women. All of the 13 colonies prohibited sexual relations between black men (both freemen and slaves) and white women (but not between white men and black women). Although black men who were convicted of raping white women were usually hanged, most colonies also allowed vigilantes, as well as the courts, to castrate black men who raped, attempted to rape, or had consensual sex with white women.

In this century, castration has been imposed by the courts for men and sterilization for women who were judged mentally retarded. The courts eventually declared this "treatment" unconstitutional. The current debate over chemical and surgical castration revolved around its use as a substitute for costly long-term imprisonment of child molesters and rapists.

In September 1996 California became the first state to require *chemical* castration of child molesters who have been convicted of committing a second sexual assault against a child under 13 years of age. Within a few months, Montana and Georgia became the second and third states to require chemical castration of child molesters. Other states are trying to pass similar measures.

In May 1997 Texas became the first state to make *surgical* castration available as an option for repeat child molesters serving time in prison. Governor George W. Bush signed into law a bill that allows voluntary surgical castration for inmates 21 or older who have been convicted of sexual offenses against children two or more times. In signing the law, Bush predicted that it will reduce child sex offenses in Texas, where an estimated 7,000 people are imprisoned for sex crimes.

Advocates of surgical castration are quick to point out that 50–60 percent of convicted sex offenders who go through the standard prison rehabilitation program become repeat offenders after they are paroled. Also, whereas untreated sex offenders have an 80 percent recidivism rate, only 3 percent of surgically castrated sex offenders repeat their offenses. California legislators were reminded that repeat offender rates among child molesters in Europe dropped from almost 100 percent to just 2 percent when chemical castration was instituted.

Among the arguments cited against chemical castration is the fact that sex offenders who undergo this treatment as a condition for parole can walk into almost any training gym and buy steroids to counter the effects of the

Depo-Provera treatment. This argument says that taxpayers will be paying millions of dollars for treatment that has not been proven to work, can easily be circumvented, and will wear off quickly at the end of the offender's parole.

Sorting out the facts and finding comparable examples of the effectiveness of chemical and surgical castration is only part of resolving this controversial issue. It is an issue that society is just beginning to deal with. The arguments raised by Besharov and Vachhs provide us with a starting point for debate, but more facts and much more discussion is needed before this issue can be resolved.

Suggested Readings

"Castration or Incarceration?" *New Scientist* (September 21, 1996).

V. T. Cheny, *A Brief History of Castration, vol. 1,* trans. Alan H. Peterson (American Focus Publishing Company, 1996).

A. J. Malcomb et al., "Should a Sexual Offender Be Allowed Castration?" *British Medical Journal* (September 25, 1993).

J. Money, *Love and Love Sickness: The Science of Sex, Gender Differences and Pairbonding* (John Hopkins University Press, 1980).

J. Money, *The Lovemap Guidebook: A Definitive Statement* (Continuum Press, 1999).

R. Wille and K. M. Beier, "Castration in Germany," *Annals of Sex Research* (1989).

ISSUE 19

Should Schools Pay Damages for Student-on-Student Sexual Harassment?

YES: Bernice Sandler, from "Without Lawsuits, Schools Will Tolerate Serious Misbehavior That Hurts All Students," *Insight on the News* (August 9, 1999)

NO: Sarah J. McCarthy, from "Don't Bankrupt Our School Systems With the Quick-Fix Solution of Punitive Damages," *Insight on the News* (August 9, 1999)

ISSUE SUMMARY

YES: Bernice Sandler, a senior scholar at the National Association for Women in Education, maintains that schools should pay damages for student-on-student sexual harassment. She cites several cases in which school authorities ignored blatant and pervasive sexual harassment of students by other students until the parents of the harassed students forced action by filing lawsuits seeking compensation for damages.

NO: Author Sarah J. McCarthy objects to schools paying damages for student-on-student sexual harassment, stating that Congress and lawmakers often jump to legislation as a quick-fix solution. She asserts that new laws authorizing the filing of lawsuits would empty taxpayers' pockets, bankrupt school districts, and lead to centralized thought control, an Americanized version of Chairman Mao's cultural revolution in China.

In the fall of 1991 stories of sexual harassment suddenly became very hot news in newspaper headlines, popular magazines, and television news broadcasts. The issue emerged with law professor Anita Hill's charge that Judge Clarence Thomas had sexually harassed her while he served as chair of the Equal Employment Opportunity Commission. The allegation came close to derailing Thomas's nomination to the United States Supreme Court. In the sports world, three members of the New England Patriots football team (and the team itself) were fined nearly $50,000 for lewd gestures and remarks to *Boston Herald* reporter Lisa Olson in their locker room.

Sexual harassment charges were also leveled at America's political leaders. The majority leader of Florida's House of Representatives lost his position for allowing an "offensive, degrading and inappropriate" atmosphere of sexual innuendo amongst his staff. The 18-year career of U.S. senator Brock Adams, a recognized leader on women's issues, ended with charges that he had sexually harassed and even raped eight women who worked with him. U.S. senator Robert Packwood also faced attack, as a congressional ethics committee investigated charges that he had regularly sexually harassed female colleagues. As a result, Packwood was forced to resign from the Senate in September 1995.

In late 1991 and throughout most of 1992, the infamous Tailhook Association convention of Navy and Marine Corps pilots made national news. After interviewing more than 1,500 officers and civilians, investigators implicated more than 70 officers in sexual harassment and assaults against at least 26 women and several men. Charged with participating in or covering up the affair, the officers were referred for disciplinary review and possible dismissal from the service. Top admirals were charged with tacitly approving this activity for years, and major promotions for two admirals were lost because of questions of sexual harassment.

In 1993 the American Association of University Women Education Foundation polled 1,632 teenagers in grades 8 to 11 in 79 schools on sexual harassment. They found that 76 percent of the girls and 56 percent of the boys reported being on the receiving end of unwanted sexual comments or looks. Two-thirds of the girls and 42 percent of the boys said they were touched, grabbed, or pinched in a sexual way. Some researchers questioned whether or not all the behaviors included in the survey should be legitimately considered sexual harassment. Christina Hoff Sommers at Clark University in Massachusetts stated, "They're committed to finding gender bias everywhere, behind every door, in every hallway, and they find it. What this is going to invite is we're going to begin litigating high-school flirtation. In order to find gender bias against girls, they had to ask questions so broad that they invited complaints from boys." Countering this criticism, Maryka Biaggio at Pacific University in Oregon defended the broad, inclusive nature of the questions. "We know that people in general tend to underreport or minimize occurrences of sexual harassment, so in order to get a good sense of an individual's experience, you have to put forth a fairly inclusive definition."

Billie Wright Dziech, coauthor of *The Lecherous Professor: Sexual Harassment on Campus* (Beacon Press, 1984) and an opponent of student-professor sexual relationships, says, "We need clear definitions. We need to recognize that they are not hard and fast. They will differ for different individuals. This is slippery terminology." Dziech suggests distinguishing between what is considered normal flirting and "horseplay between men and women," a "sexual hassle," and "sexual harassment." But even that distinction will differ with different people and with the same person in different situations.

In the following selections, Bernice Sandler asserts that schools should pay damages for student-on-student sexual harassment as a way to curb serious student misbehavior. Sarah J. McCarthy counters that punishment should be focused on the wrongdoers, not the school district as a whole.

Bernice Sandler

 **YES**

Without Lawsuits, Schools Will Tolerate Serious Misbehavior That Hurts All Students

In May the Supreme Court decided a case involving a fifth-grade girl who continually had been asked for sexual intercourse by a classmate who sat next to her. The court ruled in *Davis vs. Monroe County Board of Education* that schools could be required to pay punitive damages for sexual harassment of students by other students. For five months the boy continually tried to touch his classmate's breasts and genitals, saying he wanted to have sex with her. He rubbed up against her in the classroom and hallways of the elementary school they attended. Although the girl's mother complained to the school after each incident, the school would not even reassign the girl's seat. The girl's grades dropped, and her father found a suicide note. Finally, when it became clear that the school would do nothing, the mother filed a criminal complaint against the boy, who pleaded guilty.

The court confirmed that student-to-student harassment is prohibited by Title IX, the law that prohibits sex discrimination in schools receiving federal dollars. Schools must respond to sexual harassment by students or face the possible loss of federal funds and/or a lawsuit and damages.

Many people are not aware of the extent to which student-to-student sexual harassment is common in many educational institutions. Growing up always has been a difficult time but, in recent years, for whatever reasons, behaviors even among kindergartners and throughout high schools and colleges are worse than ever, and bad behavior occurs more often. Many more youngsters are the victims of behaviors which are far more aggressive, obscene, more insistent and invasive than the behaviors many of us remember when we were in our teens or younger.

There are verbal slurs—8-year-olds are called "whores," "sluts" and worse. There is a lot of sexual touching and grabbing. One 6-year-old girl continually was told by fourth-grade boys on the school bus to have oral sex with her father (in far less polite terms); a 13-year-old girl faced a daily gauntlet of 15 to 20 boys, who would stare at her large breasts and together call her a "cow" and follow her around as they "mooed" at her; one boy had a girl put her hand down his pants; some boys and girls continually are asked for sexual activity; and there are children of all ages who have had their crotches grabbed. There are schools in which boys and girls will not wear pants with elastic waists because other children pull them down, often along with underwear. And crotch-grabbing is not a rarity in many schools. One teenager in a magnet school in one the richest counties in the country said that she "hated it when the guys would grab your genitals as you walk up the stairs. You never know who it is because the stairways are crowded."

These behaviors are a blight in all kinds of schools, public and private, and in the best and worst neighborhoods. School buses, outdoor playgrounds, stairways and cafeterias often are hotbeds of sexual harassment, since supervision either is lax or missing.

At one prestigious, small, liberal-arts college, two first-year male students worked in pairs: One would block a female from going forward while the other grabbed her crotch from behind. When the two men were brought before the dean, they said they could not understand what the fuss was about, stating, "But everybody does this in high school!"

If you have children or access to them, don't ask if these things happen to them or if they do any of these things. Instead, tell the child something such as, "Boys [or children] used to do a lot of teasing when I was in school. What kinds of things do they do in your school?" You may be surprised at what they tell you.

Sexual harassment is not simply boys-will-be-boys behavior. It is a form of sexual bullying, using sexuality as a form of power to dominate or terrorize another person. Just as we no longer allow bosses or coworkers to put pressure on employees for sex, whether it is a pat on the rear or a breast being grabbed, schools should not allow their students to suffer the same behaviors that are illegal in the workplace and often rise to the level of sexual abuse. The Supreme Court has ruled that such behaviors no longer can be tolerated in our schools.

In a study of nearly 2,000 students in Texas public schools in grades seven through 12, nearly six in 10 girls reported that they were harassed every other day, and a large number reported they were harassed on average once a week. Boys were responsible for 70 percent of the incidents reported by all children. When the results for boys and girls were combined, 89 percent of the students experienced some form of sexual harassment. Few reported it to their parents or teachers. Of those who reported an incident to a teacher, two-thirds said that nothing happened to the harasser.

The impact of sexual harassment is substantial. Children exposed to such severe and pervasive student-to-student behaviors often find it difficult to concentrate on learning. They may avoid certain areas of the school or cut classes if they are older. Grades may drop. Many of the severely harassed children become depressed. Some children, especially girls, even contemplate suicide. Boys are more likely to turn their anger out toward others, often in violent behavior. Harassment is upsetting—even more so when children ask for help and their teachers, counselors and principals ignore their pleas to stop such behaviors. Kids need to be able to trust the adults in their world.

Students of all ages have a right to feel safe in school, safe from sexual intrusions, safe from unwanted and inappropriate behaviors. Teachers often don't intervene when bad behaviors occur, erroneously believing that kids need to "learn" to handle this kind of behavior "on their own." Why should we expect children to be able to handle abusive behaviors which even adults find challenging?

Understandably, some people are worried that as a result of the Supreme Court's decision, schools will be sued for the slightest infractions such as the usual teasing between boys and girls. We remember the 6-year-old North Carolina boy who kissed a girl and then was suspended for the day—a case of overkill, to be sure. This is not what the Supreme Court has in mind. Its concern is about behavior that is "severe, pervasive and objectively offensive," behaviors that interfere with students' ability to learn or receive the benefits of their education. The court added that "damages are not available for simple acts and teasing and name-calling among school children, however, even when these comments target differences in gender." Additionally, for a school to be liable for money damages, it must have been "deliberately indifferent to known acts of student-to-student sexual harassment and the harasser is under the school's disciplinary authority."

Good schools don't need the specter of a lawsuit to respond quickly and adequately to sexual-harassment complaints, but not all schools are good.

Will some schools be sued when children sexually harass each other? Most schools never will face a lawsuit because they will act to stop sexual harassment when it occurs. Most schools will initiate some sort of training for teachers and students addressing appropriate and inappropriate behavior in school and ways teachers and other employees (such as bus drivers and cafeteria workers) should respond.

What we have learned from the workplace, colleges and schools is that the vast majority of people do not want to sue. Also, with few exceptions, almost all complaints can be handled informally either by various kinds of intervention by school personnel or by helping the student who is harassed to deal with the harassment. For example, in some elementary schools children have written letters to the children who have harassed them, asking that the behavior stop. The letter then is delivered and read to the harassing child by an adult.

A high tolerance for sexual bullying certainly can lead to lawsuits. Certainly, some schools will be sued, however—not because a student sexually harasses another but only because a school has allowed the harassment to continue and ignored children who were hurting and needed help.

Schools that handle sexual harassment like other behavior problems are not likely to be sued at all. For example, schools rarely, if ever, are sued because students hit each other—teachers usually intervene to stop that kind of behavior. Similarly, schools in which adults intervene to stop sexually harassing behaviors are not likely to be sued.

Will it be hard to distinguish between "simple teasing" and "severe, pervasive and offensive behavior?" It may not be hard most of the time, but even if the behavior does not rise to the legal level, as in the case of a one-time sexual joke, a single comment about another teenager's breast or penis or an act of mean-spirited name-calling, schools should not look the other way. They need to teach students how to grow up respecting other people and that some behaviors simply are not appropriate in school. Ignoring any kind of bad behavior implies that either the behavior is acceptable or that the teacher is weak and unable to deal with it. Ignoring such behaviors almost always leads to more behaviors of the same kind.

As a result of the Supreme Court's decision, most schools will take more seriously all kinds of bad behaviors, including other forms of harassment and bullying, and school personnel will have to learn how to intervene to stop them. It is not unrealistic to teach children that hurtful behaviors are not tolerated in schools or to encourage children to respect each other. Of course, good schools have been doing that for a long time. Now others can catch up.

Remember the old nursery rhyme, "Georgie Porgie, pudding and pie, kissed the girls and made them cry"? Georgie Porgie is in big trouble these days. He is recognized as a sexual harasser because he made girls miserable to the point of tears. Georgie Porgie had better watch out.

Sarah J. McCarthy

 **NO**

Don't Bankrupt Our School Systems With the Quick-Fix Solution of Punitive Damages

N ow that Congress has inserted the ghost of Anita Hill into every adult male-female interaction, the Supreme Court has decided it's time to go after the kids. Though school officials say that student sexual harassment is a delicate issue, given the raging hormones that cause teens to perform acts of super-human stupidity, the court is blurring the line between adolescent bungling and criminal behavior by making school districts liable for punitive damages if anyone crosses the line. Parents and teachers have been trying to stop teenage stupidity since the beginning of time, but Justice Sandra Day O'Connor and four other members of the divided Supreme Court think they have found the cure—punitive damages, which is their usual standby and the legal profession's Johnny-One-Note-Magic-Bullet-Cure for everything: Sue for $2 million and call me in the morning.

In May the court ruled in *Davis vs. Monroe County Board of Education* that a fifth-grade girl could proceed with a lawsuit seeking damages against her school district for ignoring sexual battery by a fifth-grade boy who had been found guilty in juvenile court. The court ruled that the school district must have been informed of the harassment and indifferent to it before they could be liable. (By contrast, private businesses are liable even if they have no idea that harassment is occurring in the workplace under the legal standard that they "should have known" about it.) Certainly schools have an obligation to protect students from criminal activity. But it's not clear why, unlike physical assault or bullying among same-sex students, unwanted sexual advances should be treated as a federal civil-rights matter rather than a question of school discipline.

Following classmates in the halls, riding past their houses, boys chasing girls and pony-tail pulling once were signs of teenagers in love. The smooth operators in my high school used to snap off girls' plastic pop-it beads and try for slam-dunks by tossing them down the girls' blouses. Today, any male peacock strutting his stuff by cruising past a girl's house risks being turned in as a stalker.

Back in the days before we knew these guys were stalkers and harassers, we thought their escapades were funny—even romantic. We used to thrill to songs like "Born to Run," about "dying on Highway 9 in an everlasting kiss," and "Leader of the Pack." These are real American memories like the things that happened in the movie *American Graffiti*—memories we never could have had in a place like China, where government killjoys at the time were outlawing public hand-holding. Who would've thought it could've happened here?

The best-kept secret in America is that being sexually harassed can be one of the peak experiences of our lives. When I was 16, my boyfriend Harry and his gang, the Mad Mechanics, who had low-slung cars that made a lot of noise, had heard on the school grapevine that I was going to a party at the home of a guy in my neighborhood. The Mad Mechanics drove by the party house in a male-dominance display much like the chest-pounding behaviors they inherited from the great apes. The neighborhood guys turned out the lights and hid under the furniture at the first roar of the engines, but in reality, no one was too scared. The party guys used the darkened house as a chance to kiss the girls while the Mad Mechanics roared by.

Sexual harassment? Maybe, but it was the only time I felt like Natalie Wood in *West Side Story* in the middle of a rumble between the Jets and the Sharks. For Harry, who went on to fly hundreds of bombing missions in Vietnam, I'm glad he could go onto adulthood with his career untarnished by his teenage capers. Harry and I broke up a few months later when, upon arriving at our school picnic, I discovered he'd been riding the Tilt-A-Whirl with some girl he'd probably convinced she was the star of *West Side Story.*

In his *Newsday* column "Lunatic Feminists Arise on the Right," Robert Reno, an ardent supporter of the Supreme Court's ruling to protect girls from sexist language and hostile environments, rails against what he calls the new conservative "female TV gas bags"—women he says who are "fetching, wall-to-wall right wing and blond to their roots, like Laura Ingraham and Monica Crowley," women he designates as "silly," "lunatic," "dumb" and "deeply snide." (You have to wonder what would happen to American womanhood without chivalrous defenders such as Reno.)

But these women, bad as they are, are just "irrelevant distractions" compared with the objects of Reno's real wrath—Boston-based attorney and Independent Women's Forum, or IWF, member Jennifer Braceras, who wrote a *Wall Street Journal* article saying that for kids "a kiss on the cheek, a sexually suggestive remark, the persistent pursuit of a romantic relationship with someone who is not interested, even unwanted sexual touching, all may be normal parts of growing up when the individuals are peers."

"Who raised this woman?" Reno howls. "You'd never hear Phyllis Schlafly come out for kissing or touching in the classroom. She'd cane the whole lot of them."

"What a mouthful," he roars on, surmising that the IWF is a group of right-wing female renegades defending the rights of third-grade harassers. Her article, says Reno, "savages the Supreme Court decision that prohibits boorish little schoolboys from making repulsive pests of themselves by being sexually obnoxious to the girls in their class." The court decision "seems the least we can do for the girls who are going to grow up to run this country," he wails, "the way they have run more socially advanced nations." Reno glosses over the fact that these future presidents someday will have to compete with male candidates who have been toughened in wars such as in Vietnam and the Persian Gulf.

What Reno and other punitive-damage aficionados miss is that those of us who argue against lawsuits as the magic bullet for undesirable behaviors are not in favor of harassment but are concerned about the collateral damage caused by these penalties. The threat of financial annihilation via lawsuits is not the best environment in which freedom can thrive. Schools that could have their budget wiped out by a single child-against-child or employee-against-employee lawsuit would be pushed to go overboard in trying to control speech or behavior that could appear actionable to a creative trial lawyer.

"This is already the normal state of affairs in the workplace," says columnist John Leo. "Sexual-harassment law has given employers a powerful incentive to act in a defensive manner, warning workers against comments, gestures, office chitchat about the latest joke on a sitcom." Many schools already ban hand-holding, passing romantic notes and chasing members of the opposite sex during recess. One teacher's manual says that a child's comment of "You look nice" could be sexual harassment, depending on the "tone of voice" and "who else is around." ("You look nice" as sexual harassment! So much for the Land of the Free.) "Next year, kids will be suspended for behavior nobody's ever been suspended for," said Bruce Hunter of the American Association of School Administrators.

Beyond concerns about emptying taxpayers' pockets and bankrupting school districts, we have to wonder what effect this centralized behavior control will have on the kids. Squelching spontaneous behaviors such as teasing, joking and chasing members of the opposite sex is an outrageous thing to do to an entire nation of schoolchildren because a few have gone out of bounds. Instead, third-graders who create a hostile environment can be punished with suspensions without involving the entire school population of the United States in an Americanized version of Mao's Cultural Revolution.

The nonchalance with which Congress passes sexual-harassment laws, combined with an impassioned preference for overblown fines, is frightening. Laws are passed with a casualness about the definitions of the acts they are criminalizing and with drifting definitions such as the broadening of sexual assault to mean any unwanted touching. How can someone be sure a touch or a kiss is unwanted before it occurs?

In an article, "Could You Be the Next Monica?" by Nurith Aizenman in the July 1999 *New Woman* magazine, GOP former representative Susan Molinari of New York says she didn't "set out to make Monica Lewinsky's life miserable" when she pushed through ground-breaking sexual-assault legislation five years ago. Molinari only wanted to give a woman accusing a man of sexual assault the chance to bolster her case by showing that he also had attacked other women. Sensible enough—but the law defined sexual assault so broadly (essentially any attempt at unwanted touching) that it allowed lawyers in the Paula Jones case to probe President Clinton's past for other violations. That investigation, in turn, set an unexpected precedent: Now any woman who's had a consensual relationship with a man accused of harassment could find herself subpoenaed just as Lewinsky was. Molinari was astonished to learn that her law was behind Lewinsky's interrogation. "The law was supposed to target sexual assault," Molinari says.

And consider, if you can, the import of this revealing admission by Democratic former representative Patricia Schroeder of Colorado: "It was so much more fun to legislate than oversee. You could find many reasons to put more regulations on. We didn't feel accountable as much as we should have to make sure regulations were being applied reasonably."

It would be an oversimplification to claim that most school harassment is like the madcap adventures in *American Graffiti* or that high-school harassers are harmless. There are serious cases of harassment that need to be remedied.

In Pittsburgh, fraternity brothers at a university held "Pig Parties," inviting the ugliest dates they could find. The guy with the ugliest date would win. The girls soon realized why they were invited and would flee the party in tears. In cases such as these, the punishment should be placed at the door of the offending students rather than with the school or with the student body at large in the form of higher tuition payments to cover lawsuit expenses.

How can justice be achieved for victims of pig parties and sexual assault without trampling freedoms for everyone else? Penalties that focus punishments on the wrongdoers and minimize them for others would be the optimal solution. Current penalties do exactly the opposite. It would be a good start for the Supreme Court and American law schools to explore alternatives to threats of financial annihilation as a wholesale method of behavioral control. At least when the Mad Mechanics showed up, they had more than one tool in their box.

POSTSCRIPT

Should Schools Pay Damages for Student-on-Student Sexual Harassment?

The high cost of fighting sexual harassment often makes suffering in silence more appealing for women. "Many strong, successful professional women have made conscious decisions to ignore sexual harassment in their offices," maintains feminist Naomi Wolf, "because they know that as soon as they complained, there would be 50 other [women] waiting to take their jobs." Camille Paglia, author of *Sexual Personae: Art and Decadence from Nefertiti to Emily Dickenson* (Yale University Press, 1990), counters, "Women allow themselves to become victims when they don't take responsibility. If getting the guy to stop means putting a heel into his crotch, then just do it. Don't complain about it 10 years later." Yet, as Deborah Tannen, author of *You Just Don't Understand: Women and Men in Conversation* (Morrow, 1990), asserts, "Women have learned that confrontation is to be avoided and they don't have the verbal tools to attack this kind of problem head-on as a man would."

This issue continues to return time and again to the American conscience in television series episodes, such as *Law & Order, Ally McBeal, The Practice,* and *Sex and the City* because American society is still trying to deal with the conflicting issues posed by a recently awakened awareness of sex harassment. The issue is having a chilling effect on everyday male-female relations, on dating and courtship, in the workplace, on college campuses, and even in elementary and high schools. Anthropologist Lionel Tiger predicts a "return to a kind of Victorian period" in which men will be reluctant to try developing a relationship with any woman who initially seems aloof.

The Tailhook incident, which made headlines around the world, seems to have had some global influence. The Belgian and Dutch governments have launched public information campaigns on sexual harassment, and the Spanish and French governments have recently passed laws making sexual harassment a crime. The European Commission, the administrative arm of the 12-nation European Community, has issued a code defining sexual harassment.

Sexual harassment is fast becoming a global issue that will continue to have reverberations in the ways women and men relate to each other for years to come. The selections by Sandler and McCarthy are particularly challenging because they focus attention on examples of sexual harassment of young children by their peers in elementary, intermediate, and high schools. To what extent should schools and school administrators be held responsible for monitoring and working to eliminate student-on-student sexual harassment and punishing it when it occurs? When these questions are answered, American parents and other adults will need to find the most effective ways to educate youth about the differences between healthy flirtation and unwanted and unacceptable sexual harassment.

Suggested Readings

J. B. Brandenburg, *Confronting Sexual Harassment: What Schools and Colleges Can Do* (Teachers College Press, 1997).

L. Greenhouse, "Court Rules Schools Can Be Liable for Unchecked Sexual Harassment," *The New York Times* (May 25, 1999).

L. Greenhouse, "In Coming Term, High Court Will Add to Sex Harassment Rulings," *The New York Times* (September 30, 1998).

L. Greenhouse, "School Districts Are Given a Shield in Sex Harassment," *The New York Times* (June 23, 1998).

L. Greenhouse, "Schools May Be Sued for Student-On-Student Harassment, Divided Court Rules," *The New York Times* (May 24, 1999).

J. Larkin, *Sexual Harassment: High School Girls Speak Out* (Second Story Press, 1994).

L. McMillen, "Misleading Studies Seen on Sexual Harassment," *Chronicle of Higher Education* (September 27, 1996).

R. J. Shoop and D. Edwards, *How to Stop Sexual Harassment in Our Schools: A Handbook and Curriculum Guide for Administrators and Teachers* (Allyn & Bacon, 1994).

Contributors to This Volume

EDITORS

WILLIAM J. TAVERNER is the director of education for Planned Parenthood of Greater Northern New Jersey and is an adjunct professor of human sexuality at Fairleigh Dickinson University in Madison, New Jersey. He facilitates professional development workshops nationwide on a wide range of human sexuality subjects, from helping early childhood educators respond to young children's sexual questions and behaviors to helping those working with adolescents develop skills to educate about sexuality and relationships. Coeditor of the last three editions of *Taking Sides: Clashing Views on Controversial Issues in Human Sexuality* (McGraw-Hill/Dushkin, 1996, 1998, 2000), he is also the author of *Sexuality and Substance Abuse* (Phoenix Foundation, 1997), and the coauthor of three sexuality education manuals: *Positive Images: Teaching Abstinence, Contraception, and Sexual Health* (2001); *Educating About Abortion* (2001); and *Streetwise to Sex-Wise: Sexuality Education for High-Risk Youth* (2001), all published by Planned Parenthood of Greater Northern New Jersey. In addition, he contributed to the development of *The International Encyclopedia of Sexuality, vol. 4, vol. 5* (Continuum, 2000) and *Unequal Partners: Teaching About Power and Consent in Adult-Teen and Other Relationships* (Planned Parenthood of Greater Northern New Jersey, 2000). He received his B.A. in psychology from SUNY Albany and his M.A. in human sexuality from New York University. He can be contacted at BillTaverner@netscape.net.

STAFF

Theodore Knight List Manager
David Brackley Senior Developmental Editor
Juliana Gribbins Developmental Editor
Rose Gleich Administrative Assistant
Brenda S. Filley Director of Production/Design
Juliana Arbo Typesetting Supervisor
Diane Barker Proofreader
Richard Tietjen Publishing Systems Manager
Larry Killian Copier Coordinator

AUTHORS

ASHTON APPLEWHITE is the New York City–based author of *Cutting Loose: Why Women Who End Their Marriages Do So Well* (HarperCollins, 1998) and writes frequently on issues of marriage and divorce.

DIANE D. ARONSON is executive director of RESOLVE, the National Infertility Association, a nonprofit consumer advocacy and patient support organization in Somerville, Massachusetts.

JOHN BANCROFT is the director of the Kinsey Institute, and was trained in medicine at the University of Cambridge and served in Oxford University's psychiatry department.

DOUGLAS J. BESHAROV is a resident scholar at the American Enterprise Institute in Washington, D.C., and a professor at the University of Maryland School of Public Affairs.

ROBERT H. BORK, a former federal appeals court judge and solicitor general, is a fellow at the American Enterprise Institute.

JAMES BOVARD is the 1996 Warren T. Brookes Fellow in Environmental Journalism with the Competitive Enterprise Institute, a free market public policy group in Washington, D.C. He is a frequent contributor to the editorial pages of the *Wall Street Journal, Playboy, The American Spectator,* and other publications. He is the author of several books, including *Shakedown: How Government Screws You From A to Z* (Viking Penguin, 1995) and *Lost Rights: The Destruction of American Liberty* (St. Martin's Press, 1994).

GEORGE W. BUSH is the 43rd president of the United States and was formerly the governor of Texas.

PAT CALIFIA has described herself as a dyke, a feminist, a pornographer, a sadomasochist, a poet, a storyteller, an omnivore, a pagan, a social critic, a sex educator, and an activist. A prolific writer in a number of mediums, she has published hundreds of articles, reviews, poems, short fictional pieces, and books, including *Public Sex: The Culture of Radical Sex* (Cleis Press, 1994) and *The Second Coming,* coedited with Robin Sweeney (Alyson Publications, 1996).

MARTHA CORNOG, manager of membership services at the American College of Physicians in Philadelphia, Pennsylvania, was on the panel "For Sex: See Librarian" at the American Library Association Annual Conference in New Orleans. She is the editor of *Libraries, Erotica, and Pornography* (Oryx, 1991).

ELIZABETH CRAMER is an author who writes about the abuse of women.

BARRY M. DANK is professor of sociology at California State University at Long Beach. His research intrests include sexual behavior and deviance.

EDWIN J. DELATTRE is dean of the School of Education and a professor of education and philosophy in the College of Liberal Arts at Boston University in Boston, Massachusetts. He is also president emeritus of St. John's College, and he is well known nationally for his work on ethics in daily public and private life. His publications include *Education and the Public Trust: The Imperative for Common Purposes* (Ethics and Public Policy, 1988) and *Character and Cops: Ethics in Policing* (American Enterprise Institute, 1989).

DON FEDER is a nationally syndicated author who writes editorials for the *Boston Herald*. He is the author of *Who's Afraid of the Religious Right?* (Jameson Books, 1998). Feder graduated from the Boston University College of Liberal Arts in 1969 and received his law degree from the Boston University Law School in 1972. He is admitted to the practice of law in New York and Massachusetts.

JOSEPH S. FULDA is a contributing editor of *The Freeman* and an associate editor of *Sexuality and Culture: An Interdisciplinary Annual* as well as a columnist for *Computers and Society*.

SALLY GUTTMACHER is an associate professor in the Department of Health Studies at New York University. Her research interests include policy and prevention of chronic and infectious diseases, poverty and public health, and women's health.

TERENCE M. HINES is a professor of psychology at Pace University in Pleasantville, New York.

JUDITH KLEINFELD is a professor of psychology at the University of Alaska at Fairbanks and author of *Gender Tales: Tensions in the Schools* (St. Martins Press, 1995) and "The Myth That Schools Shortchange Girls," a paper prepared for the Women's Freedom Network (1998).

LORETTA M. KOPELMAN is a professor in and chair of the Department of Medical Humanities in the School of Medicine at East Carolina University in Greenville, North Carolina. She is coeditor, with John C. Moskop, of *Children and Health Care: Moral and Social Issues* (Kluwer Academic Publishers, 1989).

SHARON LAMB is an associate professor of psychology at St. Michael's College in Colchester, Vermont. She is a member of the American Psychological Association and the American Professional Society on the Abuse of Children. Her research interests include early moral development, sexual abuse and victimization, and coping with trauma.

BRIAN MARTIN is an associate professor of science, technology, and society at the University of Wollongong in Australia. He was a member of university committees against sexual harassment for over 15 years.

MERRILL MATTHEWS, JR. is a medical ethicist and a vice president of domestic policy at the National Center for Policy Analysis, a nonpartisan, nonprofit research institute in Dallas, Texas.

SARAH J. McCARTHY is the coauthor, with Ralph R. Reiland, of *Mom & Pop vs. the Dreambusters: The Small Business Revolt Against Big Government* (McGraw-Hill, 1999) and often writes on lawsuit abuse.

MARSHALL MILLER is a speaker, writer, and researcher on unmarried relationships. In 1998 Miller and his partner, Dorian Solot, founded the Alternatives to Marriage Project, a national nonprofit organization for unmarried people. The Alternatives to Marriage Project Web site is located at http://www.unmarried.org. Miller was named a Person to Watch in 2001 by *USA Today* for his work as an advocate for the rights of the unmarried.

JOHN MONEY is a profesor of medical psychology and pediatrics at Johns Hopkins University and Hospital in Baltimore, Maryland, where he cofounded and directed the Psychohormonal Research Unit. His research interests include hermaphrodites, transsexuals, and paraphilias, and he is the author of nearly 400 scientific papers and two dozen books on sexology and psychoendocrinology, including *Venuses Penuses* (Prometheus Books, 1986) and *Reinterpreting the Unspeakable: Human Sexuality 2000* (Continuum, 1994).

DOUGLAS F. MUNCH is founder and president of DFM, Ltd., a strategic management consulting firm specializing in the health care industry. He has more than 20 years of senior health care experience encompassing pharmaceuticals, medical products, and diagnostics. His corporate experiences include Ortho Pharmaceuticals Advanced Care Products (vice president and board member) and Sphinx Pharmaceuticals (president, CEO, and director).

P. MASILA MUTISYA is an assistant professor in the Department of Curriculum and Instruction in the School of Education at Fayetteville State University in Fayetteville, North Carolina. He teaches courses on foundations of education, human development, and multicultural education.

BEVERLY R. NEWMAN teaches at Ivy Tech College in Indianapolis, counsels survivors of sexual abuse, and has testified before the Indiana Legislature about children's issues.

DAVID POPENOE is professor of sociology at Rutgers University in New Brunswick, New Jersey, where he is also codirector of the National Marriage Project and former social and behavioral sciences dean.

JONATHAN RAUCH is a senior writer for *National Journal* and is the vice president of the Independent Gay Forum. He is the author of *Government's End: Why Washington Stopped Working*, 2d ed. (Public Affairs, LLC, 1999).

DEBORAH M. ROFFMAN, the author of *Sex and Sensibility: The Thinking Parent's Guide to Talking Sense About Sex* (Perseus Books Group, 2000), has taught human sexuality education at the Park School of Baltimore and other Baltimore-Washington area schools since 1975.

BERNICE SANDLER, a senior scholar at the National Association for Women in Education, consults with educational institutions on gender, including sexual harassment.

JAMES L. SAUER is a librarian at Eastern College in Phoenixville, Pennsylvania.

LAURA SCHLESSINGER is the host of the radio talk show "The Dr. Laura Schlessinger Show." She is also the author of *The Ten Commandments: The Significance of God's Laws in Everyday Life* (Macmillan Library Reference, 1999).

GARY SCHUBACH is a sex educator, lecturer, and writer. He is an associate professor for the Institute for the Advanced Study of Human Sexuality in San

Francisco, California, and moderates the Web site http://www.doctorg.org.

DORIAN SOLOT is the executive director of the Alternatives to Marriage Project, a national nonprofit organization for unmarried people. The Alternatives to Marriage Project Web site is located at http://www.unmarried.org. A speaker, writer, and researcher, Solot has appeared on CNN, the NBC Nightly News, and MSNBC.

KATHERINE SHAW SPAHT is a professor of law at Louisiana State University at Baton Rouge and was the chief consultant for legislators who sponsored the state's marriage covenant law.

NADINE STROSSEN is a professor in the School of Law at New York University in New York City and a general counsel for the American Civil Liberties Union.

ANDREW VACHHS is a juvenile advocate and widely praised crime novelist.

ANASTASIA VOLKONSKY is a writer and researcher based in San Francisco, California, and a founding director of PROMISE, an organization dedicated to combating sexual exploitation.

JANICE WEINMAN is the executive director of the American Association of University Women.

BARBARA DAFOE WHITEHEAD speaks and writes about family and child well-being. Her work has appeared in many publications, including the *American Enterprise, Commonweal,* the *Woodrow Wilson Quarterly, Slate,* the *Times Literary Supplement,* the *New York Times,* the *Wall Street Journal,* the *Washington Post, Reader's Digest,* the *Los Angeles Times,* and the *Boston Globe.* She is the author of *The Divorce Culture* (Alfred A. Knopf, 1997).

Index